Michael
8/4/16

discovering
MATHEMATICS 7B
Common Core

a Singapore Math® Program

 STAR PUBLISHING PTE LTD

 Singapore Math Inc®

STAR PUBLISHING PTE LTD

Star Publishing Pte Ltd
115A Commonwealth Drive #05-12
Singapore 149596
Tel: (65) 64796800
Website: www.starpub.com.sg
Email: contactus@starpub.com.sg

in association with

 Singapore Math Inc®

Singapore Math Inc
Website: www.SingaporeMath.com
Email: customerservice@singaporemath.com

Based on the original series entitled
Discovering Mathematics, approved by
Ministry of Education, Singapore.

ISBN 978-981-4250-53-5
ISBN 978-981-4250-57-3 (Hardcase)

PREFACE

DISCOVERING MATHEMATICS COMMON CORE is a series of textbooks designed for students in middle schools. Developed in collaboration between Star Publishing Pte Ltd and Singapore Math Inc., this series follows the Singapore Mathematics Framework and also covers the topics in the Common Core State Standards.

The emphasis of this series is on empowering students to learn mathematics effectively. Depending on the topics covered, different approaches are adopted for the presentation of concepts to facilitate understanding and internalization of concepts by students and to instill in them an interest to explore the topics further.

Each book includes appropriate examples, class activities, and diagrams to understand the concepts and apply them. Information technology skills are incorporated as appropriate.

With this comprehensive series, we hope that students will find learning mathematics an interesting and fun experience so that they will be motivated to study the subject, discover mathematical features and apply them in real-life situations.

Our special thanks to Richard Askey, Professor Emeritus (University of Wisconsin-Madison) for his indispensable advice and suggestions in the production of Discovering Mathematics Common Core series.

We wish to express our sincere thanks to all those who have provided valuable feedback and great assistance in the production of this series.

The Writing Team
Discovering Mathematics Common Core

TEXTBOOK FEATURES

The textbooks provide a solid well-balanced, comprehensive, and systematic approach to the teaching of mathematics. A combination of different approaches has been adopted in the presentation of mathematical concepts to motivate students and empower them to become independent learners. Examples and questions have been carefully designed to ensure that students not only understand the concepts, but are also able to apply them.

Example
Helps students understand and master a concept through a worked example

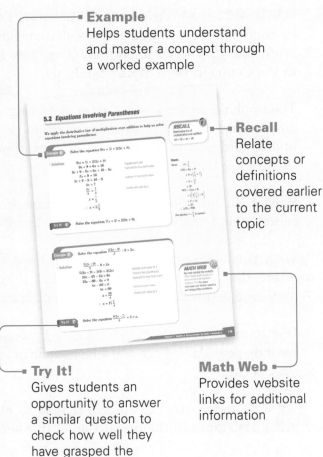

Recall
Relate concepts or definitions covered earlier to the current topic

Try It!
Gives students an opportunity to answer a similar question to check how well they have grasped the concept

Math Web
Provides website links for additional information

Chapter Opener
Introduces the topic through real-life applications and identifies the chapter's learning outcomes

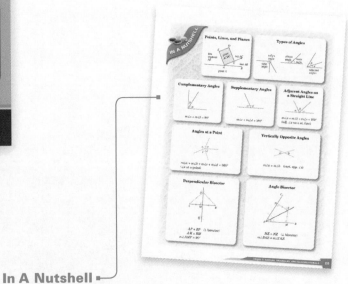

In A Nutshell
Consolidates important rules and concepts for quick and easy review

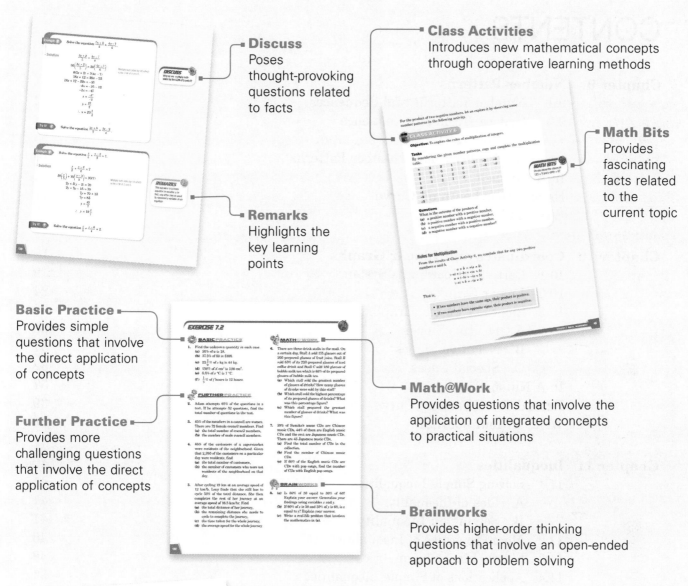

Discuss
Poses thought-provoking questions related to facts

Remarks
Highlights the key learning points

Class Activities
Introduces new mathematical concepts through cooperative learning methods

Math Bits
Provides fascinating facts related to the current topic

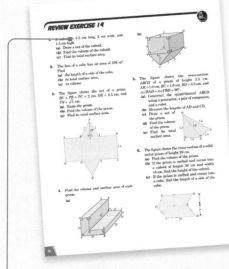

Basic Practice
Provides simple questions that involve the direct application of concepts

Further Practice
Provides more challenging questions that involve the direct application of concepts

Math@Work
Provides questions that involve the application of integrated concepts to practical situations

Brainworks
Provides higher-order thinking questions that involve an open-ended approach to problem solving

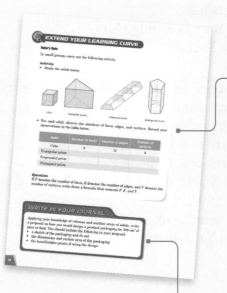

Extend Your Learning Curve
Extends and applies concepts learned to problems that are investigative in nature and engages the students in independent research

Review Exercise
Gives students the opportunity to apply the concepts learned in the chapter through a variety of integrated questions

Write In Your Journal
Encourages reflective learning

CONTENTS

9 NUMBER PATTERNS

Playing

LET'S LEARN TO...

1. understand the idea of a sequence
2. find the terms of a sequence
3. find the formula for the general term of a sequence
4. solve problems involving sequences and number patterns

Many plants show the Fibonacci sequence in the arrangements of the leaves around their stems. If we look down on a plant, the leaves are often arranged so that leaves above do not hide leaves below. This means that each gets a good share of the sunlight and catches the most rain to channel down to the roots as it runs down the leaf to the stem. Do you know what is Fibonacci sequence? Where else can you find the Fibonacci numbers in nature?

9.1 *Number Patterns and Sequences*

Look at the following four patterns of dots.

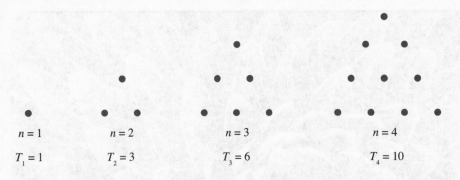

$n = 1$ $n = 2$ $n = 3$ $n = 4$

$T_1 = 1$ $T_2 = 3$ $T_3 = 6$ $T_4 = 10$

What do you observe about the number of dots in each pattern?

The number of dots form an ordered list which is 1, 3, 6, and 10.

An ordered list of numbers is called a **sequence** and it may be generated from shapes, patterns, or rules. In this case, the numbers of dots generate the sequence

$$1, 3, 6, 10.$$

Each number in a sequence is called a **term** and it is identified by its position in the ordered list. The terms are usually denoted by $T_1, T_2, T_3, \ldots$ or $a_1, a_2, a_3, \ldots$. For the above sequence,

the first term $\quad = T_1 = 1,$

the second term $= T_2 = 3,$

the third term $\quad = T_3 = 6,$

the fourth term $= T_4 = 10.$

CLASS ACTIVITY 1

Objective: To observe number patterns.

Questions

1. In each case, the first four terms of a sequence are given. Find the 5th and 6th terms of each sequence.
   (a) 2, 5, 8, 11, ...
   (b) 30, 25, 20, 15, ...
   (c) 1, 3, 9, 27, ...
   (d) 96, 48, 24, 12, ...

2. Look at the following patterns of dots.

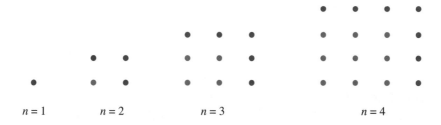

$n = 1$ $n = 2$ $n = 3$ $n = 4$

Let a_n be the number of green dots and T_n be the total number of dots in the nth pattern of the figure.
   (a) Write down the terms T_1, T_2, T_3, and T_4.
   (b) What will T_5 and T_6 be?
   (c) How are the numbers T_n related in the sequence?
   (d) Write down the terms a_1, a_2, a_3, and a_4.
   (e) What will a_5 and a_6 be?
   (f) How are the numbers a_n related in the sequence?

Example 1   Find the next two terms of the sequence 12, 5, −2, −9, ...

Solution   Observe that in the given sequence

$$12, \quad 5, \quad -2, \quad -9, \ ... \ ,$$
$$\qquad -7 \quad -7 \quad -7$$

a term is obtained by adding (−7) to the previous term.
∴   the 5th term = −9 + (−7)
                   = −16
and   the 6th term = −16 + (−7)
                   = −23

DISCUSS

What are the sequences in Class Activity 1 that can be generated by the method used in Example 1?

Try It! 1   Find the next two terms of the following sequences.
   (a) 2, 6, 10, 14, ...   **(b)** 7, 1, −5, −11, ...

Example **2**

Find the next two terms of the following sequences.
(a) 3, 6, 12, 24, ...
(b) 54, −18, 6, −2, ...

Solution

(a) Observe that in the given sequence

$$3, \quad 6, \quad 12, \quad 24, \ldots,$$
$$\times 2 \quad \times 2 \quad \times 2$$

a term is obtained by multiplying the previous term by 2.
$\therefore$ the 5th term $= 24 \times 2$
$= 48$
and the 6th term $= 48 \times 2$
$= 96$

(b) Observe that in the given sequence

$$54, \quad -18, \quad 6, \quad -2, \ldots,$$
$$\times \left(-\frac{1}{3}\right) \quad \times \left(-\frac{1}{3}\right) \quad \times \left(-\frac{1}{3}\right)$$

a term is obtained by multiplying the previous term by $\left(-\frac{1}{3}\right)$.

$\therefore$ the 5th term $= -2 \times \left(-\frac{1}{3}\right)$
$= \dfrac{2}{3}$
and the 6th term $= \dfrac{2}{3} \times \left(-\frac{1}{3}\right)$
$= -\dfrac{2}{9}$

DISCUSS

What are the sequences in Class Activity 1 that can be generated by the method used in Example 2?

Try It! 2

Find the next two terms of the following sequences.
(a) 2, 6, 18, 54, ...
(b) 625, −250, 100, −40, ...

Example 3

The figures below are a sequence of patterns formed by matchsticks.

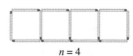

$n = 1$ $n = 2$ $n = 3$ $n = 4$

Each matchstick is 3 cm long and the matchsticks are arranged as shown. Let the number of matchsticks in the nth pattern be T_n and the perimeter of the nth pattern be P_n cm.

(a) Complete the following table.

n	1	2	3	4
T_n	4			
P_n	12			

(b) Find T_5 and P_5.

Solution

(a) We add three matchsticks to the 1st pattern to form the 2nd pattern.
$$\therefore\ T_2 = 4 + 3$$
$$= 7$$
Perimeter of the 2nd pattern
$$= (1 + 2) \times 2 \times 3 \text{ cm}$$
$$= 18 \text{ cm}$$
$$\therefore\ P_2 = 18$$

The 2nd pattern is two matches long and one match high.

Similarly, we can complete the table as follows:

n	1	2	3	4
T_n	4	7	10	13
P_n	12	18	24	30

(b) In the sequence of T_n, we observe that the next term is obtained by adding 3 to the previous term.
$$\therefore\ T_5 = T_4 + 3$$
$$= 13 + 3$$
$$= 16$$

In the sequence of P_n, we observe that the next term is obtained by adding 6 to the previous term.
$$\therefore\ P_5 = P_4 + 6$$
$$= 30 + 6$$
$$= 36$$

From the figures below, study and compare the matchstick patterns.

$n = 1$ $n = 2$ $n = 3$ $n = 4$

Each matchstick is 3 cm long and the matchsticks are arranged as shown. Let the number of matchsticks in the nth pattern be T_n and the perimeter of the nth pattern be P_n cm.

(a) Complete the following table.

n	1	2	3	4
T_n	3			
P_n	9			

(b) Find T_5 and P_5.

EXERCISE 9.1

 BASIC PRACTICE

1. Write down the next two terms of each sequence.
    (a) 11, 13, 15, 17, ...
    (b) 1, 4, 7, 10, ...
    (c) 16, 12, 8, 4, ...
    (d) 49, 38, 27, 16, ...

2. Write down the next two terms of each sequence.
    (a) 1, 2, 4, 8, ...
    (b) 375, 75, 15, 3, ...
    (c) 1, −1, 1, −1, ...
    (d) −4, 12, −36, 108, ...

3. Write down the next two terms of each sequence.
    (a) 1, 8, 27, 64, ...
    (b) 1, 3, 6, 10, ...
    (c) $1, \dfrac{1}{2}, \dfrac{1}{4}, \dfrac{1}{8}, ...$
    (d) $\dfrac{1}{2}, \dfrac{2}{3}, \dfrac{3}{4}, \dfrac{4}{5}, ...$

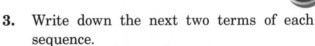 **FURTHER PRACTICE**

4. Find the 7th term of each sequence.
    (a) 2, 4, 6, 8, ...
    (b) 23, 20, 17, 14, ...
    (c) 5, 10, 20, 40, ...
    (d) 216, −144, 96, −64, ...

5. A sequence is formed by
$$2 \times 1^2, 2 \times 2^2, 2 \times 3^2, 2 \times 4^2, \ldots.$$
(a) Write down the first four terms of the sequence.
(b) Find the 8th term of the sequence.

6. A sequence is formed by
$$1 \times 2, 2 \times 3, 3 \times 4, 4 \times 5, \ldots.$$
(a) Write down the first four terms of the sequence.
(b) Find the 10th term of the sequence.

 MATH@WORK

7. The figures below show a sequence of patterns formed by small square tiles.

$n = 1$ $n = 2$

 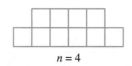

$n = 3$ $n = 4$

(a) Draw the 5th figure of the pattern.
(b) If T_n is the number of small tiles in the nth figure, find T_1, T_2, T_3, T_4, and T_5.
(c) Let P_n cm be the perimeter of the nth figure. Find P_n for $n = 1$ to 5, taking the length of each side of the square tile to be 2 cm.

8. The figures below show a sequence of patterns formed by matchsticks.

$n = 1$ $n = 2$ $n = 3$ $n = 4$

The matchsticks, 3 cm each, are arranged end to end. If T_n is the number of matchsticks in the nth figure and P_n is its respective perimeter, find
(a) T_n for $n = 1$ to 5,
(b) T_8,
(c) P_n for $n = 1$ to 5,
(d) P_8.

 BRAIN WORKS

9. Find the 7th term of the sequence 3, 4, 10, 24, 49, 88, ...

10. The sequence 1, 1, 2, 3, 5, 8, 13, ... is known as the **Fibonacci sequence**.
(a) What is the rule used to obtain the terms in the sequence?
(b) Write down the next three terms of the sequence.
(c) Complete the following where each value in the lower row is the difference of the two terms just above it.

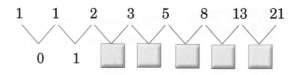

Write a paragraph to explain what you have discovered.

Note: You may access the website *www.maths. surrey.ac.uk/hosted-sites/R.Knott/ Fibonacci/fibnat.html* for more information regarding this famous sequence.

9.2 *General Term of a Sequence*

A General Term

Consider the sequence of triangular numbers 1, 3, 6, 10, ... We can find the pattern of its terms as follows:

$$T_1 = 1$$
$$T_2 = 1 + 2$$
$$T_3 = 1 + 2 + 3$$
$$T_4 = 1 + 2 + 3 + 4$$
$$\vdots$$

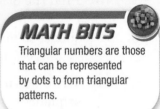

MATH BITS

Triangular numbers are those that can be represented by dots to form triangular patterns.

Hence, the nth term = $T_n = 1 + 2 + 3 + 4 + ... + n$.

It can be shown that

$$1 + 2 + 3 + ... + n = \frac{1}{2}n(n + 1).$$ (Refer to Question 9 in Exercise 9.2.)

$\therefore$ the nth term of the sequence is given by the formula:

$$T_n = \frac{1}{2}n(n + 1)$$

The nth term of a sequence is called the **general term** of the sequence. If we know the formula for the general term, we can find any term in the sequence by substituting the corresponding value for n.

For example, the 6th term of the triangular sequence is

$$T_6 = \frac{1}{2} \times 6 \times (6 + 1)$$ Substitute $n = 6$ into the formula.
$$= 21$$

Example 4

The general term of a sequence is $T_n = n^2 + 2n - 1$. Find its 1st term and 10th term.

Solution

$$T_n = n^2 + 2n - 1$$
The 1st term and 10th term of the sequence are T_1 and T_{10} respectively.

Substituting $n = 1$ into the formula, we get
$$T_1 = 1^2 + 2(1) - 1$$
$$= 2$$

Substituting $n = 10$ into the formula, we get
$$T_{10} = 10^2 + 2(10) - 1$$
$$= 119$$

Try It! 4

The general term of a sequence is $T_n = n(n + 3)$. Find its 2nd term and 9th term.

Example 5

Consider the sequence 4, 10, 16, 22, ...
(a) Find its general term.
(b) Hence, find its 25th term.

Solution

(a) $T_1 = 4$
$T_2 = 10 = 4 + 6$ $= 4 + 6 \times 1$
$T_3 = 16 = 4 + 6 + 6$ $= 4 + 6 \times 2$
$T_4 = 22 = 4 + 6 + 6 + 6 = 4 + 6 \times 3$
$\therefore$ the general term $= T_n$
$= 4 + 6 \times (n - 1)$
$= 4 + 6n - 6$
$= 6n - 2$

(b) Substituting $n = 25$ into the formula, we get
the 25th term $= 6(25) - 2$
$= 148$

Try It! **5**

Consider the sequence 4, 7, 10, 13, ...
(a) Find its general term.
(b) Hence, find its 15th term.

Example 6

The figures below show a sequence of dot patterns.

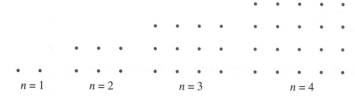

$n = 1$ $\qquad$ $n = 2$ $\qquad$ $n = 3$ $\qquad$ $n = 4$

T_n is the number of dots in the nth pattern.
(a) Find the general term T_n of the sequence.
(b) Find the 17th term T_{17}.

Solution

(a) $T_1 = 1 \times 2 = 2$
$T_2 = 2 \times 3 = 6$
$T_3 = 3 \times 4 = 12$
$T_4 = 4 \times 5 = 20$
$\therefore T_n = n \times (n + 1)$
$= n(n + 1)$

(b) The 17th term $= T_{17}$
$= 17(17 + 1)$
$= 306$

The figures below show a sequence of dot patterns.

$n = 1$ $n = 2$ $n = 3$ $n = 4$

Let T_n be the number of dots in the nth pattern.
(a) Find the general term T_n of the sequence.
(b) Find the 18th term T_{18}.

B Application of Number Patterns

We can solve some application problems by observing the number patterns and generalizing them to find the general term of a sequence. Let us explore the skills used to solve such problems.

 CLASS ACTIVITY 2

Objective: To observe number patterns and write down the general term of a sequence.

Questions

1. The first three members of a family of hydrogen and carbon compounds have bonding structures as shown below. (CH_4 stands for C_1H_4.)

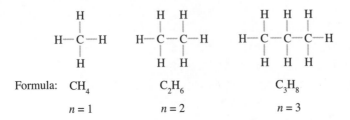

Formula: CH_4 C_2H_6 C_3H_8

$n = 1$ $n = 2$ $n = 3$

> **REMARKS**
>
> C stands for carbon atoms and H stands for hydrogen atoms. CH_4 denotes the bonding of one carbon atom with four hydrogen atoms.

(a) Draw the structures for the 4th and 5th members of the family.

(b) Copy and complete the following table.

n	Number of carbon atoms	Number of hydrogen atoms
1		
2		
3		
4		
5		

(c) Write down a general formula for the nth member in the family.

(d) How many hydrogen atoms does a member have when it has 100 carbon atoms?

2. The figures below show a sequence of patterns. Each pattern is formed by using joiners to connect identical short sticks. The joiners used are corner joiner ($\ulcorner$), edge joiner ($\dashv$), and cross joiner ($+$). Let C_n, E_n, and R_n be the numbers of corner, edge, and cross joiners used in the nth figure respectively.

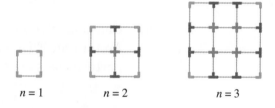

$n = 1$ $n = 2$ $n = 3$

(a) Draw the 4th figure in the sequence, showing clearly the types of joiners used.

(b) Copy and complete the following table.

n	1	2	3	4	5
C_n					
E_n					
R_n					

(c) Find the general terms for C_n, E_n, and R_n.

(d) Find the total number of joiners needed for the 10th figure.

After going through Class Activity 2, we can summarize the main steps used in problem solving as follows:

Problem-solving Strategy

1. Understand the problem.

2. Look for a pattern. Draw figures to gain some insight if necessary.

3. Generalize the results obtained.

4. Look back and check the validity of your solution.

EXERCISE 9.2

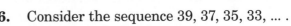

BASIC PRACTICE

1. Find the first three terms of each sequence from the given general term T_n.
   - (a) $T_n = 2n + 1$
   - (b) $T_n = 7 - 3n$
   - (c) $T_n = 2(n-1)^2$
   - (d) $T_n = \dfrac{n}{n+2}$

2. The general term of a sequence is
   $$T_n = n(n+3).$$
   Find its 11th term.

3. The general term of a sequence is
   $$T_n = n^3 - 1.$$
   Find its 7th term.

4. The general term of a sequence is
   $$T_n = 108 \times \left(\frac{2}{3}\right)^n.$$
   Find its 3rd term.

FURTHER PRACTICE

5. If the general term of a sequence is
   $$T_n = 7n + 4,$$
   find the sum of its 5th term and 6th term.

6. Consider the sequence 39, 37, 35, 33, ...
   - (a) Find its general term.
   - (b) Hence, find its 18th term.

7. Consider the sequence 4, 10, 18, 28, ... Adam and Elisa observe different number patterns as shown in the table.

n	Term	Adam's pattern	Elisa's pattern
1	4	1×4	$1^2 + 3 \times 1$
2	10	2×5	$2^2 + 3 \times 2$
3	18	3×6	$3^2 + 3 \times 3$
4	28	4×7	$4^2 + 3 \times 4$

   - (a) Find the general term a_n based on Adam's number patterns.
   - (b) Find the general term T_n based on Elisa's number patterns.
   - (c) Is $a_n = T_n$? Explain your answer.

8. The figures below show a sequence of patterns.

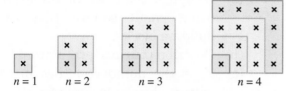

n = 1   n = 2   n = 3   n = 4

(a) Observe the patterns. Find the missing numbers in the parentheses.

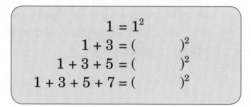

$$1 = 1^2$$
$$1 + 3 = (\quad)^2$$
$$1 + 3 + 5 = (\quad)^2$$
$$1 + 3 + 5 + 7 = (\quad)^2$$

(b) Express the sum $1 + 3 + 5 + 7 + 9$ as a square number.

(c) Express the sum
$$1 + 3 + 5 + \ldots + (2n - 1)$$
as a square number, where n is a positive integer.

9. The figures below show a sequence of rectangular array of dots.

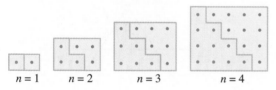

n = 1   n = 2   n = 3   n = 4

(a) Observe the patterns and complete the following table.

n	Number of red dots	Total number of dots
1	1	1×2
2	$1 + 2$	2×3
3		
4		
5		

(b) What is the ratio of the number of red dots to the total number of dots in each pattern?

(c) Hence, find a formula for the sum $1 + 2 + 3 + \ldots + n$.

(d) Evaluate the sum
$$51 + 52 + 53 + \ldots + 200$$
using the result in **(c)**.

MATH@WORK

10. Study the rectangles formed by small square tiles in the figures below.

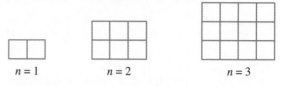

n = 1   n = 2   n = 3

Each side of a small tile is 2 cm and P_n cm is the perimeter of the nth rectangle.

(a) Find P_1, P_2, and P_3.

(b) State the general term P_n.

(c) Hence, find the perimeter of the 15th rectangle.

11. The figures below show a sequence of tiling patterns formed by small white and red tiles.

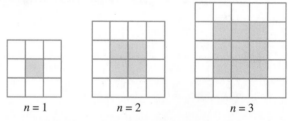

n = 1   n = 2   n = 3

(a) R_n is the number of red tiles in the nth square. Find
  (i) R_4,   **(ii)** R_n.

(b) W_n is the number of white tiles in the nth square. Find
  (i) W_4,   **(ii)** W_n.

12. The first three members of a family of hydrogen (H) and carbon (C) compounds have bonding structures as shown below.

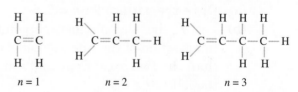

n = 1   n = 2   n = 3

(a) Draw the structure for the 4th member of the family.

(b) Copy and complete the following table.

n	Number of carbon atoms	Number of hydrogen atoms
1		
2		
3		
4		

(c) The formulas for the first three members are written as C_2H_4, C_3H_6, and C_4H_8 respectively. Write down a general formula for the nth member of the family.

13. The figures below show a sequence of patterns formed by lines joining the markings on the horizontal and vertical axes.

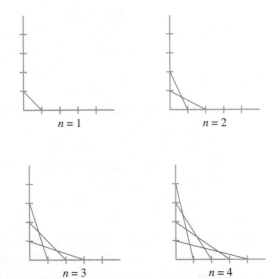

$n = 1$ $n = 2$

$n = 3$ $n = 4$

(a) Draw the pattern for $n = 5$.

(b) Let T_n be the number of points of intersection of the line segments other than the two axes. Copy and complete the following table.

n	1	2	3	4	5
T_n					

(c) Find T_6 and T_7.

14. (a) Design a sequence of tiling patterns using small square tiles as your building blocks.

    (b) Describe your pattern in words.

    (c) T_n is the number of tiles in the nth pattern. Find a formula for T_n.

15. Study the figures below. It shows the maximum number of parts obtained when one line, two lines, and three lines divide a plane respectively.

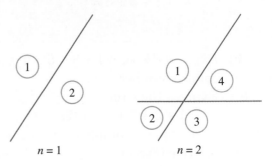

$n = 1$ $n = 2$

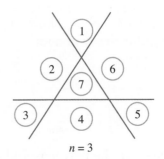

$n = 3$

Find the maximum number of parts that can be obtained when five lines divide a plane.

Sequence

A sequence is an ordered list of numbers.

E.g., 2, 3, 5, 7, ...

3rd term

2nd term

1st term

General Term

The nth term T_n of a sequence is its general term.

E.g., if $T_n = \dfrac{n}{n+1}$,

then $T_1 = \dfrac{1}{2}$,

and $T_2 = \dfrac{2}{3}$.

Sequences with Some Rules

(a) Sequences with a common difference

E.g., 2, 5, 8, 11, ...

+3 +3 +3

13, 10, 7, 4, ...

+(−3) +(−3) +(−3)

(b) Sequences with a common ratio

E.g., 1, 2, 4, 8, ...

× 2 × 2 × 2

36, 12, 4, $\dfrac{4}{3}$, ...

× $\dfrac{1}{3}$ × $\dfrac{1}{3}$ × $\dfrac{1}{3}$

Sequences from Patterns

(a) Square numbers

1, 4, 9, 16, ..., n^2, ...

(b) Cube numbers

1, 8, 27, 64, ..., n^3, ...

(c) Even numbers

2, 4, 6, 8, ..., $2n$, ...

(d) Odd numbers

1, 3, 5, 7, ..., $2n-1$, ...

1. Find the next two terms in each sequence.
    (a) 25, 27, 29, 31, ...
    (b) 41, 35, 29, 23, ...
    (c) 1, 4, 16, 64, ...
    (d) 5, –10, 20, –40, ...

2. If the general term T_n of a sequence is $T_n = n(n + 2)$, find T_3 and T_{20}.

3. If the general term T_n of a sequence is $T_n = \dfrac{1}{2n+1}$, find the sum of the first three terms.

4. Find the general term T_n of each sequence in terms of n.
    (a) 2, 3, 4, 5, ...
    (b) 2, 6, 18, 54, ...
    (c) $\dfrac{1}{4}, \dfrac{2}{5}, \dfrac{3}{6}, \dfrac{4}{7}, ...$
    (d) $1 \times 2, 2 \times 3, 3 \times 4, 4 \times 5, ...$

5. Study the patterns formed by green and white tiles in the figures below.

    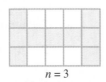

    $n = 1$ $n = 2$ $n = 3$

    (a) Draw the pattern for $n = 4$.
    (b) Let G_n be the number of green tiles and W_n be the number of white tiles in the nth pattern. Copy and complete the following table.

n	1	2	3	4
G_n				
W_n				

    (c) Find the general term of G_n.
    (d) Find the general term of W_n.

6. Study the square patterns formed by matchsticks in the figures below. T_n is the number of matchsticks in the nth pattern.

    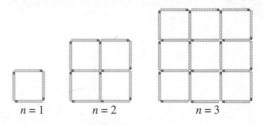

    $n = 1$ $n = 2$ $n = 3$

    (a) Copy and complete the following table.

n	1	2	3	4
T_n				

    (b) Express T_n in terms of n.
    (c) How many matchsticks are required for a 10×10 square pattern?

7. The figures below show a sequence of triangle patterns. Each small triangle in a pattern is the same size as the small triangle for $n = 1$.

    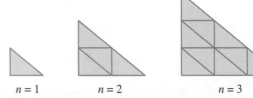

    $n = 1$ $n = 2$ $n = 3$

    T_n is the number of small triangles in the nth pattern. P_n cm is the perimeter of the nth pattern. Suppose $P_1 = 7$.
    (a) Draw the 4th pattern.
    (b) Copy and complete the following table.

n	1	2	3	4
T_n				
P_n				

    (c) Find the general term of T_n.
    (d) Find the general term of P_n.

EXTEND YOUR LEARNING CURVE

Fibonacci Sequence

The Fibonacci sequence 1, 1, 2, 3, 5, ... is formed by the rules:

$$T_1 = 1, T_2 = 1 \text{ and } T_n = T_{n-2} + T_{n-1} \text{ for } n \geqslant 3.$$

The numbers in this sequence often appear in nature.

Use the Internet to explore the properties of this sequence.

WRITE IN YOUR JOURNAL

1. What are your views on number patterns?

2. Reflect on the different methods used to find the general terms of sequences.

Playing

LET'S LEARN TO...

1. construct the Cartesian coordinate system and state the coordinates of points on it
2. plot a graph of a set of ordered pairs
3. draw the graph of a linear relationship
4. define linear relationships between two variables
5. find the slopes of linear graphs

If a ship encounters a heavy storm in the sea, how could the captain identify his location and ask for help? We use a system of coordinates to locate positions on the Earth's surface.

10.1 *Cartesian Coordinate System*

René Descartes (1596–1650), a French mathematician, came up with a system known as the **Cartesian coordinate system** to describe the positions of points and lines in a plane. Through this Cartesian coordinate or **rectangular coordinate system**, we can link and study the problems of geometry and algebra together.

You can construct a Cartesian coordinate system by placing two number lines perpendicular to each other as shown in the diagram.

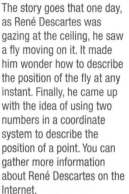
In the Cartesian coordinate system, the horizontal and vertical number lines are called the *x*-**axis** and the *y*-**axis** respectively. Collectively, they are the **coordinate axes**. The two lines intersect at right angles at the point *O* known as the **origin**. The axes divide the plane into four parts known as the **first**, **second**, **third**, and **fourth quadrants**. The plane thus formed is called the **coordinate plane**, **Cartesian plane**, or *x-y* **plane**.

The position of any point, say *P*, on the plane can be described by an ordered pair (a, b) of real numbers. We obtain the value of a when the vertical line through *P* intersects the *x*-axis and the value of b when the horizontal line through *P* intersects the *y*-axis. We call a the *x*-**coordinate** and b the *y*-**coordinate** of *P*. We say that *P* has **coordinates** (a, b) and refer the point *P* as $P(a, b)$. Hence, we can locate a point in a plane if we know its *x*- and *y*-coordinates.

Example *1*

REMARKS

In this coordinate plane, we say that the scale of both the *x*-axis and the *y*-axis is 1 cm to 1 unit.

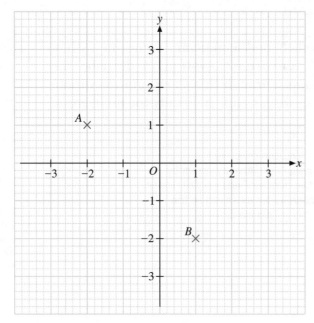

(a) State the coordinates of the points *A* and *B* in the above diagram.

(b) State the quadrants in which *A* and *B* lie.

(c) Plot the points $C(2, 3)$, $D(0, 2)$, $E(-3, 0)$, and $F(-2, -3)$ on the diagram.

Solution (a)

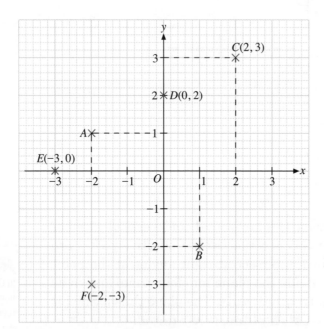

REMARKS

Have you ever noticed how a seat in a theater is numbered? What about the location of a place on a map?

We drop the perpendiculars from *A* to the *x*-axis and *y*-axis.

The perpendiculars meet the *x*-axis at −2 and the *y*-axis at 1 respectively.

∴ the coordinates of $A = (-2, 1)$.

Similarly, the coordinates of $B = (1, -2)$.

(b) $A(-2, 1)$ lies in the second quadrant.
$B(1, -2)$ lies in the fourth quadrant.

(c) Draw a dotted line perpendicular to the x-axis at $x = 2$.
Draw a dotted line perpendicular to the y-axis at $y = 3$.
The point of intersection of the above lines is $C(2, 3)$.
Similarly, we can plot the points $D(0, 2)$, $E(-3, 0)$, and
$F(-2, -3)$ as shown in the diagram in part **(a)**.

Note: • The points $(-2, 1)$ and $(1, -2)$ are different because
they refer to different locations on the coordinate
plane. Thus, the order in which the coordinates
are written in an ordered pair is important.
• The point $D(0, 2)$ is on the y-axis while the point
$E(-3, 0)$ is on the x-axis.

Try It! ➊

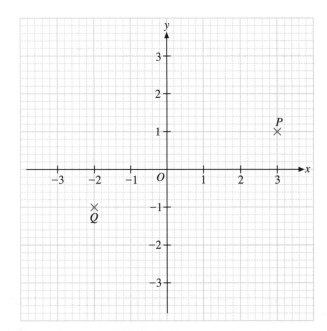

(a) State the coordinates of the points P and Q in the above diagram.

(b) State the quadrants in which P and Q lie.

(c) Using a scale of 1 cm to 1 unit on both axes, draw a coordinate plane on a sheet of graph paper and plot the points $R(1, 3)$, $S(-2, 3)$, $T(0, -1)$, and $U(2, -2)$.

EXERCISE 10.1

![gear icon] **BASIC**PRACTICE

1. **(a)** Write down the coordinates of the points *A* to *J* shown in the diagram below.
    (b) Which points are in the first quadrant?
    (c) Which points are in the fourth quadrant?
    (d) Which points are on the *y*-axis?

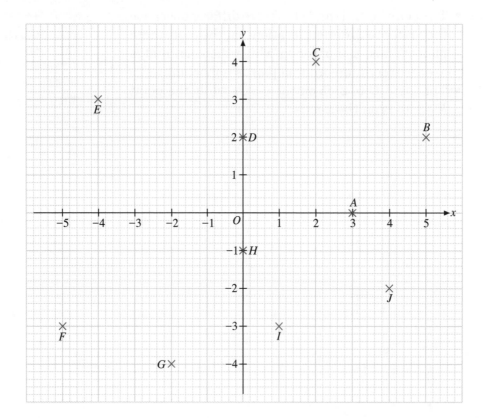

2. Write down the *x*-coordinate of each point.
    (a) *A*(3, −2)   **(b)** *B*(−2, 7)
    (c) *C*(−1, 4)   **(d)** *D*(0,0)

3. Write down the *y*-coordinate of each point.
    (a) *P*(4, −5)   **(b)** *Q*(3, 2)
    (c) *R*(−6, 7)   **(d)** *S*(9, 0)

4. Using a scale of 1 cm to 1 unit on both axes, draw a coordinate plane on a sheet of graph paper. Then plot and label the following points.

    A(0, 4), *B*(5, 3), *C*(1, 3), *D*(0, 6),
    E(−3, 2), *F*(−2, 0), *G*(−5, −2), *H*(3, −4)

 FURTHERPRACTICE

5. **(a)** Plot the points *A*(3, 3), *B*(0, 3), and *C*(−3, 3) on a coordinate plane.
    (b) Which point(s) is/are in the second quadrant?
    (c) Join *OA* and *OC*. Then measure ∠*AOB* and ∠*BOC*.
    (d) Give at least two relationships between the line segments *OA* and *OC*.

6. **(a)** Plot the points $P(1, -2)$ and $Q(-4, -2)$ on a coordinate plane.
    (b) State the quadrant in which P lies.
    (c) State the quadrant in which Q lies.
    (d) Join OP and OQ. Then measure $\angle POQ$.
    (e) Find the coordinates of a point R such that the x-axis is the perpendicular bisector of the line segment QR.

7. **(a)** Plot the points $S(-5, 0)$ and $T(0, 2)$ on a coordinate plane.
    (b) Join ST. Find the area of $\triangle SOT$.
    (c) Mark the midpoint of S and T with the letter M, and state its coordinates.
    (d) State the relationship between the lengths of MO, MS, and MT.

8. **(a)** Plot the points $A(-3, 1)$, $B(0, -1)$, $C(1, -1)$, and $D(4, -1)$ on a coordinate plane.
    (b) Which of the above points are in the fourth quadrant?

(c) If a point is in the fourth quadrant, what is the sign of its
    (i) x-coordinate,
    (ii) y-coordinate?

MATH@WORK

9. **(a)** On a sheet of graph paper, draw a coordinate plane using a scale of 1 cm to represent 2 units on both axes and plot the following points.

    $A(6, 0)$, $B(3, 1)$, $C(2, 6)$, $D(0, 2)$, $E(-4, 2)$, $F(-2, 0)$, $G(-6, -6)$, $H(-1, -3)$, $I(4, -6)$, $J(2, -2)$

    (b) Draw the design formed by joining the points successively by line segments, and the points A and J.

BRAINWORKS

10. Study the pattern of squares in the diagram on the right. Each square is drawn with its vertices on the axes. The lengths of the diagonals of Square 1, Square 2, and Square 3 are 2 units, 4 units, and 6 units respectively.
    (a) Find the area of each square.
    (b) What is the area of Square 10?
    (c) Express, in terms of n, the area of Square n.

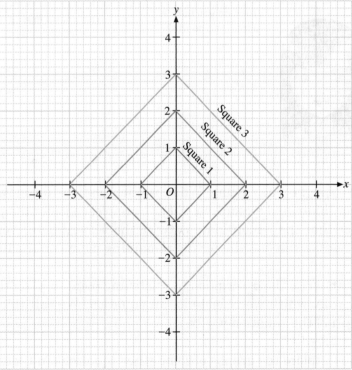

10.2 *Linear Graphs*

In real-life situations, we often investigate whether there is any relationship between two variables, x and y. One method is to obtain some corresponding values of x and y and then plot them as ordered pairs (x, y) on a coordinate plane.

Let us plot the points $(0, 0)$, $(1, 2)$, $(2, 4)$, $(3, 6)$, and $(4, 8)$ on a coordinate plane as shown below.

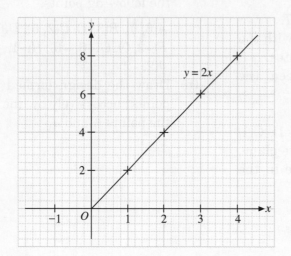

REMARKS
We should always label a graph with its equation.

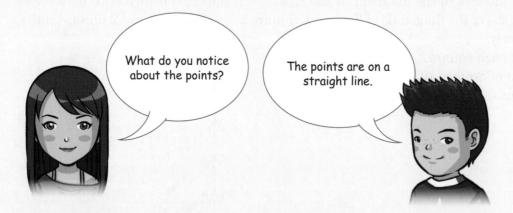

What do you notice about the points?

The points are on a straight line.

Now observe each point. What is the relationship between each pair of x-coordinate and y-coordinate? For example, consider the point $(1, 2)$. Do you notice that the y-coordinate is twice the x-coordinate? Verify for yourself if the relationship is valid for the remaining points on the line.

We can write the description to relate any point (x, y) on this particular line as $y = 2x$ which we refer to as an equation. We call this straight line the **graph** of the equation $y = 2x$.

Let us explore the graphs of some other equations in Class Activity 1.

Objective: To explore the graphs of linear functions.

Questions

1. **(a)** Copy and complete the following table of values for x and y.

x	−4	−2	0	2	4
$y = x$	−4				
$y = -x + 2$	6				
$y = \frac{1}{2}x + 1$	−1				

   (b) Using a scale of 1 cm to 1 unit on both axes, draw and label the graph of the following equations on a sheet of graph paper.

$$y = x, \ y = -x + 2, \text{ and } y = \frac{1}{2}x + 1$$

   (c) What do you observe about the graphs of these equations?

2. **(a)** Using a scale of 1 cm to 1 unit on both axes and the following tables of values for x and y, draw and label the graphs of $y = 3$ and $y = -1$ on a sheet of graph paper.

x	−3	−1	1	3
$y = 3$	3	3	3	3

x	−3	−1	1	3
$y = -1$	−1	−1	−1	−1

REMARKS

The line $y = 3$ can be considered as $y = (0)x + 3$.

For different values of x, y is always equal to 3.

How about the line $y = -1$?

   (b) What do you observe about the graphs of $y = 3$ and $y = -1$?

   (c) Using the following tables of values for x and y, draw and label the graphs of $x = 2$ and $x = -\frac{3}{2}$ on the same axes in **(a)**.

$x = 2$	2	2	2	2
y	3	1	0	−1

$x = -\frac{3}{2}$	$-\frac{3}{2}$	$-\frac{3}{2}$	$-\frac{3}{2}$	$-\frac{3}{2}$
y	3	1	0	−1

REMARKS

The line $x = -\frac{3}{2}$ can be considered as $x = (0)y - \frac{3}{2}$.

For different values of y, x is always equal to $-\frac{3}{2}$.

How about the line $x = 2$?

   (d) What do you observe about the graphs of $x = 2$ and $x = -\frac{3}{2}$?

   (e) What are the equations of the x-axis and the y-axis?

From Class Activity 1, we can observe that:

> The graph of an equation of the form $y = mx + b$ is a straight line, where b and m are constants.

The graph of an equation that is a straight line is called a **linear graph**.

Note: • The graph of $y = c$ is a horizontal straight line which is parallel to the x-axis.

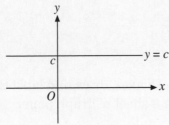

• The graph of $x = c$ is a vertical straight line which is parallel to the y-axis.

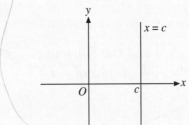

Example 2

(a) Draw the graph of $y = -\dfrac{1}{3}x + 2$ for values of x from -3 to 6.

(b) Does the point $A\left(1, 1\dfrac{3}{5}\right)$ lie on the graph?

(c) Use the graph to estimate the value of y when $x = 2$.

Solution

(a) First, we set up a table of values for x and y to help us plot the points on the graph.

x	-3	0	3	6
$y = -\dfrac{1}{3}x + 2$	3	2	1	0

Next, we join all the points to obtain the graph of $y = -\dfrac{1}{3}x + 2$ on the next page.

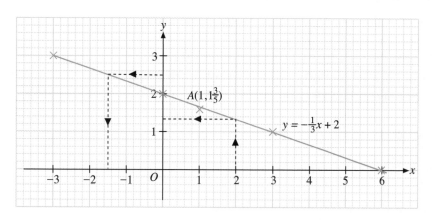

(b) To check if the point $A\left(1, 1\frac{3}{5}\right)$ lies on the graph, we can substitute $x = 1$ into $y = -\frac{1}{3}x + 2$.

When $x = 1$, $y = -\frac{1}{3}(1) + 2 = 1\frac{2}{3}$.

As $1\frac{2}{3} \neq 1\frac{3}{5}$, the coordinates of the point A do not satisfy the equation $y = -\frac{1}{3}x + 2$.

Therefore, point A does not lie on the graph.

(c) To find the value of y when $x = 2$:

STEP ❶ Draw a vertical line from the x-axis where $x = 2$ to meet the graph.

STEP ❷ Draw a horizontal line from the point of intersection to meet the y-axis.

STEP ❸ Read the value of y on the y-axis.

From the graph, when $x = 2$, $y = 1.3$ approximately.

Try It! ② **(a)** Draw the graph of $y = -\frac{1}{2}x - 1$ for values of x from -4 to 4.

(b) Does the point $B(1, -1)$ lie on the graph?

(c) Using the graph, find the value of y when $x = -3$.

Example **3**

The charge $y of a plumber for a job is $y = 20t + 30$ where t is the number of hours spent on the job.

(a) Draw the graph of $y = 20t + 30$ from $t = 0$ to $t = 4$.

(b) The charge for a job is $80. Use the graph to find the time taken to complete the job.

Solution

(a)

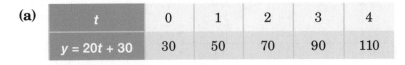

t	0	1	2	3	4
$y = 20t + 30$	30	50	70	90	110

The graph of $y = 20t + 30$ is shown below.

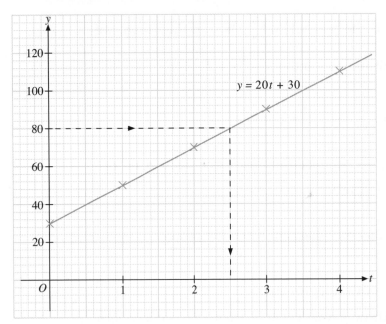

(b) Draw a horizontal line at $y = 80$ to meet the graph and then drop a perpendicular from the point of intersection to the t-axis. The value of t where the perpendicular meets the t-axis is the required value.

∴ the time taken to complete the job is 2.5 hours.

Note: • The labels on the two axes depend on the variables used. In this example, the horizontal axis is the t-axis.

• When the graph of two variables is a straight line, the two variables are said to have a **linear relationship**.

Water is being drained from a tank. The water level h cm at time t minutes is given by $h = 40 - 5t$.

(a) Draw the graph of $h = 40 - 5t$ from $t = 0$ to $t = 8$.

(b) From your graph, find the time when the water level is 15 cm.

EXERCISE 10.2

BASIC PRACTICE

1. **(a)** Copy and complete the following table.

x	–3	0	2	4
y = x – 2				

   (b) Draw the graph of $y = x - 2$ for values of x from –3 to 4.

2. **(a)** Copy and complete the following table.

x	–2	0	1	3
y = –2x + 1				

   (b) Draw the graph of $y = -2x + 1$ from $x = -2$ to $x = 3$.

3. **(a)** Draw the graph of $y = \frac{1}{2}x + 3$ from $x = -4$ to $x = 4$.
   (b) Does the point $A(1, 3)$ lie on the graph?

4. **(a)** Draw the graph of $y = 3 - x$ from $x = -1$ to $x = 4$.
   (b) Does the point $B(2, 1)$ lie on the graph?
   (c) From your graph, find the value of x when $y = 0$.

5. **(a)** Draw the graph of $y = 3(x - 1)$ for values of x from –3 to 3.
   (b) Find the coordinates of the point at which the graph cuts the x-axis.

6. **(a)** Draw the graph of $y = \frac{x + 2}{4}$ from $x = -8$ to $x = 4$.
   (b) Find the coordinates of the points at which the graph cuts the axes.

7. **(a)** Draw the following lines on the same coordinate plane.
   (i) $x = 1$ **(ii)** $x = 3$
   (iii) $y = 2$ **(iv)** $y = -3$
   (b) Label the coordinates of the points of intersection of the lines.
   (c) Find the area of the rectangle formed by the lines in **(a)**.

FURTHER PRACTICE

8. **(a)** Draw the following lines on the same coordinate plane for values of x from –3 to 3.
   (i) $y = x + 1$
   (ii) $y = \frac{1}{3}x + 1$
   (iii) $y = -\frac{1}{2}x + 1$
   (iv) $y = 1$
   (b) What is the common property of the graphs of the above lines?
   (c) What is the common property of the equations of the above lines?

9. **(a)** Draw the following lines on the same coordinate plane for values of x from –3 to 3.
   (i) $y = -x$
   (ii) $y = -x + 1$
   (iii) $y = -x - 2$
   (iv) $y = -x + 3$
   (b) What is the common property of the graphs of the above lines?
   (c) What is the common property of the equations of the above lines?

10. **(a)** Draw the graph of $y = 12 - 3x$ from $x = -2$ to $x = 5$.
    (b) The points $(a, 0)$, $(1, b)$, and $(c, 5)$ are some points on the graph. Find the values of a, b, and c from the graph.

MATH@WORK

11. The volume V cm^3 of a gas formed in a chemical reaction at time t minutes is given by $V = 5t$.
    (a) Draw the graph of $V = 5t$ from $t = 0$ to $t = 6$.
    (b) Use your graph to find the time taken to produce 20 cm^3 of the gas.

12. Steven is driving to a city. His distance d miles from the city at time t hours after starting is given by

$$d = 180 - 60t \text{ for } 0 \leqslant t \leqslant 3.$$

(a) Draw the graph of $d = 180 - 60t$ for $0 \leqslant t \leqslant 3$.

(b) Use your graph to find the time when Steven is 30 miles from the city.

13. On a coordinate plane where values of x and of y are from -5 to 5, plot five different locations of a point (x, y)

(a) if the y-coordinate is one unit greater than the x-coordinate,

(b) if the y-coordinate is the additive inverse of the x-coordinate.

10.3 *Slopes of Linear Graphs*

To measure the steepness of a straight line, we need to define the term **slope**. We can draw a right-angled triangle with its hypotenuse (the side opposite the right-angle) along each line as shown in the diagram. The slope of a line is a measure of the ratio of the vertical **rise** to the horizontal **run**.

> **REMARKS**
> The slope of a line may also be referred as the **gradient**.

$$\text{Slope of a line} = \frac{\text{Rise}}{\text{Run}} = \frac{\text{Vertical change}}{\text{Horizonal change}}$$

A Positive Slopes

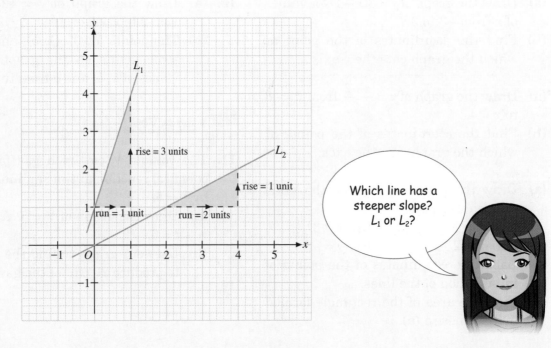

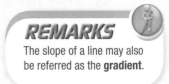

For the lines L_1 and L_2, we work out the respective slopes as follows:

Rise of $L_1 = 4 - 1$
$= 3$

Rise of $L_2 = 2 - 1$
$= 1$

Run of $L_1 = 1 - 0$
$= 1$

Run of $L_2 = 4 - 2$
$= 2$

Slope of $L_1 = \dfrac{\text{Rise of } L_1}{\text{Run of } L_1}$

$= \dfrac{3}{1}$

$= 3$

Slope of $L_2 = \dfrac{\text{Rise of } L_1}{\text{Run of } L_1}$

$= \dfrac{1}{2}$

Since $3 > \dfrac{1}{2}$, the line L_1 is steeper than the line L_2.

Observe that as we move along the x-axis from left to right, the respective y-coordinate increases in value for both lines L_1 and L_2. We say that the graphs are **increasing** and their slopes are **positive**.

B Negative Slopes

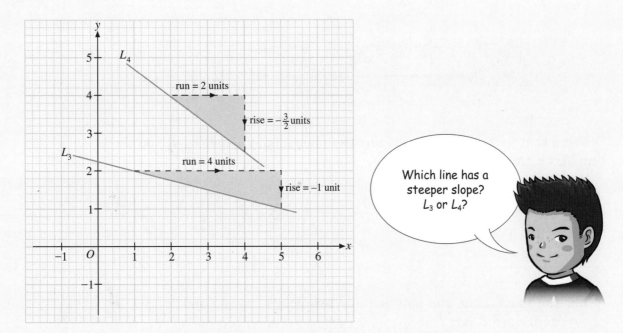

The diagram above shows two lines with **negative** slopes. For such lines, as we move along the x-axis from left to right, their respective y-coordinate decreases in value. These graphs are said to be **decreasing**.

For the lines L_3 and L_4, we work out the respective slopes as follows:

Rise of $L_3 = -1$
Run of $L_3 = 4$

Slope of $L_3 = \dfrac{\text{Rise of } L_3}{\text{Run of } L_3}$

$= \dfrac{-1}{4}$

$= -\dfrac{1}{4}$

Rise of $L_4 = -\dfrac{3}{2}$

Run of $L_4 = 2$

Slope of $L_4 = \dfrac{\text{Rise of } L_4}{\text{Run of } L_4}$

$= \dfrac{-\dfrac{3}{2}}{2}$

$= -\dfrac{3}{4}$

C Special Cases

In the diagram below, the line L_5 is a horizontal line and L_6 is a vertical line. It is not possible for us to draw triangles as before to find the slopes of these lines.

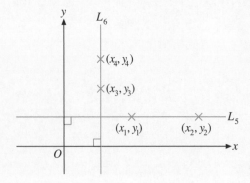

Observe that for the run between any two points, (x_1, y_1) and (x_2, y_2), on the line L_5, we have $y_1 = y_2$.

$\therefore$ rise of $L_5 = y_2 - y_1$

$= 0$

Slope of $L_5 = \dfrac{0}{\text{Run of } L_5}$

$= 0$

As for the line L_6, the run between any two points, (x_3, y_3) and (x_4, y_4), is always zero since $x_3 = x_4$.

Slope of $L_6 = \dfrac{\text{Rise of } L_6}{0}$ which is undefined.

We can conclude as follows:

- The slope of a horizontal line is zero.
- The slope of a vertical line is undefined.

Example **4**

The vertices of $\triangle ABC$ are $A(1, 1)$, $B(-2, 3)$, and $C(3, 3)$. Find the slopes of the sides of $\triangle ABC$.

Solution

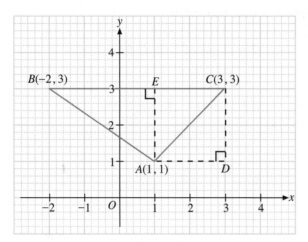

Draw a right-angled $\triangle ABE$ along AB as shown.

Rise of side $AB = -AE$
$$= -2$$

Run of side $AB = BE$
$$= 3$$

$\therefore$ slope of side $AB = \dfrac{\text{rise of } AB}{\text{run of } AB}$

$$= \dfrac{-2}{3}$$

$$= -\dfrac{2}{3}$$

Draw a right-angled $\triangle ACD$ along AC as shown.

Rise of side $AC = CD$
$$= 2$$

Run of side $AC = AD$
$$= 2$$

$\therefore$ slope of side $AC = \dfrac{\text{rise of } AC}{\text{run of } AC}$

$$= \dfrac{2}{2}$$

$$= 1$$

Since the y-coordinates of the points B and C are equal, BC is a horizontal line.
$\therefore$ slope of side $BC = 0$.

Try It! 4

The vertices of $\triangle PQR$ are $P(-2, -1)$, $Q(3, -1)$, and $R(1, 2)$. Find the slopes of the sides of $\triangle PQR$.

Example 5

(a) Plot the points $A(-1, -4)$, $B(0, -2)$, and $C(3, 4)$ on a coordinate plane, and draw the straight line, L, that passes through the three points.

(b) Find the slope of the line L using the points
  (i) A and B,   **(ii)** B and C,   **(iii)** A and C.

(c) What do you observe about the slope of line L found in **(b)**?

Solution

(a) The straight line graph which passes through the three points is shown below.

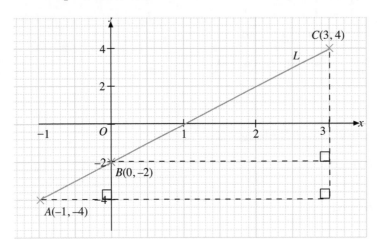

(b) (i) Slope of $AB = \dfrac{\text{Rise of } AB}{\text{Run of } AB}$

$= \dfrac{-2 - (-4)}{0 - (-1)}$

$= \dfrac{2}{1}$

$= 2$

(ii) Slope of $BC = \dfrac{\text{Rise of } BC}{\text{Run of } BC}$

$= \dfrac{4 - (-2)}{3 - 0}$

$= \dfrac{6}{3}$

$= 2$

(iii) Slope of $AC = \dfrac{\text{Rise of } AC}{\text{Run of } AC}$

$= \dfrac{4 - (-4)}{3 - (-1)}$

$= \dfrac{8}{4}$

$= 2$

(c) The slope of the line L which passes through A, B, and C can be found using any two of the given points on the line, that is

slope of AB = slope of BC = slope of AC.

REMARKS

Since it is the same using any triangle on a line to get its slope, it would be easier to use those whose points have whole number coordinates.

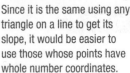

Note: As the slope of a straight line found using any two points on the line has the same value, we said that the slope of a straight line is uniform.

Try It! 5

(a) Draw a straight line which passes through the points $E(-2, 5)$, $F(0, 1)$, $G(1, -1)$, and $H(3, -5)$ on a coordinate plane.

(b) Find the slope of the line using the points
 (i) E and G,
 (ii) F and H,
 (iii) G and H,
 (iv) E and H.

EXERCISE 10.3

BASIC PRACTICE

1. Find the slopes of the lines L_1, L_2, and L_3 in the following diagram.

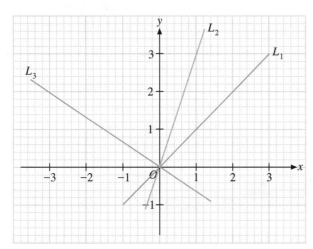

2. Find the slopes of the lines L_4, L_5, and L_6 in the following diagram.

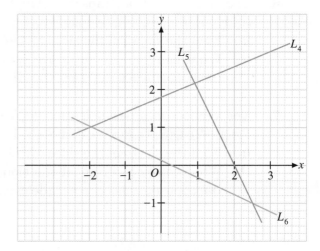

3. Find the slopes of the sides of $\triangle ABC$ in the following diagram.

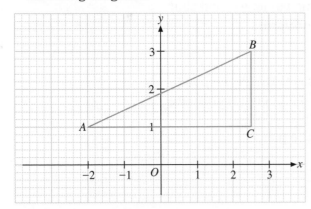

4. In each case, draw the line through the given pair of points and find its slope.
   (a) $O(0, 0)$, $A(2, 2)$
   (b) $B(1, 2)$, $C(3, 3)$
   (c) $D(-2, 3)$, $E(2, 1)$
   (d) $F(-5, 2)$, $G(1, -3)$
   (e) $H(-2, 1)$, $I(3, 1)$
   (f) $J(-3, 2)$, $K(-3, -2)$

5. The vertices of $\triangle ABC$ are $A(-2, 0)$, $B(3, -2)$, and $C(0, 2)$. Find the slopes of the sides of $\triangle ABC$.

6. The vertices of a trapezoid $ABCD$ are $A(-1, -1)$, $B(7, 3)$, $C(4, 6)$, and $D(0, 4)$.
   (a) Find the slopes of the sides of $ABCD$.
   (b) What can you say about the slopes of the opposite sides of a trapezoid?

7. The vertices of a parallelogram $PQRS$ are $P(-4, -2)$, $Q(5, 1)$, $R(6, 4)$, and $S(-3, 1)$.
   (a) Find the slopes of the sides of $PQRS$.
   (b) What can you say about the slopes of the opposite sides of a parallelogram?

8. The following diagram shows a straight line passing through the points $P(-4, 8)$, $Q(a, 5)$, $R(3, b)$ and $S(4, -4)$.

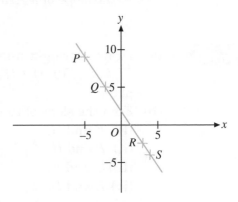

   (a) Find the slope of the line.
   (b) Find the values of a and b.

 MATH@WORK

9. The distance y meters of a boy at time t seconds from a fixed point F is given by
$$y = 3 + 0.5t \text{ for } 0 \leqslant t \leqslant 10.$$
   (a) Draw the graph of $y = 3 + 0.5t$ for $0 \leqslant t \leqslant 10$.
   (b) Find the slope of the graph.
   (c) What is the physical meaning of the slope in this case?

10. The volume V cm^3 of a piece of melting ice at time t minutes is given by
$$V = 24 - 3t \text{ for } 0 \leqslant t \leqslant 8.$$
   (a) Draw the graph of $V = 24 - 3t$ for $0 \leqslant t \leqslant 8$.
   (b) Find the slope of the graph.
   (c) What is the physical meaning of the slope in this case?
   (d) What is the physical meaning of 24 in the equation $V = 24 - 3t$?

 BRAINWORKS

11. (a) Name three public buildings that have access ramps at the entrance for people in wheelchairs.
   (b) Do an online search of the maximum slope for wheelchair ramps.
   (c) Based on your result in **(b)**, find the horizontal run required for a vertical rise of 0.5 m.

Cartesian Coordinate System

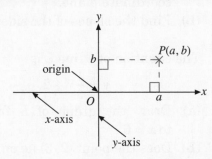

Coordinates of P = Ordered pair (a, b)

x-coordinate

y-coordinate

Graph

A graph connects a set of ordered pairs on a coordinate plane.

Linear Graph

The graph of an equation that is a straight line is called a linear graph.

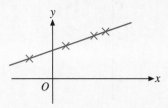

Linear Relationship

Two variables, x and y, are in a linear relationship if the graph of the equation in x and y is a straight line.

Slope

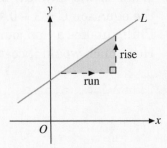

Slope of the line $L = \dfrac{\text{Rise}}{\text{Run}}$

Signs of Slope

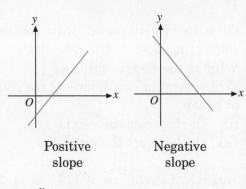

Positive slope   Negative slope

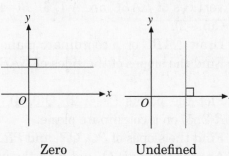

Zero slope   Undefined slope

1. Refer to the given diagram.

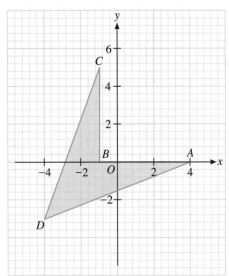

   (a) State the coordinates of A, B, C, and D.
   (b) Which point is in the second quadrant?
   (c) Find the slopes of
      (i) AB,
      (ii) BC,
      (iii) CD.
   (d) State the equations of the lines
      (i) AB,   **(ii)** BC.

2. **(a)** On a coordinate plane, draw the line connecting $A(-3, 5)$ and $B(4, -2)$.
   (b) What is the slope of the line?
   (c) Write down the coordinates of the point at which
      (i) the line cuts the x-axis.
      (ii) the line cuts the y-axis.

3. The vertices of $\triangle ABC$ are $A(1, 6)$, $B(-4, 3)$, and $C(5, -2)$.
   (a) Draw $\triangle ABC$ on a coordinate plane.
   (b) Find the slopes of the sides of $\triangle ABC$.

4. **(a)** Plot the points $P(-4, 2)$, $Q(0, 4)$, and $R(2, 5)$ on a coordinate plane.
   (b) Find the slopes of PQ, QR, and PR.
   (c) Are the points P, Q, and R on the same straight line?
   (d) Find the slopes of the lines OP and OQ, where O is the origin.

5. The vertices of a quadrilateral $ABCD$ are $A(-3, -2)$, $B(-5, 1)$, $C(2, 3)$, and $D(4, 0)$.
   (a) Draw the quadrilateral $ABCD$ on a coordinate plane.
   (b) Find the slopes of the sides of $ABCD$.

6. The equation of a line L is
   $$y = \frac{1}{3}x + 2.$$
   (a) Draw the graph of L from $x = -6$ to $x = 6$.
   (b) Does the point $(2, 3)$ lie on the line L?
   (c) Find the slope of the line L.
   (d) State the coordinates of the point at which the line L cuts the y-axis.

7. The cost, $\$C$, for traveling a distance of x miles on a taxi in Garden City, is given by $C = 3 + 0.4x$.
   (a) Draw the graph of $C = 3 + 0.4x$ for values of x between 0 and 10.
   (b) Find the slope of the graph.
   (c) What is the physical meaning of the slope in this case?
   (d) What is the physical meaning of 3 in the equation $C = 3 + 0.4x$?
   (e) Philip makes a taxi journey of 7 miles. How much would it cost him?

EXTEND YOUR LEARNING CURVE

Global Positioning System

Global Positioning System (GPS) is a satellite navigation system used to locate the position of an object that bears a GPS receiver. It has wide applications in defence, navigation, and tracking. Find out more about GPS on the Internet and briefly describe how it relates to the coordinate system.

WRITE IN YOUR JOURNAL

1. Describe in your own words how the slope of a straight line can be found.

2. Discuss two quantities which have a linear relationship in your daily life.

11 INEQUALITIES

Playing

LET'S LEARN TO...

1. understand the basic properties of inequalities
2. solve simple linear inequalities, such as $ax + b > c$
3. compare and constrast the solutions of inequalities with different inequality signs such as $x > 3$ and $x \geqslant 3$
4. represent the solution of a linear inequality on a number line
5. formulate simple problems into inequalities
6. apply linear inequalities to solve word

One of the main attractions of an amusement park is the thrill rides. However, some rides have minimum height or maximum weight requirements. The situation is an example of mathematical inequalities that exists in everyday life.

11.1 *Solving Simple Inequalities*

A   Idea of Inequality

Wow! There's a big sale at the bookshop. Some of the books cost $3 each.

That's wonderful! How many books can I buy for $10 at $3 per book?

REMARKS

An inequality is a statement which indicates that one quantity is less than or greater than another. You can write inequalities using symbols such as "$<$", "$>$", "$\leqslant$", or "$\geqslant$".

Suppose Vicky can buy x books at $3 each with $10. Then the total cost of the books bought must not exceed $10. Thus $\$3x$ is less than $10. Mathematically, we write

$$3x < 10.$$

We call "$3x < 10$" an **inequality**. It is a linear inequality with one variable x. All values of x that satisfy the inequality are called the **solutions** of the inequality.

RECALL

$a < b$ means a is on the left of b on the number line.

What are the values of x that will satisfy the above inequality?
By inspection,

$$3 \times 1 = 3 < 10, \ 3 \times 2 = 6 < 10, \ 3 \times 3 = 9 < 10 \text{ but } 3 \times 4 = 12 > 10.$$

Therefore, $x = 1, 2,$ and 3 are solutions of the inequality $3x < 10$ but $x = 4$ is not a solution.

So Vicky can buy either 1, 2, or 3 books.

MATH BITS

Thomas Harriot (1560–1621) was the person who introduced the symbols, "$<$" and "$>$". Pierre Bouguer introduced the symbols "$\leqslant$" and "$\geqslant$" much later.

B   Solving an Inequality

Unlike the equation $3x = 10$ which has only one solution, $x = \dfrac{10}{3}$, the inequality $3x < 10$ has more than one solution. Through Class Activity 1, we will learn how to solve a simple inequality of the form $ax < b$.

Objective: To explore the properties of simple inequalities.

Questions

1. Copy and complete the following table. Fill the "solutions" column in your table from the following selection of numbers.

$$-3, 0, 2, 7.9, 8, 8\frac{1}{4}, 10, 13$$

Inequality	Read as	Solutions
$x \leq 8$	x is less than or equal to 8	
$x < 8$		
$x \geq 8$		
$x > 8$	x is greater than 8	

2. Fill in each ⬚ with either ">" or "<" to make it a true statement.

(a) $8 > 6$, $\quad 5 \times 8 \;\boxed{}\; 5 \times 6$

(b) $8 > 6$, $\quad \dfrac{1}{2} \times 8 \;\boxed{}\; \dfrac{1}{2} \times 6$

(c) $9 \;\boxed{}\; -18$, $\quad 2 \times 9 \;\boxed{}\; 2 \times (-18)$

(d) $9 \;\boxed{}\; -18$, $\quad \dfrac{2}{3} \times 9 \;\boxed{}\; \dfrac{2}{3} \times (-18)$

(e) $-21 \;\boxed{}\; 14$, $\quad 3 \times (-21) \;\boxed{}\; 3 \times 14$

(f) $-21 \;\boxed{}\; 14$, $\quad \dfrac{4}{7} \times (-21) \;\boxed{}\; \dfrac{4}{7} \times 14$

(g) $-20 \;\boxed{}\; -15$, $\quad 4 \times (-20) \;\boxed{}\; 4 \times (-15)$

(h) $-20 \;\boxed{}\; -15$, $\quad \dfrac{1}{5} \times (-20) \;\boxed{}\; \dfrac{1}{5} \times (-15)$

(i) If $a > b$ and $k > 0$, then $ka \;\boxed{}\; kb$.

(j) If $a < b$ and $k > 0$, then $ka \;\boxed{}\; kb$.

Since $8 > 6$, $\qquad 8 - 6 > 0$. $\qquad$ Subtract 6 from both sides.

We know that $5 > 0$ and the product of two positive numbers is positive.
Hence, $\qquad 5(8 - 6) > 0$.

Using distributive property,
$$5 \times 8 - 5 \times 6 > 0.$$
Hence, $\qquad 5 \times 8 > 5 \times 6.$ $\qquad$ Add 5×6 to both sides.

In general, if $\qquad a > b,$
then $\qquad a - b > 0.$

If $k > 0$, we have
$$k(a - b) > 0,$$
that is $\qquad ka - kb > 0$
$$\therefore \; ka > kb$$

The same argument works when $a < b$ and $k > 0$. Thus, we have

REMARKS

If $a < b$, then $b - a > 0$.
If $k > 0$, we have
$$k(b - a) > 0,$$
that is $kb - ka > 0$
$$kb > ka$$
$$\therefore \; ka < kb$$

> If $a > b$ and $k > 0$, then $ka > kb$.
> If $a < b$ and $k > 0$, then $ka < kb$.

The above property also holds when $a \geqslant b$ and $a \leqslant b$.

To solve an inequality of the form $ax > b$, $ax < b$, $ax \geqslant b$ or $ax \leqslant b$, where $a > 0$, we can use the above property.

In general, a variable x in an inequality can be a real number. For example, the solution of $x > c$ includes all the real numbers greater than c. Similarly, the solution of $x < c$ includes all the real numbers less than c.

DISCUSS

Why are the solutions of $x \leqslant b$ different from the solutions of $x < b$?

Example 1 $\qquad$ Solve the inequality $4x < 28$.

Solution $\qquad\qquad 4x < 28$

Multiplying both sides by $\dfrac{1}{4}$, we have

$\dfrac{1}{4}$ and 4 are reciprocal of each other. The product of a number and its reciprocal yields 1.

$$\frac{1}{4}(4x) < \frac{1}{4} \times 28$$

$$\therefore \; x < 7$$

The solution includes all the real numbers less than 7.

Try It! 1 $\qquad$ Solve the inequality $3x < 36$.

REMARKS

This argument shows that if $4x < 28$, then $x < 7$. To show that $x < 7$ implies $4x < 28$, we can just multiply both sides of $x < 7$ by 4. Thus, every $x < 7$ satisfies $4x < 28$.

Example 2 Solve the inequality $\frac{3}{5}x \geqslant -9$.

Solution

$$\frac{3}{5}x \geqslant -9$$

Multiplying both sides by $\frac{5}{3}$, we have $\frac{5}{3}$ and $\frac{3}{5}$ are reciprocal of each other.

$$\frac{5}{3}\left(\frac{3}{5}x\right) \geqslant \frac{5}{3} \times (-9)$$

$$\therefore \ x \geqslant -15$$

The solution includes all the real numbers greater than or equal to -15.

Try It! 2 Solve the inequality $\frac{2}{7}x \geqslant -6$.

EXERCISE 11.1

BASIC PRACTICE

1. Determine whether the value of x in each case is a solution of the given inequality.
   (a) $x < 6$; $x = 3$
   (b) $x \geqslant 4$; $x = 2$
   (c) $x > -5$; $x = -1$
   (d) $x \leqslant -3$; $x = -3$
   (e) $x \geqslant 0$; $x = -8$
   (f) $x < 7$; $x = 7$
   (g) $2x < -1$; $x = -\frac{3}{2}$
   (h) $\frac{1}{4}x > -5$; $x = \frac{1}{3}$

2. Solve the following inequalities.
   (a) $2x < 10$ (b) $3x > 18$
   (c) $4x \leqslant 6$ (d) $5x \geqslant 11$
   (e) $6x > -9$ (f) $8x \leqslant -30$
   (g) $14x \geqslant -35$ (h) $15x < -40$

FURTHER PRACTICE

3. Solve the following inequalities.
   (a) $\frac{1}{2}x > 5$ (b) $\frac{1}{3}x < -4$
   (c) $\frac{5}{8}x < -\frac{15}{4}$ (d) $\frac{11}{9}x \leqslant \frac{22}{27}$
   (e) $\frac{12}{7}x \geqslant -3$ (f) $\frac{4}{15}x > 2\frac{2}{3}$

4. Solve the following inequalities.
   (a) $x + x \geqslant 3$
   (b) $5x - 2x < -24$
   (c) $\frac{1}{2}x + \frac{1}{3}x > -10$
   (d) $\frac{4}{5}x - \frac{2}{7}x \leqslant 1 + \frac{1}{2}$

MATH@WORK

5. Find the greatest integer x that satisfies each inequality.
   (a) $11x < 36$ (b) $8x \leqslant 72$
   (c) $3x \leqslant -8$ (d) $5x < -30$

44

6. Find the smallest integer x that satisfies each inequality.

    (a) $4x \geqslant 12$

    (b) $\dfrac{2}{3}x > \dfrac{4}{7}$

    (c) $\dfrac{5}{6}x > -\dfrac{7}{3}$

    (d) $\dfrac{9}{4}x \geqslant -\dfrac{15}{2}$

 **BRAIN**WORKS

7. Write down an inequality of the form $ax > b$, where $a \neq 1$, such that its solution is $x > 7$.

8. Write down an inequality of the form $ax \leqslant b$, where $a \neq 1$, such that its solution is $x \leqslant -\dfrac{3}{4}$.

11.2 *More Properties of Inequalities*

We have learned that real numbers can be represented on a number line and how to decide their orders based on their relative positions on the number line.

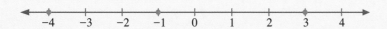

For example,

    -4 is on the left of -1, $\therefore$ -4 is less than -1 and is denoted by $-4 < -1$;
    3 is on the right of -1, $\therefore$ 3 is greater than -1 and is denoted by $3 > -1$.

Therefore, to compare two numbers, we have the following relationship:

> For any two numbers, a and b, one and only one of the following relationships holds:
>
> $$a < b \quad \text{or} \quad a = b \quad \text{or} \quad a > b$$

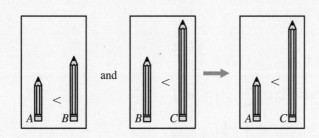

If pencil A is shorter than pencil B, and pencil B is shorter than pencil C, it is therefore obvious that pencil A is shorter than pencil C. Thus, we have the following property:

If $a < b$ and $b < c$, then $a < c$.

Example 3   It is given that $a < 5$. Is $a < 9$?

Solution   Since $a < 5$
and $5 < 9$,
$\therefore \ a < 9$

Try It! 3   It is given that $p < 0$. Is $p < 2$?

CLASS ACTIVITY 2

Objective: To explore other properties of inequalities.

Questions

1. Fill in each ⬜ with either "<" or ">" to make it a true statement.

    (a)   3 ⬜ 5,   3 + 6 ⬜ 5 + 6

    (b)   −9 ⬜ 2,   −9 + 3 ⬜ 2 + 3

    (c)   7 ⬜ 10,   7 − 8 ⬜ 10 − 8

    (d) If $a < b$, then $a + k$ ⬜ $b + k$.

2. **(a)**   2 ⬜ 8,   5 × 2 ⬜ 5 × 8

    (b)   −3 ⬜ −1,   7 × (−3) ⬜ 7 × (−1)

    (c)   −12 ⬜ 6, $\frac{1}{2} \times (−12)$ ⬜ $\frac{1}{2} \times 6$

    (d) If $a < b$ and $k > 0$, then ka ⬜ kb.

3. **(a)**   4 ⬜ 7,   (−3) × 4 ⬜ (−3) × 7

    (b)   −15 ⬜ 10, $\left(-\frac{2}{5}\right) \times (−15)$ ⬜ $\left(-\frac{2}{5}\right) \times 10$

    (c)   −28 ⬜ −14, $\left(-\frac{3}{7}\right) \times (−28)$ ⬜ $\left(-\frac{3}{7}\right) \times (−14)$

    (d) If $a < b$ and $k < 0$, then ka ⬜ kb.

From the results of Class Activity 2, we see that when a number is added to or subtracted from both sides of an inequality, the inequality still holds.

$$\text{If } a < b, \text{ then } a + k < b + k.$$

Since subtracting k is equivalent to adding $-k$, it is not necessary to write the law for subtraction separately.

When both sides of an inequality are multiplied by a non-zero number k, the inequality holds for $k > 0$, but the inequality sign is reversed for $k < 0$.

$$\text{If } a < b \text{ and } k > 0, \text{ then } ka < kb.$$
$$\text{If } a < b \text{ and } k < 0, \text{ then } ka > kb.$$

REMARKS
The same type of argument given at the start of page 43 can be given here to show that these inequalities are true.

The properties are similar for the cases, $a \leq b$, $a > b$, and $a \geq b$. Try to write them down yourself.

Example 4

It is given that $a < b$. Compare the values of the following pairs of numbers and write an inequality statement for each pair.
(a) $a + 3$ and $b + 3$
(b) $\frac{1}{2}a$ and $\frac{1}{2}b$
(c) $-a$ and $-b$

Solution

(a) Since $\quad a < b$,
$$\therefore \ a + 3 < b + 3$$

(b) Since $\quad a < b$ and $\frac{1}{2} > 0$,
$$\therefore \ \frac{1}{2}a < \frac{1}{2}b$$

(c) Since $\quad a < b$ and $-1 < 0$,
$$\therefore \ (-1)a > (-1)b \qquad \text{The inequality sign is reversed.}$$
i.e., $\quad\quad -a > -b$

Try It! 4

It is given that $p < q$. Compare the values of the following pairs of numbers and write an inequality statement for each pair.
(a) $p - 1$ and $q - 1$
(b) $-4p$ and $-4q$
(c) $\frac{1}{5}p$ and $\frac{1}{5}q$

BASIC PRACTICE

1. If $a < 7$, determine whether the following inequalities are true.
   (a) $a < 10$ (b) $a < 2$
   (c) $a + 2 < 9$ (d) $-a < -7$

2. If $p > -5$, determine whether the following inequalities are true.
   (a) $p > -3$ (b) $p > -9$
   (c) $p + 5 > 0$ (d) $-p < -5$

3. Copy and fill in each box with an inequality sign.
   (a) If $a < b$, then $a - 6$ ☐ $b - 6$.
   (b) If $p > q$, then $p + 7$ ☐ $q + 7$.
   (c) If $r \leqslant s$, then $2r$ ☐ $2s$.
   (d) If $x \geqslant y$, then $-\frac{1}{3}x$ ☐ $-\frac{1}{3}y$.

FURTHER PRACTICE

4. Copy and fill in each box with an inequality sign.
   (a) If $a < b$, then
      (i) $4a$ ☐ $4b$,
      (ii) $4a + 3$ ☐ $4b + 3$.

   (b) If $m \geqslant n$, then
      (i) $-m$ ☐ $-n$,
      (ii) $-m + 1$ ☐ $-n + 1$.

5. If $p \leqslant q$, write an appropriate inequality statement for each of the following pairs of numbers.
   (a) $2p - 7$ and $2q - 7$
   (b) $-4 - \frac{1}{5}p$ and $-4 - \frac{1}{5}q$

MATH@WORK

6. (a) If $a < b$ and $c < d$, what is the inequality relationship between
      (i) $a + c$ and $b + c$,
      (ii) $b + c$ and $b + d$,
      (iii) $a + c$ and $b + d$?
   (b) If Mr. and Mrs. Smith's monthly salaries are more than \$4,000 and \$3,500 respectively, what can you say about their combined monthly salary?

BRAIN WORKS

7. If $a < b$ and $c < d$, is it necessary that $a - c < b - d$? If it is not true, give a counterexample.

8. If $a < b$, must a^2 be less than b^2?

11.3 Simple Linear Inequalities

We can apply the properties of inequalities learned in the previous sections to solve simple linear inequalities in one variable, such as

$$3x + 5 < 17 \quad \text{and} \quad 4x - 9 \geqslant 7x + 8.$$

Example 5

Solve the inequality $3x + 5 < 17$.

Solution

(a)
$$3x + 5 < 17$$
$$3x + 5 - 5 < 17 - 5 \qquad \text{Subtract 5 from both sides.}$$
$$3x < 12$$
$$\frac{3x}{3} < \frac{12}{3} \qquad \text{Divide both sides by 3.}$$
$$\therefore \qquad x < 4$$

Try It! 5

Solve the inequality $2x + 3 < 15$.

The solution of an inequality can be represented by an interval on a number line. For example, the number line below shows the solution $x < 4$.

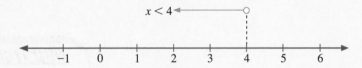

The small **hollow circle** indicates that the solution **does not include** the value $x = 4$.

Example 6

Solve the inequality $2x - 19 \leqslant 7x + 6$ and represent the solution on a number line.

Solution

$$2x - 19 \leqslant 7x + 6$$
$$2x - 19 + 19 \leqslant 7x + 6 + 19 \qquad \text{Add 19 to both sides.}$$
$$2x \leqslant 7x + 25$$
$$2x - 7x \leqslant 7x + 25 - 7x \qquad \text{Subtract 7x from both sides.}$$
$$-5x \leqslant 25$$
$$\frac{-5x}{-5} \geqslant \frac{25}{-5} \qquad \text{Divide both sides by } -5.$$
$$\qquad\qquad\qquad\qquad \text{(Note the reversal of the inequality sign.)}$$
$$\therefore \ x \geqslant -5$$

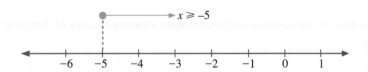

The number line above shows the solution $x \geqslant -5$. The **solid circle** indicates that the solution **includes** the value $x = -5$.

Try It! 6

Solve the inequality $3x - 8 \leqslant 7x + 16$ and represent the solution on a number line.

Example 7

Solve the inequality $\dfrac{2x+3}{4} \geqslant \dfrac{5x-1}{6}$ and represent the solution on a number line.

Solution

$$\dfrac{2x+3}{4} \geqslant \dfrac{5x-1}{6}$$

$$12 \times \dfrac{2x+3}{4} \geqslant 12 \times \dfrac{5x-1}{6}$$ Multiply both sides by 12, as 12 is the LCM of the denominators 4 and 6.

$$3(2x+3) \geqslant 2(5x-1)$$
$$6x+9 \geqslant 10x-2$$
$$6x \geqslant 10x-11$$ Subtract 9 from both sides.
$$-4x \geqslant -11$$ Subtract 10x from both sides.
$$x \leqslant \dfrac{-11}{-4}$$ Divide both sides by −4.
$$x \leqslant \dfrac{11}{4}$$
$$\therefore\ x \leqslant 2\dfrac{3}{4}$$

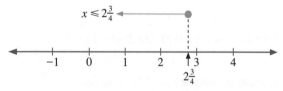

The number line above shows the solution $x \leqslant 2\dfrac{3}{4}$.

DISCUSS

What is the difference between the following inequalities?
- x is greater than 2.
- x is not smaller than 2.

Try It! 7

Solve the inequality $\dfrac{x-4}{5} \geqslant \dfrac{2x+1}{7}$ and represent the solution on a number line.

EXERCISE 11.3

BASIC PRACTICE

1. Solve each of the following inequalities and represent its solution on a number line.
   (a) $x-2 < 7$
   (b) $x+3 \geqslant 4$
   (c) $\dfrac{1}{5}x \leqslant 2$
   (d) $-4x > 12$
   (e) $3x+5 \geqslant 2$
   (f) $7x-13 < 1$
   (g) $9x-2 < 4x+8$
   (h) $6x+7 \geqslant 8x-5$

2. Solve each of the following inequalities and represent its solution on a number line.
   (a) $5(2x + 3) > 4(x - 2) - 13$
   (b) $11 - 2(3x - 7) \leqslant 6(9 - 2x)$
   (c) $2(x + 3) \geqslant 19 - 3(5 - 2x)$
   (d) $\dfrac{1}{3}x + 1 > \dfrac{5}{6}$
   (e) $\dfrac{2x - 1}{5} < \dfrac{x}{2}$
   (f) $\dfrac{2}{7} + \dfrac{1}{4}x \leqslant \dfrac{3}{4}x - \dfrac{5}{7}$
   (g) $\dfrac{2(3x + 1)}{5} \geqslant \dfrac{3(x - 1)}{8}$
   (h) $\dfrac{4x - 5}{3} - \dfrac{1}{4} > \dfrac{1 - x}{9}$
   (i) $\dfrac{x - 3}{2} > \dfrac{4}{13}(2x + 5) - 1$
   (j) $\dfrac{x + 1}{2} - \dfrac{x - 1}{3} \leqslant \dfrac{2x - 7}{4}$

 MATH@WORK

3. The maximum loading of electric current on a power strip is 13 amperes (A). A lamp of $\dfrac{1}{2}$ A is already plugged into it. How many hairdryers of 3A can be plugged into the power strip and turned on without overloading it?

power strip

 BRAIN WORKS

4. Write a linear inequality in the form $ax + b < cx + d$ such that the solution is $x > 8$, where a, b, c, and d are constants.

11.4 *Applications of Simple Inequalities*

The steps for solving a word problem involving an inequality or an equation are similar. The difference is that we set up an inequality instead of an equation. Let us go through some examples to learn the steps involved in solving word problems on inequalities.

Problem-solving Strategy

1. Read the question carefully. Identify the unknown quantity.
2. Use a letter, say x, to represent the unknown.
3. Express some other quantities in the question in terms of x.
4. Set up an inequality using the given information.
5. Solve the inequality.
6. Write down the solution of the problem in words.

Example 8

The maximum load of an elevator is 828 lb. If we assume that the weight of each boy is 92 lb, find the possible numbers of boys who can use the elevator at any one time.

Solution

STEP ❶ Identify what we have to solve. In this case, we have to find the possible numbers of boys who can use the elevator at any one time.

STEP ❷ Let x be the possible number of boys.

STEP ❸ Load of the elevator = Total weight of the boys
= $92x$ lb

STEP 4   Maximum load = 828 lb

$$\therefore \ 92x \leqslant 828$$

STEP 5   Multiplying both sides by $\dfrac{1}{92}$, we have

$$\dfrac{1}{92} \times 92x \leqslant \dfrac{1}{92} \times 828$$

$$x \leqslant 9$$

STEP 6   The possible numbers of boys who can use the elevator at any one time are 1, 2, 3, ... 9.

Note: In this example, x should be a positive integer.

Try It! **8**   The maximum load that a small cart can carry is 40 kg. If the mass of each box of goods is 5 kg, find the possible numbers of boxes the cart can carry at any one time.

Estimate: Is the answer reasonable?
Take $x = 9$:
$9 \times 92 \approx 9 \times 90$
$ = 810$
$ < 828$

Take $x = 10$:
$10 \times 92 \approx 10 \times 90$
$ = 900$
$ > 828$
So, the answer $x \leqslant 9$ is reasonable.

Example **9**   One ham-and-egg sandwich contains 16 g of protein. Suppose the minimum daily intake of a man is 46 g of protein. Find the least whole number of ham-and-egg sandwiches that the man should eat per day to meet his minimum daily protein requirement.

Solution   **STEP 1**   Identify what we have to solve. In this case, we have to find the least number of ham-and-egg sandwiches the man should eat.

STEP 2   Let x be the number of sandwiches the man is required to eat in a day.

STEP 3   Total mass of protein in sandwiches = $16x$ g

STEP 4   Minimum daily protein requirement = 46 g

$$\therefore \ 16x \geqslant 46$$

STEP 5   Multiplying both sides by $\dfrac{1}{16}$, we have

$$\dfrac{1}{16} \times 16x \geqslant \dfrac{1}{16} \times 46$$

$$x \geqslant 2\dfrac{7}{8}$$

STEP 6   The man should eat at least 3 ham-and-egg sandwiches per day.

Estimate: Is the answer reasonable?
A sandwich has 16 g of protein and a man needs 46 g of protein.
$16 \times 3 = 48$, so he would get enough protein from 3 sandwiches.

Try It! **9**   An 8-inch submarine roll contains 70 g of carbohydrate. Suppose the recommended daily carbohydrate intake of a woman is 130 g, find the minimum whole number of submarine rolls that the woman should eat per day to meet her recommended daily carbohydrate intake.

Example 10

A potted plant is 11 in. tall and grows 3 in. a week. After how many complete weeks will it first be taller than 40 in.?

Solution

Let x be the number of weeks after the current date.
The height of the plant after xth week $= (11 + 3x)$ in..

$$11 + 3x > 40$$
$$3x > 29$$
$$x > \frac{29}{3}$$
$$x > 9\frac{2}{3}$$

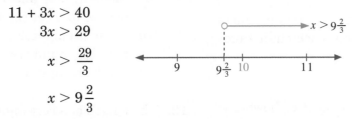

$\therefore$ the smallest integer value of x is 10.
$\therefore$ the plant will first be taller than 40 in. after 10 weeks.

Try It! 10

Sally has $70 in her money box. She saves $40 every month in her money box. What is the minimum number of complete months required in order for Sally to have more than $500 in her money box?

Estimate: Is the answer reasonable?

From 11 in. to 40 in., the plant has to grow another about 30 in. At 3 in. a week, that will take about 10 days.

EXERCISE 11.4

 BASIC PRACTICE

1. Jane works in a store and is paid by the hour. Her hourly rate of pay is $15.
   (a) If she works for x hours, how much does she get?
   (b) What are the possible numbers of hours she has worked if she earns less than $75?

2. The price of a concert ticket is $50.
   (a) Find the total price for x tickets.
   (b) Henry has $200 to spend on buying the concert tickets. Find the possible numbers of concert tickets he can buy.

3. The weight of a book is $1\frac{1}{5}$ lb.
   (a) Find the total weight of x books.
   (b) If the weight of a pile of books is more than 18 lb, find the minimum number of books in the pile.

4. Josh took two math tests. He scored 57 out of 100 on the first test. If his total score has to be at least 120 to pass both tests, what is the minimum points he should score on the next test?

5. Mr. Lee wants to travel more than 130 miles in $2\frac{1}{2}$ hours. What should his average speed of driving be?

6. How many chairs can a carpenter make in 7 hours assuming that each chair takes $\frac{3}{4}$ of an hour to make?

7. The selling price of a bouquet of flowers is $25. Find the minimum number of bouquets of flowers a florist must sell if she wants her total sales to be more than $360.

8. Mr. Haris has six $10 bills and some $20 bills in his wallet. If the total value of the bills is less than $150, how many $20 bills are there?

9. In a chemical reaction, the mass of a product grows 11 g in every hour. The current mass of the product is 46 g. When will the mass of the product first exceed 101 g?

10. Rachael weighed 164 lb. After joining a weight-loss program, she lost 6 lb a month. Find the number of months Racheal has to be in this program if she continues to lose 6 lb a month and wants her weight to become less than 128 lb.

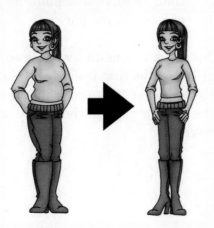

11. A school needs to raise $45,000 to equip a multimedia room. The school has 800 students.
    (a) If every student donates the same amount, how much must each student donate to meet the target?
    (b) If each computer costs $1,700, find the possible numbers of computers that can be bought with $45,000.

12. The length of a rectangle is twice its width. Suppose the width is x cm.
    (a) Express the perimeter of the rectangle in terms of x.
    (b) If the perimeter of the rectangle is 102 cm, find its width.
    (c) If the perimeter of the rectangle is less than 120 cm, what are the possible values of its width?

 **BRAIN** WORKS

13. Company A quotes a rental rate for a car at $45 per day. Company B quotes a rate of $38 per day, but with an initial charge of $75. Find the minimum number of complete days of rental required such that the charges by Company B will become lower than those by Company A.

14. The sum of three consecutive odd numbers is between 90 and 100. Find two possible sets of the three consecutive odd numbers.

Simple Inequalities

(a) Examples of simple inequalities:
$$3x < 6, 2x > 8, 5x \leq 11, ax \geq b,$$
where x is the variable, a and b are constants and $a \neq 0$.

(b) $x = x_0$ is a solution of $3x < 6$
if $\quad 3x_0 < 6$.
For example, $x = 0$ and 1 are solutions.

Basic Properties of Inequalities

1. If $a < b$, then $a + k < b + k$.

2. If $a < b$ and $k > 0$, then $ka < kb$.

3. If $a < b$ and $k < 0$, then $ka > kb$.

Linear Inequalities in One Variable

If $a > 0$, the solution of $ax < b$ is
$$x < \frac{b}{a}.$$
If $a \neq 0$, the solution of $ax + b < c$ is
$$x < \frac{c-b}{a} \quad \text{(if } a > 0\text{)}$$
$$\text{or} \quad x > \frac{c-b}{a} \quad \text{(if } a < 0\text{)}.$$

Solving Word Problems

(a) Understand the word problem, set up an inequality, and solve it.

(b) Note that some solutions require positive integers or positive values.

1. State whether each of the following statements is **true** or **false**. If it is false, give a numerical example to support your claim.
   (a) If $x > 0$, then $x^2 > x$.
   (b) If $x < 0$, then $\dfrac{1}{x} > 0$.
   (c) If $x > 0$, then $-\dfrac{1}{x} < 0$.
   (d) If $a < 0$ and $b < 0$, then $a + b < 0$.
   (e) If $a < b$, then $\dfrac{1}{a} > \dfrac{1}{b}$.

2. If $a < 7$, state which of the following statements are **true**?
   (a) $a < 17$ (b) $-a < -7$
   (c) $3a + 4 < 25$ (d) $a^2 < 49$

3. Solve each of the following inequalities and represent the solution on a number line.
   (a) $3x < 24$ (b) $-5x \geqslant 75$
   (c) $\dfrac{4}{9}x > -\dfrac{8}{3}$ (d) $-\dfrac{1}{7}x \leqslant -\dfrac{10}{21}$

4. Find the greatest integer x that satisfies each inequality.
   (a) $8x \leqslant 32$ (b) $2x + x < -31$

5. Find the smallest integer x that satisfies each inequality.
   (a) $2x > -9$ (b) $\dfrac{2}{3}x + \dfrac{1}{4}x > 15$

6. (a) Simplify $3(5x - 4) + 2(x + 6)$.
   (b) Hence, solve the inequality
   $$3(5x - 4) + 2(x + 6) \geqslant -51.$$

7. Solve each of the following linear inequalities and represent the solution on a number line.
   (a) $4x + 9 < -11$
   (b) $15 - 2x \geqslant 23$
   (c) $7(3x - 5) > 6(2x + 1)$
   (d) $\dfrac{5x - 8}{11} \leqslant 2$

8. Solve the following linear inequalities.
   (a) $\dfrac{1}{5}x - 2(x - 3) < 4$
   (b) $\dfrac{1}{2}x - \dfrac{1}{3}x \geqslant -13$
   (c) $\dfrac{7 - x}{4} \leqslant \dfrac{1 - 3x}{6}$
   (d) $(x - 1)^2 < (x + 9)^2$

9. The Chan family consumes $\dfrac{3}{10}$ kg of rice a day. If the family has 15 kg of rice, what is the maximum number of days the family can consume the rice such that at least 4 kg of it is left?

10. A swimming club charges a monthly membership fee of $20 and an admission fee of $3 per entry. Cathy paid more than $50 to the club last month. Find the minimum number of times she had swum in the club last month.

11. (a) Solve the inequalities
    (i) $8x > 40$, (ii) $6y \leqslant -42$.
    (b) $P(x, y)$ is a point on the coordinate plane such that $8x > 40$ and $6y \leqslant -42$. In which quadrant does the point P lie?

12. The diagram shows a square $OABC$ of side n units. It has a perimeter that is not more than 20 units.
    (a) Express the perimeter of the square in terms of n.
    (b) Find the possible values of n.
    (c) Suppose the square has a maximum possible area, find
    (i) the coordinates of A, B, and C,
    (ii) the slopes of the side AB and the diagonal OB.

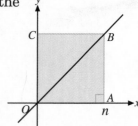

13. Consider the sequence 3, 6, 9, 12, ...
  (a) Find the general term of the sequence.
  (b) Find the 11th term of the sequence.
  (c) What is the largest term of the sequence that is less than 101?

14. A store offers $x\%$ discount on goods such that $4x \leqslant 60$.
  (a) Find the maximum percentage discount.
  (b) A desk lamp and a magazine rack are sold at the maximum percentage discount.
    (i) If the marked price of the desk lamp is $200, find its selling price.
    (ii) If the selling price of the magazine rack is $51, find its marked price.

15. A game center offers two charge schemes, A and B, for using its stations.

  Scheme A: $6 per game
  Scheme B: $0.75 per minute (time of play is counted in seconds)

  Let $y be the charge for a game that lasts t minutes.
  (a) **(i)** Find y under scheme A.
    (ii) Express y in terms of t under scheme B.
  (b) On the same diagram, draw the graphs of the equations involving y obtained in **(a)** for $0 \leqslant t \leqslant 12$.
  (c) What is the minimum duration of a game if the charge on scheme A is not more than that on scheme B?

EXTEND YOUR LEARNING CURVE

Purchasing Power

Ann plans to spend not more than $39 on fish and chickens from a supermarket. The price of a fish is $7 and the price of a chicken is $5. What are the combinations of different numbers of fish and chickens can she buy? Assume that the fish and chickens are bought whole. You may wish to present your answers in a list or table.

WRITE IN YOUR JOURNAL

1. In what way is an inequality different from an equation?

2. Give some examples of real-life situations where you have applied mathematical inequalities.

12 PERIMETERS AND AREAS OF PLANE FIGURES

Playing

LET'S LEARN TO...

1. solve problems involving perimeters and areas of squares, rectangles, and triangles

2. find the circumference and area of a circle

3. find the area of a parallelogram

4. find the area of a trapezoid

5. solve problems involving perimeters and areas of composite plane figures

Greenland, which has a land area of more than 2,100,000 km², is the biggest island in the world. With a long coastline of about 44,087 km, Greenland is located between the Artic Ocean and the North Atlantic Ocean. Do you know how many times is Greenland larger than Alaska in land area?

12.1 Perimeters and Areas of a Square, a Rectangle, and a Triangle

Let us recall the formulas for finding the perimeters and areas of squares, rectangles, and triangles.

Figure	Perimeter	Area
square	Perimeter $= 4x$ where $x =$ the length of a side	Area $= x^2$
rectangle	Perimeter $= 2(l + w)$ where $\quad l =$ length and $\quad w =$ width	Area $= lw$
triangle	Perimeter $= a + b + c$ where $\quad b =$ base and $\quad h =$ height	Area $= \frac{1}{2}bh$

Example 1

The length and width of a rectangle are 9 cm and 4 cm respectively. A square of side x cm has the same area as the rectangle. Find
(a) the area of the rectangle,
(b) the value of x,
(c) the perimeter of the square.

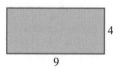

Solution

(a) Area of the rectangle $= 9 \times 4$
$$= 36 \text{ cm}^2$$

(b) Suppose A cm^2 is the area of the square.
Then $\qquad A = x^2$
$$\therefore \; x^2 = 36$$
$$x = \sqrt{36}$$
$$= 6 \quad \text{or} \quad -6 \quad \text{(rejected)}$$

(c) Perimeter of the square $= 4x$
$$= 4 \times 6$$
$$= 24 \text{ cm}$$

Note: In **(b)**, $x = -6$ is not applicable as x represents the length of the square.

Try It! **1** The length and width of a rectangle are 40 cm and 10 cm respectively. A square of side y cm has the same area as the rectangle. Find
(a) the area of the rectangle,
(b) the value of y,
(c) the perimeter of the square.

Example **2** In the figure, $AB = 3$ cm, $AC = 5$ cm, and $CD = 2$ cm. Find
(a) the area of $\triangle ABC$,
(b) the length of BN.

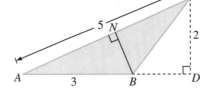

Solution **(a)** Area of $\triangle ABC = \dfrac{1}{2} \times AB \times CD$
$$= \dfrac{1}{2} \times 3 \times 2$$
$$= 3 \text{ cm}^2$$

(b) Area of $\triangle ABC = \dfrac{1}{2} \times AC \times BN$
$$\therefore \dfrac{1}{2} \times 5 \times BN = 3$$
$$BN = \dfrac{6}{5}$$
$$= 1\dfrac{1}{5} \text{ cm}$$

Try It! **2** In the figure, $AB = 5$ cm, $BC = 4$ cm, and $AC = 3$ cm. Find
(a) the area of $\triangle ABC$,
(b) the length of CD.

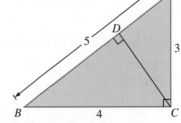

EXERCISE 12.1

 BASICPRACTICE

1. Find the area and the perimeter of each square whose length is given in inches.

(a)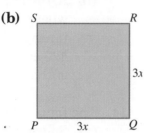

(b)

2. Find the area and the perimeter of each rectangle whose dimensions are given in centimeters.

(a) **(b)**

3. Find the area of each shaded triangle whose dimensions are given in centimeters.

(a)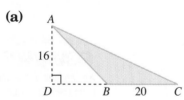

(b)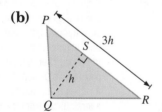

 FURTHERPRACTICE

4. The perimeter of a square is 24 cm. Find
   (a) the length of a side,
   (b) the area of the square.

5. The area of a square is 529 cm². Find
   (a) the length of a side,
   (b) the perimeter of the square.

6. The area of a rectangle is 120 m². If the width is 7.5 m, find
   (a) the length,
   (b) the perimeter
   of the rectangle.

7. The rectangle has a perimeter of 98 cm and its length is two and a half times as long as its width. Find
   (a) the width,
   (b) the area
   of the rectangle.

8. In the figure, $BC = 9$ cm, $AC = 6$ cm, and the area of $\triangle ABC$ is 15 cm². Find the value of
   (a) h,
   (b) k.

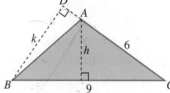

 MATH@**WORK**

9. A picture frame 30 cm by 21 cm has a picture centrally placed in it, leaving a uniform border of 2 cm around it. Find
   (a) the perimeter of the picture,
   (b) the area of the border.

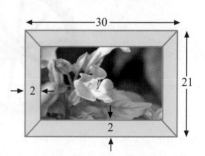

10. A garden *ABCDEF*, as shown in the figure, has a triangular-shaped pond in it. The dimensions are given in meters.
    (a) Find the area of the garden.
    (b) What is the percentage of the garden that is occupied by the pond? Give your answer correct to 1 decimal place.

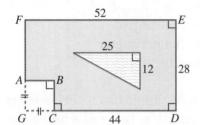

11. A workman has two pieces of wire, each of length 26 m. One piece is to be bent into a square. The other piece is to be bent into a rectangle whose width is 3 m shorter than its length.
    (a) What is the length of a side of the square?
    (b) What are the dimensions of the rectangle?
    (c) Which shape has the greater area?

 **BRAIN** WORKS

12. Draw two triangles whose areas are 12 cm² each.

13. (a) Find the prime factorization of 420.
    (b) A rectangle measures *x* cm by *y* cm, where *x* and *y* are relatively prime integers. The area of the rectangle is 420 cm². Find two possible dimensions of the rectangle.

14. The figure shows a square *ABCD*.
    (a) Suggest how you can draw two line segments from vertex *A* to divide the area of *ABCD* into three equal parts.
    (b) Where are the other end points of these segments?

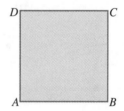

12.2 *Circumference and Area of a Circle*

A **circle** is an important shape in the field of geometry. Let us first look at the definition of a circle and its parts.

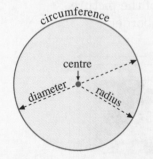

A circle is a shape with all points having the same distance from a given point, the **center**. Some real-life examples of a circle are a wheel and the surface of a coin. The **radius** of a circle is the distance from the center of a circle to any point on its edge. The spoke of a wheel is a real-life example of a radius.

The **diameter** of a circle is the distance across the circle through the center. Thus, the diameter of a circle is twice as long as the radius. It is the largest distance between any two points on the circle.

Diameter = 2 × Radius

The perimeter or the distance around the edge of the circle is called the **circumference**. In the following class activity, we will see how the circumference and the area of a circle is related to its radius and diameter.

 **CLASS ACTIVITY 1**

Objective: To explore the formulas for the circumference and area of a circle using Sketchpad.

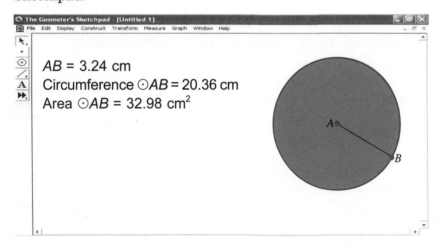

Tasks

(a) Use the **Compass** tool to create a circle with center A.

(b) Use the **Segment** tool to construct a radius from center A to a point B on the circle.

(c) Select the points A and B. Then select **Measure | Distance**.

(d) Select the circle. Then select **Measure | Circumference**.

(e) Select center A. Then select **Construct | Circle Interior** to shade the circle.

(f) Select the shaded circle. Then select **Measure | Area** to calculate the area of the circle.

(g) Repeat the steps with additional circles. Record the radius, circumference, and area of each circle.

Questions

1. Determine the diameter of each circle.

2. Find the ratio of the circumference to the diameter for each circle. What do you observe?

3. Determine the square of the radius of each circle.

4. Find the ratio of the area to the square of the radius for each circle. What do you observe?

From Class Activity 1, we observe that the ratio of the circumference of a circle to the diameter is a fixed constant for any circle. This fixed constant is the same as the ratio of the area of a circle to the radius squared. In Questions 2 and 4 of Class Activity 1, the values of both the ratios are approximately equal to 3.14159.

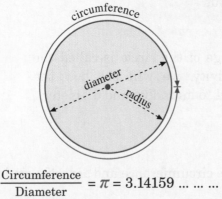

$$\frac{\text{Circumference}}{\text{Diameter}} = \pi = 3.14159 \ldots \ldots \ldots$$

The value of this ratio is actually an irrational number which is represented by the Greek letter π (pronounced as "pi"). The value of π is approximately 3.14159265358979323846.

We can express the relationships discovered in Class Activity 1 as

$$\frac{C}{d} = \pi \quad \text{or} \quad \frac{C}{2r} = \pi$$

and
$$\frac{A}{r^2} = \pi$$

where C is the circumference,
$\quad A$ is the area,
$\quad d$ is the diameter, and
$\quad r$ is the radius
of a circle.

Thus, we have the following formulas for circles:

- Circumference of a circle = πd
$$= 2\pi r$$
- Area of a circle = πr^2

Note:
- The value 3.14 or $\frac{22}{7}$ is often used as an approximation of π in calculations.
- With the use of computers, π has been calculated to over one trillion digits past the decimal point.

In Class Activity 1, we found the ratio of the area, calculated by The Geometer's Sketchpad, to the square of the radius to show that the result is π. Why did we use the square of the radius? To better understand how the formula for the area of the circle is derived, let us try the following class activity.

Objective: To derive the formula for the area of a circle.

Tasks

(a) Draw a circle on a piece of card or paper. The exact size does not matter; for instance you may draw a circle with a radius of 5 cm.

(b) Use your protractor to divide the circle into 12 equal sectors or wedges. Divide just one of the sectors into two equal parts. You now have 13 sectors. Number each sector from 1 to 13.

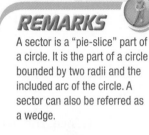

REMARKS

A sector is a "pie-slice" part of a circle. It is the part of a circle bounded by two radii and the included arc of the circle. A sector can also be referred as a wedge.

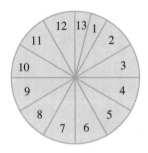

(c) Cut out the 13 sectors using the scissors.

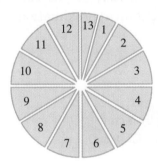

(d) Rearrange the 13 sectors as follows (you can glue them onto a piece of paper).

Now the shape resembles a rectangle as shown below.

(e) What are the approximate width and length of the rectangle formed? Notice that its width is the radius of the circle and its length is half of the curved parts along the edge of the circle. In other words, the length is half the circumference of the original circle. We have learned that "circumference = 2 × π × radius", so the length of the rectangle is π × radius.

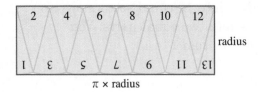

π × radius

Hence, the area of the rectangle above is

$$(\pi \times \text{radius}) \times \text{radius} \text{ or } \pi r^2.$$

Do you remember where this rectangle comes from?

Thus, the area of the circle = πr^2.

(f) Measure the length of this rectangle as accurately as you can using a ruler. Divide by the radius (5 cm) to get an approximation for π.

Record your answer here:

Length of the rectangle	Divide by 5 cm (approximation for π)

Recall that π is about 3.14159. How close was your answer?

Note: You could probably get a more accurate answer if you used a bigger circle or divided your circle into more sectors.

Example 3

The diameter of a circle is 14 cm. Find its circumference and area by taking

(a) π as 3.14,

(b) π as $\dfrac{22}{7}$,

(c) the value of π on your calculator, giving your answer correct to 2 decimal places.

Solution

(a) Circumference = 3.14×14

$= 43.96$ cm

Area = $3.14 \times \left(\dfrac{14}{2}\right)^2$

$= 3.14 \times 7^2$

$= 153.86$ cm^2

Circumference = $\pi \times$ Diameter

Radius = $\dfrac{\text{Diameter}}{2}$

Area = $\pi \times (\text{Radius})^2$

(b) Circumference = $\dfrac{22}{7} \times 14$

$= 44$ cm

Area = $\dfrac{22}{7} \times 7^2$

$= 154$ cm^2

(c) Circumference = $\pi \times 14$

$= 43.98$ cm   (correct to 2 d.p.)

Area = $\pi \times 7^2$

$= 153.94$ cm^2 (correct to 2 d.p.)

Try It! 3

The radius of a circle is 15 cm. By using the value of π on your calculator, find the area and the circumference of the circle, giving your answers correct to 2 decimal places.

Example 4

The circumference of a circle is 6π cm. Find

(a) the radius of the circle,

(b) the area of the circle, leaving your answer in terms of π,

(c) the radius of a circle whose area is half that of the given circle, giving your answer correct to 2 decimal places.

Solution

(a) Let r cm be the radius of the given circle.

Circumference of the circle = $2\pi r$

$2\pi r = 6\pi$

$\therefore r = 3$

The radius of the circle is 3 cm.

(b) Area of the circle $= \pi r^2$

$$= \pi \times 3^2$$
$$= 9\pi \text{ cm}^2$$

(c) Let R cm be the radius of the required circle.

$$\pi R^2 = \frac{1}{2} \times 9\pi$$

$$R^2 = \frac{9}{2}$$

$$\therefore \ R = \sqrt{\frac{9}{2}}$$

$$= 2.12 \quad \text{(correct to 2 d.p.)}$$

The required radius is 2.12 cm.

 Try It! 4

The circumference of a circle is 12π cm. Find
(a) the radius of the circle,
(b) the area of the circle, leaving your answer in terms of π,
(c) the radius of a circle whose area is $\frac{1}{4}$ that of the given circle.

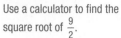

REMARKS

Use a calculator to find the square root of $\frac{9}{2}$.

Estimate: $\frac{9}{2} = 4.5$ and the square root of 4 is 2. So, the answer 2.12 is reasonable.

EXERCISE 12.2

⚙ BASIC PRACTICE

Round the answers to 2 decimal places if they are not exact values.

1. Find the area and the circumference of each circle whose dimensions are given in cm. Leave your answer in terms of π.

(a)

(b)

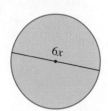

2. Find the area and the circumference of each circle with the given measurement.
(a) Diameter of 22 mm, taking π as 3.14
(b) Radius of 3.5 m, taking π as $\frac{22}{7}$
(c) Radius of 6 in., taking the value of π from your calculator

3. The circumference of a circle is 28.26 cm.
Find
(a) the diameter,
(b) the area
of the circle.

4. The area of a circle is 616 cm². Find
(a) the radius,
(b) the circumference
of the circle.

5. The diameter of a semicircle
is 3.9 m. What is the
perimeter and area of
the semicircle?

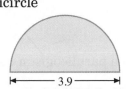

6. The figure is made up of two semicircles.
Taking π as = $\frac{22}{7}$, find its
(a) perimeter,
(b) area.
The unit of length is mm.

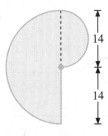

7. The area of a circular pond is 15 m². It is
surrounded by a circular path 0.5 m wide.
Find
(a) the radius of the pond,
(b) the circumference of the pond,
(c) the area of the path.

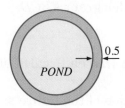

8. There are two pieces of wires, each of
length 66 cm. One wire is bent into a square
and the other wire is bent into a circle. Find
(a) the area of the square,
(b) the area of the circle.

9. A circular dance floor has a radius of 9.5 m.
The floor is to be waxed. A can of wax will
cover an area of 10 m². How many cans of
wax would be needed?

10. The diameter of a bicycle wheel is 19 inches.
What is the distance in miles covered
if the wheel makes 600 complete turns?
(1 mi = 5,280 ft)

11. A lawn sprinkler sprays water over a
distance of x meters in every direction as it
rotates. Mrs. Ford wishes to install one such
lawn sprinkler that will sprinkle at least
80 m² of her lawn. What is the least value
of x that will meet Mrs. Ford's requirement?

BRAIN WORKS

12. Circles, arcs, and curves are often used to
create beautiful designs. In the following
figures, the squares are of the same size
and the curved lines are all arcs of circles.
Which of the following shaded figures has
the greatest area? Which has the greatest
perimeter?

(a)   (b)

(c)   (d)

(e)   (f)

12.3 *Area of a Parallelogram*

A **parallelogram** is a quadrilateral in which the opposite sides are parallel and equal in length. Here are some examples of parallelograms.

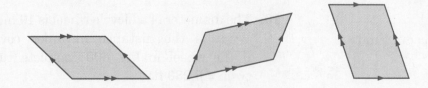

CLASS ACTIVITY 3

Objective: To explore the formula for the area of a paralleogram using Sketchpad.

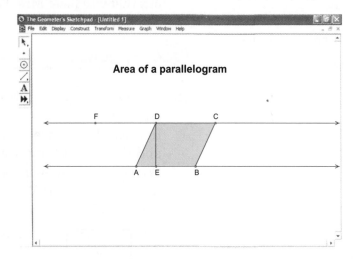

Tasks

(a) Construct two parallel lines AB and FD as shown.

(b) Construct a parallelogram $ABCD$.

(c) Construct the line segment DE perpendicular to AB with E on AB.

(d) Select the points A, B, C, and D in order. Then select **Construct | Quadrilateral Interior** to shade the parallelogram $ABCD$.

(e) Measure the lengths AB, AD, and DE.

(f) Calculate $AB \times AD$ and $AB \times DE$.

(g) Select the shaded parallelogram and then select **Measure | Area** to calculate the area of $ABCD$.

(h) Drag the point D along the line FD and observe the variation of the figure and the numerical values obtained in (e) to (g).

Questions

1. Which numerical values remain the same as the position of D changes?

2. Suggest a formula for the area of a parallelogram.

We have learned that the formula for the area of a rectangle is length × width. We can cut a parallelogram into two pieces and then rearrange them to form a rectangle as shown.

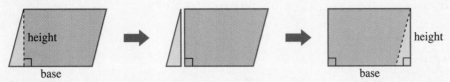

Hence based on the result of Class Activity 3 and the above illustration, we can find the area of a parallelogram as follows:

> Area of parallelogram = Base × Perpendicular height

Example 5

In the figure, $ABCD$ is a parallelogram, $AB = 8$ cm $BC = 6.4$ cm, and $DE = 6$ cm. Find

(a) the area of the parallelogram,
(b) the length of BF.

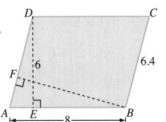

Solution

(a) Area of the parallelogram
$$= \text{Base} \times \perp \text{height}$$
$$= AB \times DE$$
$$= 8 \times 6$$
$$= 48 \text{ cm}^2$$

(b) If we take AD as the base, then BF is the corresponding perpendicular height.
Hence, $AD \times BF = 48$
$$6.4 \times BF = 48$$
$$BF = \frac{48}{6.4}$$
$$= 7.5 \text{ cm}$$
The length of BF is 7.5 cm.

REMARKS

The height and base of a parallelogram must be perpendicular to each other. The symbol "$\perp$" represents **perpendicular**.

Estimate: Is the answer reasonable?
Can you see from the figure that the length of BF would be slightly less than the length of AB?

Try It! 5

In the figure, $PQRS$ is a parallelogram, $RS = 12$ cm, $PS = 6$ cm, and $SM = 5$ cm. Find

(a) the area of the parallelogram,
(b) the length of RN.

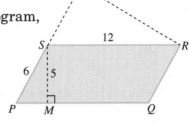

Example 6

In the figure, $ABCD$ is a parallelogram and $AB = 6$ cm. If the area of $\triangle ADE$ is $\frac{3}{4}$ that of parallelogram $ABCD$, find the length of BE.

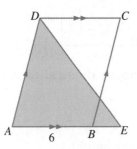

Solution

Let the length of BE be y cm and the height from D to the base AB be h cm.

Area of $\triangle ADE = \frac{3}{4} \times$ Area of $ABCD$

$\therefore \ \frac{1}{2} \times (6 + y) \times h = \frac{3}{4} \times 6 \times h$

$\qquad 6 + y = 2 \times \frac{3}{4} \times 6$

$\qquad 6 + y = 9$

$\qquad\qquad y = 3$

The length of BE is 3 cm.

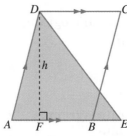

In the figure, $ABCD$ is a parallelogram and $BC = 12$ cm. If the area of $\triangle ABE$ is $\frac{1}{5}$ that of parallelogram $ABCD$, find the length of BE.

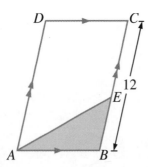

EXERCISE 12.3

BASIC PRACTICE

In this exercise, the unit of length is centimeters (cm) unless stated otherwise.

1. Find the area of each parallelogram.

(a)

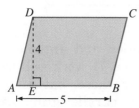

(b)

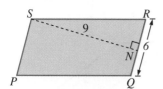

(c)

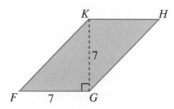

(d)

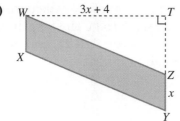

2. In the figure, *ABCD* is a parallelogram. Copy and complete the following table using the given measurements.

	AB	DE	BC	DF	Area of *ABCD*
(a)	10	6	8		
(b)	18		9	12	
(c)	15	8		10	
(d)		9	6		72

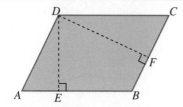

FURTHER PRACTICE

3. In the figure, *ABCD* is a parallelogram of area 20 cm².
   (a) Find the area of *ABEF*.
   (b) If *AB* = 5 cm, find the length of *AF*.

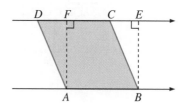

4. In the figure, *ABCD* is a parallelogram, *AB* = 4 cm, and *EF* = 6 cm.
   (a) Find the ratio of the area of △*EFG* to that of *ABCD*.
   (b) If the area of △*EFG* is 24 cm², find the area of *ABCD*.

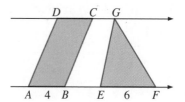

5. In the figure, *ABCD* is a parallelogram and *AD* = 18 cm. The area of △*ABE* is $\frac{5}{6}$ that of *ABCD*.
   (a) Find the length of *DE*.
   (b) If the area of *ABCD* is 450 cm², find the height from *B* to *AD*.

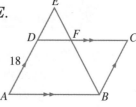

6. In the figure, *ABCD* is a rhombus, *AD* = 13 cm, *AC* = 24 cm, and *BD* = 10 cm. Find
   (a) the measure of ∠*AED*,
   (b) the area of *ABCD*,
   (c) the height from *B* to *AD*.

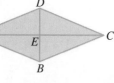

7. In the figure, *ABCD* is a vertical wall 2 m high. It casts a shadow *ABEF* on the ground. *ABEF* is a parallelogram in which the height *EN* is $1\frac{1}{2}$ times the height of the wall.
   (a) Find the height *EN*.
   (b) If the area of the wall is 7.6 m², find the area of the shadow.

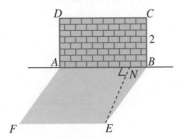

8. In the figure, *ABCD* is a square board of area 3.24 m², *M* is the midpoint of *BC*, and *AM* // *NC*. The shape *AMCN* is cut off from the board. Find
   (a) the lengths of *MC* and *AN*,
   (b) the area of *AMCN*,
   (c) the ratio of the area of △*ABM* to that of *AMCN*.

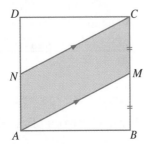

9. The figure shows a square grid in which the area of each small square is 1 cm². Copy the grid and draw two parallelograms on it such that the area of each figure is 6 cm².

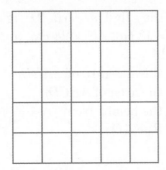

10. The figure shows one way to divide a parallelogram into two equal parts by a line segment. Find as many other ways as possible to divide the parallelogram into two equal parts.

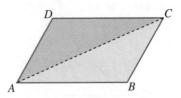

11. The illustration and argument shown on the top of page 71 work well for the given parallelogram there, but do not seem to work with a parallelogram like the one shown below.

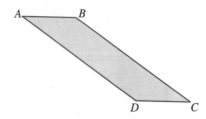

Draw parallelogram *ABCD* on a sheet of paper. Cut this parallelogram into smaller parallelograms. Investigate how you can derive the area of parallelogram *ABCD*. You may take *b* to be the length of the base of parallelogram *ABCD* and *h* to be its corresponding height.

12.4 *Area of a Trapezoid*

A **trapezoid** is a quadrilateral in which only one pair of opposite sides is parallel. Let us cut out two identical trapezoids from a sheet of cardboard or paper, and do the following activity.

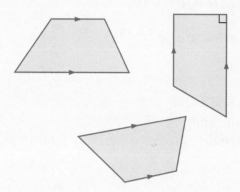

When we place two identical trapezoids together as shown below, we get a parallelogram.

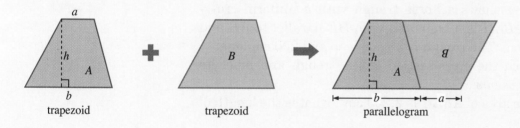

Area of the trapezoid = $\frac{1}{2}$ × Area of the parallelogram formed

$$= \frac{1}{2} \times (a + b) \times h$$

Hence, the formula is as follows:

Area of trapezoid = $\frac{1}{2}$ × Sum of parallel sides × Height

$$= \frac{1}{2} \times (a + b) \times h$$

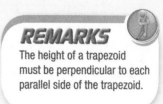

REMARKS
The height of a trapezoid must be perpendicular to each parallel side of the trapezoid.

Example 7

In the figure, *ABCD* is a trapezoid in which *AB* = 15 cm, *DC* = 9 cm, and *DE* = 8 cm. Find the area of *ABCD*.

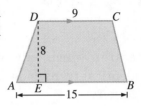

Solution

Area of trapezoid $ABCD = \frac{1}{2} \times (AB + DC) \times DE$

$$= \frac{1}{2} \times (15 + 9) \times 8$$

$$= 96 \text{ cm}^2$$

Try It! 7

In the figure, *PQRS* is a trapezoid in which *PQ* = 14 cm, *SR* = 8 cm, and *PS* = 10 cm. Find the area of *PQRS*.

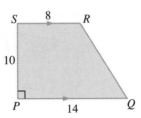

Example 8

The figure shows a horse trough with a uniform cross-section. *ABEH* is a trapezoid with *HE* parallel to *AB* and *AB* = 50 cm. The trough is 36 cm deep and 200 cm long.

(a) Sketch the cross-section of the trough and label its dimensions.

(b) If the area of *ABEH* is 2,250 cm², what is the length of *HE*?

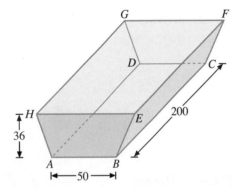

Solution

(a) The cross-section of the trough is shown below.

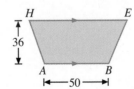

(b) Let the length of *HE* be *x* cm.

$$\frac{1}{2} \times (AB + HE) \times \text{Depth} = \text{Area of } ABEH$$

$$\frac{1}{2} \times (50 + x) \times 36 = 2{,}250$$

$$(50 + x) \times 18 = 2{,}250$$

$$50 + x = 125$$

$$x = 75$$

The length of *HE* is 75 cm.

Try It! 8

The figure shows a shed with a uniform cross-section in which *ABCD* is a trapezoid with *AD* parallel to *BC*, *AB* = 2.5 m, and *BC* = 3 m.

(a) Sketch the cross-section of the shed and label its dimensions.

(b) Find the length of *AD* if the area of *ABCD* is 5.5 m².

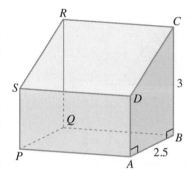

EXERCISE 12.4

BASIC PRACTICE

In this exercise, the unit of length is centimeters (cm) unless stated otherwise.

1. Find the area of each trapezoid.

(a)

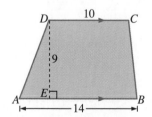

(b)

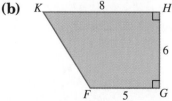

(c)

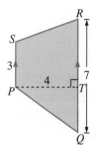

(d)

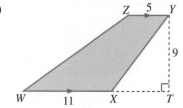

2. In the figure, *ABCD* is a trapezoid. Copy and complete the table using the given measurements.

	a	b	h	Area of *ABCD*
(a)	7	10	8	
(b)	5	9		42
(c)	13		14	231
(d)		11	10	85

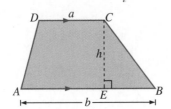

3. In the figure, *ABCD* is a trapezoid, *AE* = 3 in., *EB* = 5 in., *BC* = 5 in., and *AE* is one and a half times as long as *DC*. Find
  (a) the length of *DC*,
  (b) the ratio of the area of *AECD* to that of *ABCD*.

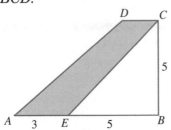

4. In the figure, *ABCD* is a parallelogram, *M* is the midpoint of *AB* and *CD* = 10 cm.
  (a) Find the length of *AM*.
  (b) If the area of *ABCD* is 60 cm², find the area of *AMCD*.

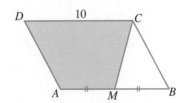

5. In the figure, *ABCD* is a parallelogram, *AN* = 6 cm, *NB* = 12 cm, and *M* is the midpoint of *CD*.
  (a) Find the length of *CM*.
  (b) Find the ratio of the area of *ANMD* to that of *NBCM*.
  (c) If the area of *ABCD* is 200 cm², find the area of *ANMD*.

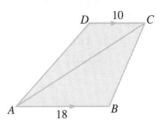

6. In the figure, *ABCD* is a trapezoid, *AB* = 18 cm, and *CD* = 10 cm. The area of △*ACD* = 75 cm². Find the area of *ABCD*.

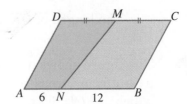

7. The figure shows a window *ABCD*.
  (a) Find the perimeter of the frame.
  (b) Find the area enclosed by the frame.
  (c) If the cost of the frame is $30 per meter and the cost of the glass panel used to fit the window is $150 per square meter, find the cost of making the window.

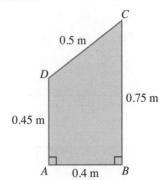

8. In the figure, *ABCD* is a rectangular board that measures 20 ft by 15 ft, and $AE = BF = x$ ft. A trapezoid *CDEF* is cut out from the rectangular board.
    (a) Express *EF* in terms of *x*.
    (b) If the area of *CDEF* is $\frac{3}{4}$ that of *ABCD*, find
        (i) the area of *CDEF*,
        (ii) the value of *x*.

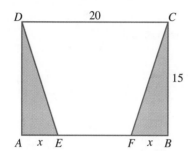

9. Draw two trapezoids whose areas are 12 cm² each.

10. You are given four identical table tops, each in the shape of a trapezoid as shown.
    (a) Sketch the shapes that can be formed if they are arranged together to form a large table.
    (b) Find the perimeter of each shape formed.

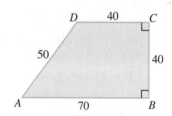

12.5 Perimeters and Areas of Composite Plane Figures

There are many shapes around us that are formed by joining two or more basic geometric shapes. Their perimeters and areas can be found by applying the formulas for the basic shapes.

Example 9   In the figure, $AD = 4$ in., $CE = 6$ in., $AE = 5$ in., and $BE = 3$ in. Find the area of the quadrilateral *ABCD*.

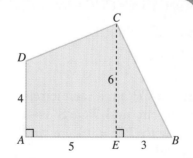

Solution   Area of *ABCD* = Area of trapezoid *AECD* + Area of $\triangle BCE$

$$= \frac{1}{2} \times (4 + 6) \times 5 + \frac{1}{2} \times 3 \times 6$$

$$= 25 + 9$$

$$= 34 \text{ in.}^2$$

In the figure, AD = 6 cm, EC = 5 cm, AE = 4 cm, and EB = 3 cm. Find the area of the quadrilateral $ABCD$.

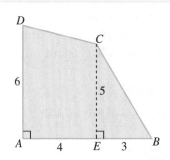

Example 10

A semicircle CDE is mounted on a parallelogram $ABCE$ as shown. If AB = 24 cm, AE = 13 cm, and EF = 12 cm, find
(a) the perimeter,
(b) the area
of the figure.
(Leave your answers in terms of π)

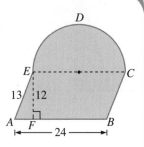

Solution

(a) $EC = AB$ (opp. sides of parallelogram)
    = 24 cm

$\therefore$ radius of semicircle $CDE = \dfrac{1}{2}EC$
                 = 12 cm

Perimeter of the figure
= Length of arc $CDE + EA + AB + BC$
= $\dfrac{1}{2} \times 2\pi \times 12 + 13 + 24 + 13$
= $(12\pi + 50)$ cm

(b) Area of the figure
= Area of semicircle CDE + Area of parallelogram $ABCE$
= $\dfrac{1}{2} \times \pi \times 12^2 + 24 \times 12$
= $(72\pi + 288)$ cm^2

Try It! **10**

In the figure, STP is a semicircle of diameter 30 cm and $PQRS$ is a parallelogram with PQ = 16 cm and SU = 15 cm. Find
(a) the perimeter,
(b) the area
of the figure.
(Take π as 3.142)

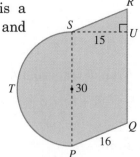

Example **11**

The figure represents a billboard in which $AD = 8$ ft, $BC = 6$ ft, $ME = 4$ ft, and $EN = 3$ ft. Find the area of the billboard.

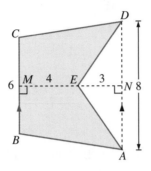

Solution

Area of the billboard
= Area of trapezoid $ABCD$ – Area of $\triangle ADE$
$= \dfrac{1}{2} \times (6 + 8) \times (4 + 3) - \dfrac{1}{2} \times 8 \times 3$
$= 49 - 12$
$= 37$ ft^2

The figure shows the cross-section of a stool in which $AD = 40$ cm, $EH = 30$ cm, $BC = 24$ cm, and $FG = 16$ cm. The distances of BC and FG from the ground are 25 cm and 15 cm respectively. Find the area of the cross-section of the stool.

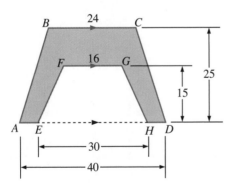

EXERCISE 12.5

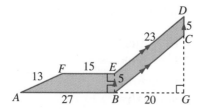 **BASIC PRACTICE**

In this exercise, the unit of length is centimeters (cm) unless stated otherwise.

1. Find the perimeter and area of each figure.

   (a)

   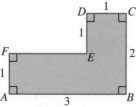

   (b)

   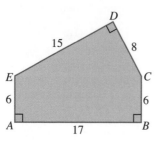

   (c)

   (d)

   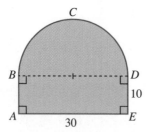

   (Take π as 3.142)

   (e)

   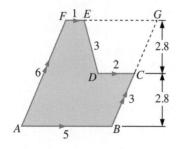

(f)

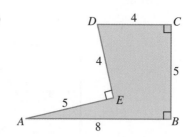

2. Each solid below has a uniform cross-section.
   (i) Sketch and label the cross-section of each solid.
   (ii) Hence, find the perimeter and area of each cross-section.

   (a)

   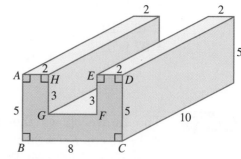

   (b) Take π as 3.142 and give your answer correct to 2 decimal places.

   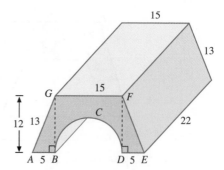

3. Find the area of each figure.

(a)

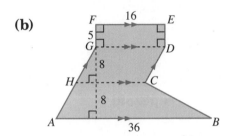

(b)

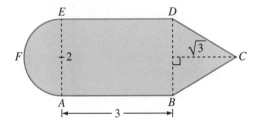

4. In the figure, the shape is made up of a semicircle *AFE*, a rectangle *ABDE*, and an equilateral triangle *BCD*. If *AE* = 2 cm, *AB* = 3 cm, and the height from *C* to *BD* is $\sqrt{3}$ cm, find
(a) the perimeter,
(b) the area
of the shape. Round your answers correct to 2 decimal places.

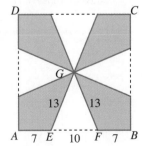

5. In the figure, four identical triangles such as △*GEF* are cut off from a square *ABCD* to form a symmetrical shape. If *EF* = 10 cm, *AE* = *FB* = 7 cm, and *GE* = *GF* = 13 cm, find
(a) the perimeter,
(b) the area
of the shape formed.

6. The figure shows a cross slot on a circular plate where a joystick stands. Each side of the cross and the diameter of the plate are 1.2 in. and 5 in. respectively. Find
(a) the perimeter of the cross,
(b) the area of the cross,
(c) the area of the plate, giving your answer correct to 2 decimal places.

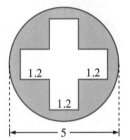

7. The figure shows a cross-section of an iron rail. The top part consists of a rectangle and two semicircles at the ends. The bottom part is a trapezoid. These two parts are joined by a rectangle in the middle. Find
(a) the perimeter,
(b) the area
of the cross-section.
(Take π as 3.142)

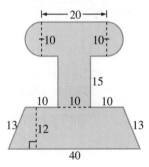

8. Name two items in our daily life which are composite plane figures and describe what shapes each of them is composed of.

9. **(a)** Sketch some closed plane figures with right-angled vertices which you can form using 12 toothpicks.
(b) Suppose each toothpick is 5 cm long, find the perimeter and the area of each figure formed.
(c) What is the maximum area obtained among your figures?

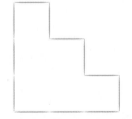

Circle

Diameter = 2 × Radius

Circumference = π × Diameter

= 2 × π × Radius

Area = π × (Radius)²

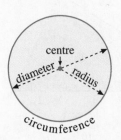

Parallelogram

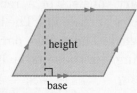

Area = Base × Perpendicular height

The base and height must be perpendicular to each other.

Trapezoid

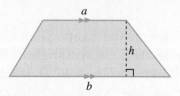

Area = $\frac{1}{2}$ × Sum of parallel sides × Height

= $\frac{1}{2}$ × (a + b) × h

Composite Figures

(a) Using Sum

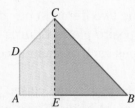

Area of ABCD
= Area of AECD + Area of △BCE

(b) Using Difference

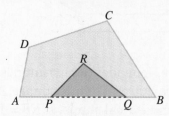

Area of APRQBCD
= Area of ABCD − Area of △PQR

1. In the figure, *ABCD* is a rectangle in which
    AB = 32 cm, *BE* = 13 cm, *EC* = 8 cm, and
    CF = 15 cm. Find
    (a) the perimeter of *ABCD*,
    (b) the area of *ABCD*,
    (c) the area of △*AEF*.

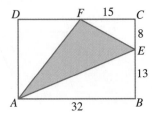

2. A circular pie was cut into five equal pieces.
    Each piece of pie has an area of 63 cm².
    Find the perimeter of each piece of pie,
    giving your answer correct to 2 decimal
    places.

3. In the figure, the shaded region is formed
    by three semicircles with *AB* = 12 cm, and
    BC = 6 cm. Find, in terms of π,
    (a) the perimeter,
    (b) the area
    of the shaded region.

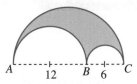

4. The figure shows a semicircle of area
    308 cm² formed by a piece of wire.
    (a) Find the radius of the semicircle.
    (b) Find the perimeter of the semicircle.
    (c) If the semicircle is cut at *A* and bent
         into a circle, find the radius of the
         circle.
    Round your answers to 2 decimal places.

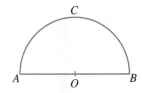

5. In the figure, *ABEF* and *BCDE* are two
    parallelograms. *CD* = 24 cm, *DE* = *EF* = 18 cm,
    and *AC* = 30 cm. Find
    (a) the perimeter of
         the figure,
    (b) the area of the
         figure,
    (c) the perpendicular
         distance from *F* to
         AB.

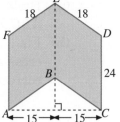

6. The figure shows the innermost line of
    a 400-meter running track, with two
    straight sides of length 100 m each and two
    semicircles of length 100 m each. Find
    (a) *d*, the distance between the two
         straight sides,
    (b) the area enclosed by the track.
    Round your answers to 2 decimal places.

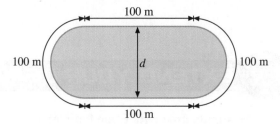

7. The figure shows a solid with a uniform
    cross-section. *CD* = *DE* = *FG* = *GH* = 1 cm,
    AH = 2 cm, and *EF* = 3 cm.
    (a) Sketch and label the cross-section of
         the solid.
    (b) Find the perimeter and area of the
         cross-section.
    (c) If a square has the same area as the
         cross-section of the given solid, what
         is the length of a side of the square?
         Round your answer to 2 decimal places.

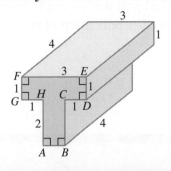

8. The figure shows the internal part of a thermal bottle. The uniform cross-section of the bottle consists of a trapezoid, a rectangle, and a semicircle. $AB = GF = 13$ cm, $CE = 20$ cm, $EF = 25$ cm, $AG = 10$ cm, and $AN = 12$ cm.
   (a) Draw and label the cross-section $ABCDEFG$ of the bottle.
   (b) Find the perimeter and area of the cross-section, giving your answer correct to the nearest integer.

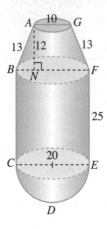

9. In the figure, $ABCD$ is a parallelogram in which $AB = 30$ cm, $AD = 20$ cm, $DE = 10$ cm, and $CN = 27$ cm. Find
   (a) the perimeter of $ABCD$,
   (b) the area of $ABCD$,
   (c) the area of $ABCE$,
   (d) the ratio of the area of $\triangle ADE$ to the area of $ABCE$.

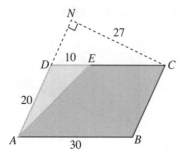

 EXTEND YOUR LEARNING CURVE

Maximum Area with Given Perimeter

1. You are given a piece of wire of a certain length. Your task is to bend the wire into a rectangle with the greatest possible area. What type of rectangle do you think it should be? Explain your answer.

2. Which shape gives the greatest possible area for a given perimeter?

WRITE IN YOUR JOURNAL

Write what you understand about the concept of area and perimeter. Describe the application of the concept of area to a real-life situation.

13 VOLUMES AND SURFACE AREAS OF SOLIDS

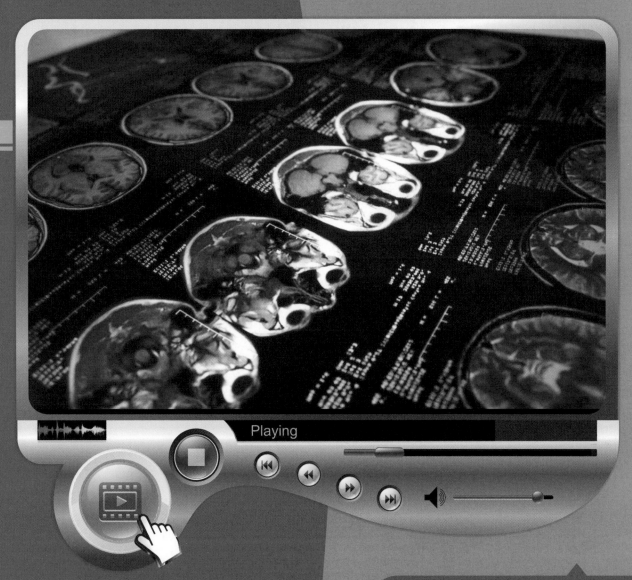

Playing

LET'S LEARN TO...

1. sketch prisms
2. use nets to visualize their surface areas
3. find the volumes and surface areas of prisms
4. convert between cm^2 and m^3, and between cm^3 and m^3
5. solve word problems involving volumes and surface areas of composite solids of prisms

Computed tomography (CT) and magnetic resonance imaging (MRI) can provide slice visualization of an organ in a human body. The slice images are transformed to a 3D view of the organ. These technologies help medical practitioners greatly in diagnosing diseases and planning a treatment for a disease.

13.1 Volumes and Total Surface Areas of a Cube and a Cuboid

A Nets of Cubes, Cuboids, and Other Prisms

We say that a plane figure, such as a rectangle which has length and width, is a **two-dimensional (2D) shape**. A solid, such as a cuboid which has length, width, and height, is a **three-dimensional (3D) shape**. In general, a 3D shape is a solid which encloses a volume. The following solids are some common 3D shapes which we will study in this chapter.

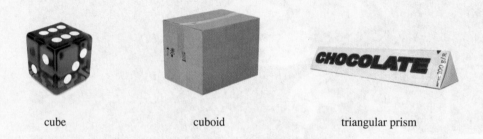

cube   cuboid   triangular prism

Imagine cutting along some edges of a solid and unfolding it to form a plane figure as shown below. The plane figure is called the **net** of the solid.

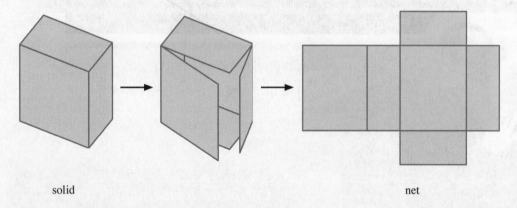

solid   net

> A net of a solid is a plane figure that can be folded up to form the solid.

We can try to cut up different containers along the seams and draw their nets. In Class Activity 1, we will learn how the nets of some basic solids look like.

Objective: To recognize the relationship between nets and the solids formed from the nets.

Tasks
- Copy the given nets on a sheet of paper.
- Cut each of them out along the solid lines.
- Fold each of them up along the dotted lines to form solids.

(a)

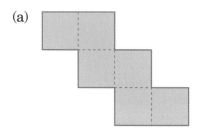

(b)

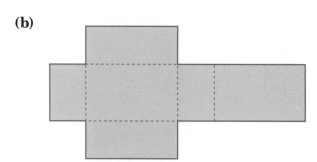

(c)

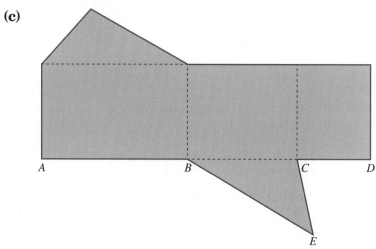

MATH WEB
You can look at the formation of solids from their nets on the following website:
http://www.learner.org/ interactives/geometry/3d_ prisms.html

Questions
1. What is the solid of each net in **(a)**, **(b)**, and **(c)**?
2. What is the relationship between *AB* and *BE*, and between *CD* and *CE* in the figure in **(c)**?
3. State a common property of these solids.
4. Can a solid have different nets? Sketch other possible nets for each of the solids formed.

The solids formed from the nets in Class Activity 1 can be drawn as follows:

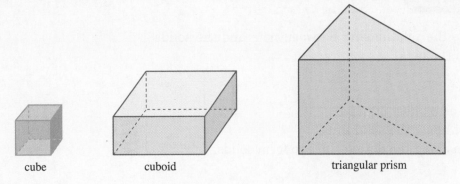

cube   cuboid   triangular prism

B | Cube

The space that a three-dimensional solid occupies is called its **volume** and the area of its net is its **total surface area**.

A cube is a rectangular prism with all its sides equal. From its net, we see that all its six faces are squares of the same area.

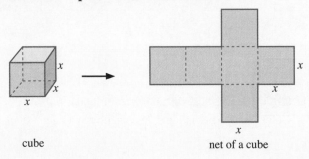

cube   net of a cube

The volume of a cube is the cube of its length and its total surface area is six times the area of one face.

Hence, we have the formulas:

$$\text{Volume of cube} = x^3$$
$$\text{Total surface area of cube} = 6x^2$$
where x is the length of a side of the cube.

Example 1 Find the volume and the total surface area of a cube of side 3 inches.

Solution Volume of the cube = 3^3
            = 27 in.^{3}

Total surface area of the cube = 6×3^2
            = 54 in.^{2}

Try It! 1 Find the volume and the total surface area of a cube of side 4 cm.

Example 2

The total surface area of a cube is 150 cm². Find
(a) the length of a side of the cube,
(b) the volume of the cube.

Solution

(a) Let the length of a side of the cube be x cm.

Thus $6x^2 = 150$
$x^2 = 25$
$x = \sqrt{25}$
$= 5 \quad$ or $\quad -5$ (rejected)

The length of a side of the cube is 5 cm.

(b) Volume of the cube $= 5^3$
$= 125$ cm³

Try It! 2

The surface area of a cube is 294 cm². Find
(a) the length of a side of the cube,
(b) the volume of the cube.

C Cuboid

A cuboid, like a cube, is a rectangular prism but with at least four of its opposite faces in the shape of a rectangle. A cuboid and its net are shown below.

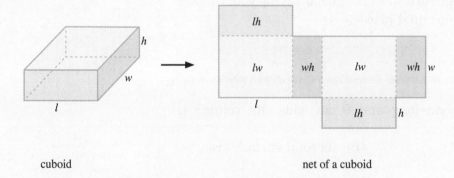

cuboid   net of a cuboid

Let us recall the formula for finding the volume of a cuboid.

> Volume of cuboid = Length × Width × Height
> $= l \times w \times h$

The formula for finding the total surface area of a cuboid is as follows:

> Total surface area of cuboid $= 2 \times (lw + lh + wh)$

Example 3

A rectangular block of metal measures 8 cm by 7 cm by 5 cm.
(a) Find the volume of the metal block.
(b) Find the total surface area of the metal block.
(c) If the metal block is melted and recast into a cube, find the length of a side of the cube, giving your answer correct to 2 decimal places.

Solution

(a) Volume of the metal block $= 8 \times 7 \times 5$
$$= 280 \text{ cm}^3$$

(b) Total surface area of the metal block
$$= 2 \times (8 \times 7 + 8 \times 5 + 7 \times 5)$$
$$= 262 \text{ cm}^2$$

(c) Let the length of a side of the cube be x cm.
Thus $x^3 = 280$
$$x = \sqrt[3]{280}$$
$$= 6.54 \quad \text{(correct to 2 d.p.)}$$
The length of a side of the cube is 6.54 cm.

Try It! 3

A rectangular block of copper is 10 cm by 9 cm by 4 cm.
(a) Find the volume of the copper block.
(b) Find the total surface area of the copper block.
(c) If the copper block is melted and recast into a cube, find the length of a side of the cube, giving your answer correct to 2 decimal places.

Example 4

A cuboid is 11 cm long and 9 cm wide. Its volume is 693 cm³. Find
(a) its height,   **(b)** its total surface area.

Solution

(a) Let the height of the cuboid be h cm.
Thus $11 \times 9 \times h = 693$
$$h = \frac{693}{11 \times 9}$$
$$= 7$$
The height of the cuboid is 7 cm.

(b) Total surface area of the cuboid
$$= 2 \times (11 \times 9 + 11 \times 7 + 9 \times 7)$$
$$= 478 \text{ cm}^2$$

Try It! 4

A cuboid is 13 cm long and 6 cm high. Its volume is 624 cm³. Find
(a) its width,   **(b)** its total surface area.

EXERCISE 13.1

BASIC PRACTICE

1. Determine whether each of the following is a net of a cube.

   (a)

   (b)

2. Draw two possible nets of the cuboid shown below, where the unit of length is centimeter.

   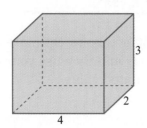

3. Sketch the solid that can be formed by each of the following nets.

   (a)

   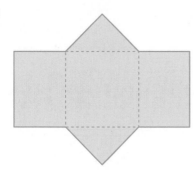

(b)

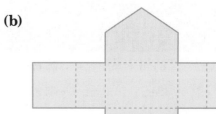

4. Find the volume and the total surface area of a cube whose side is
   (a) 6 cm,   **(b)** 11 in.,
   (c) 1.3 m.

5. Find the volume and the total surface area of a cuboid whose dimensions are
   (a) 12 cm by 8 cm by 5 cm,
   (b) 10 in. by 7 in. by 6 in.,
   (c) 4 ft by 3 ft by 2 ft.

 FURTHER PRACTICE

6. Draw a net of the solid shown below, where the unit of length is centimeter.

   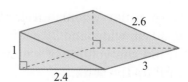

7. The area of a face of a cube is 169 cm². Find
   (a) the length of a side,
   (b) the total surface area,
   (c) the volume
   of the cube.

8. The total surface area of a cube is 486 cm². Find
   (a) the length of a side,
   (b) the volume
   of the cube.

9. Copy and complete the following table for cuboids.

	Length	Width	Height	Volume	Total surface area
(a)	9 cm	6 cm		270 cm³	
(b)		8 cm	5 cm	440 cm³	
(c)	14 cm		6 cm		608 cm²

10. The dimensions of a cuboid are 7 cm by 5cm by 4 cm.
  (a) Find its volume.
  (b) If a cube of side x cm has the same volume as the cuboid, find the value of x. Give your answer correct to 2 decimal places.

11. A rectangular copper block A measuring 10 cm by 6 cm by 5 cm, is melted and recast into a rectangular bar B, 3 cm wide and 2 cm high. Find
  (a) the length of copper bar B,
  (b) the ratio of the total surface area of block A to that of bar B.

12. A rectangular aquarium tank is 50 cm long, 30 cm wide, and 36 cm high.
  (a) Find the volume of water required to fill up the tank.
  (b) The tank is open at the top. Find the external surface area of glass required to make the tank.
  (c) If 6,000 cm³ of water is drained from the tank, find the drop in water level.

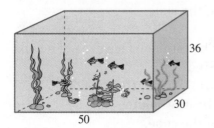

13. A rectangular tin plate measures 40 cm by 30 cm. A small square of side 8 cm is cut out from each corner as shown in the figure. The plate is then folded along the dotted lines to form an open tray. Find
  (a) the external surface area,
  (b) the volume
  of the tray.

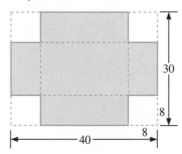

14. The external dimensions of a wooden box are 15 cm by 10 cm by 8 cm. The thickness of the wood on each side is 1.5 cm. Find
  (a) the internal dimensions of the box,
  (b) the volume of wood used to make the box.

BRAINWORKS

15. Suggest a way to estimate the volume of your body and then use your method to find an estimated value.

13.2 *Volume and Total Surface Area of a Prism*

A Prism

When a solid is sliced through by a plane, the polygon formed by the slice is a **cross-section** of the solid. In the figure, S_1 and S_2 are the cross-sections of the solid shown below and they are parallel to the end face *ABCD*.

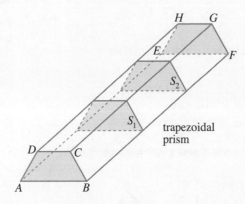

trapezoidal prism

When every cross-section parallel to an end face of a solid has the same shape and size, the solid is said to have a **uniform cross-section**.

A **prism** is a solid with two parallel polygons for its end faces and a uniform cross-section. Each end face is called a **base** of the prism. A prism is named by the shape of its base as shown below.

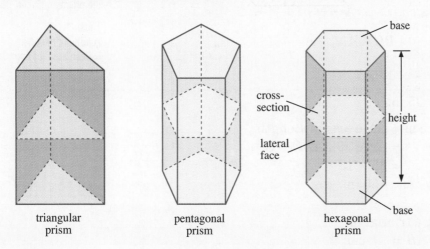

triangular prism   pentagonal prism   hexagonal prism

The perpendicular distance between the two bases of a prism is its **height**. The other faces of the prism are called **lateral faces**. In this section, we shall only consider those right prisms whose lateral faces are rectangles.

B Volume of Prism

A cuboid is a rectangular prism.

Volume of cuboid = Length × Width × Height
= (Length × Width) × Height
= Base area × Height

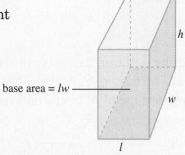

base area = lw

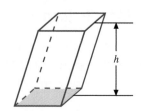
The above formula can be generalized to find the volume of a prism.

> Volume of prism = Base area × Height

Example 5

The figure shows a triangular prism in which $BC = 10$ in., $AN = 7$ in., and $CF = 13$ in. Find the volume of the prism.

Solution

Area of $\triangle ABC = \frac{1}{2} \times BC \times AN$

$= \frac{1}{2} \times 10 \times 7$

$= 35$ in.²

Volume of the prism = Base area × Length
= Area of $\triangle ABC \times CF$
= 35 × 13
= 455 in.³

Try It! 5

The figure shows a triangular prism in which $AB = 14$ cm, $CN = 6$ cm, and $BE = 8$ cm. Find the volume of the prism.

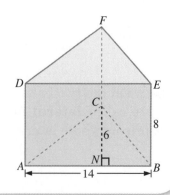

Example 6

The figure shows a swimming pool with a rectangular surface *ABCD* (not drawn to scale). The pool is 50 m long and 23 m wide. It has a depth of 1 m at the shallow end and 2 m at the deep end. Find the volume of the pool.

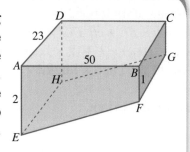

Solution

The pool can be considered as a trapezoidal prism with base *ABFE* and length *AD*.

Base area = Area of trapezoid *ABFE*

$$= \frac{1}{2} \times (1 + 2) \times 50$$

$$= 75 \text{ m}^2$$

$\therefore$ volume of the pool = base area × length

$$= 75 \times 23$$

$$= 1,725 \text{ m}^3$$

REMARKS

It is essential to identify the base and the height of a prism correctly.

Try It! 6

The figure shows a swimming pool with a rectangular surface *ABCD* (not drawn to scale). It is 25 m long and 18 m wide. Its depth is 3 m at the deep end and 2 m at the shallow end. Find the volume of the swimming pool.

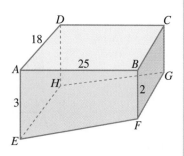

C Surface Area of Prism

The figure shows a pentagonal prism and its net.

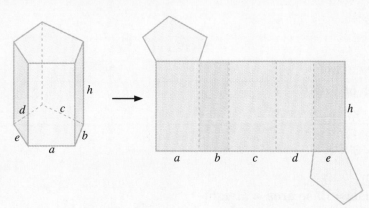

Notice that
the total surface area of the prism
= sum of areas of its lateral faces + (2 × base area)
= $ah + bh + ch + dh + eh$ + (2 × base area)
= $(a + b + c + d + e)$ × h + (2 × base area)
= perimeter of the base × height + (2 × base area)

This formula can be applied to any prism.

> **Total surface area of prism**
> = Perimeter of the base × Height + (2 × Base area)

Example 7

The figure shows a triangular prism in which AB = 5 cm, BC = 4 cm, CA = 3 cm, $m\angle ACB$ = 90°, and BE = 2.5 cm.

(a) Draw a net of the prism.
(b) Find the volume of the prism.
(c) Find its total surface area.

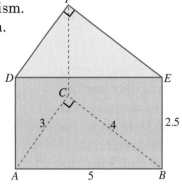

Solution

(a) The net of the prism is shown below.

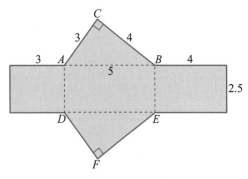

(not drawn to scale)

(b) Base area = Area of △ABC

$$= \frac{1}{2} \times AC \times BC$$

$$= \frac{1}{2} \times 3 \times 4$$

$$= 6 \text{ cm}^2$$

Volume of the prism = Base area × Height
$$= 6 \times 2.5$$
$$= 15 \text{ cm}^3$$

(c) Perimeter of the base = Perimeter of $\triangle ABC$
$$= 3 + 4 + 5$$
$$= 12 \text{ cm}$$
∴ total surface area of the prism
= perimeter of the base × height + (2 × base area)
$$= 12 \times 2.5 + 2 \times 6$$
$$= 42 \text{ cm}^2$$

Try It! 7 The figure shows a triangular prism in which $m\angle BAC = 90°$, $AB = 5$ cm, $BC = 13$ cm, $AC = 12$ cm, and $BE = 14$ cm.
(a) Draw a net of the prism.
(b) Find the volume of the prism.
(c) Find its total surface area.

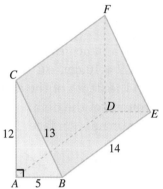

Example 8 The figure shows a trough shaped like a trapezoidal prism in which $AB = CD = 15$ cm, $BC = 20$ cm, $AD = 30$ cm, $CF = 28$ cm, and the depth of the trough is 14.1 cm.
(a) Find the volume of the trough.
(b) Find the external surface area of the trough.
(c) If the material for the trough costs $0.04 per cm^2, find the total cost of material used in making the trough.

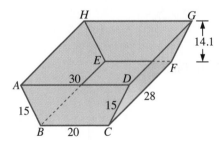

Solution
(a) Base area = Area of trapezoid $ABCD$
$$= \frac{1}{2} \times (20 + 30) \times 14.1$$
$$= 352.5 \text{ cm}^2$$
∴ volume of the trough $= 352.5 \times 28$
$$= 9,870 \text{ cm}^3$$

REMARKS
A trapezoid with two equal non-parallel opposite sides is called an isosceles trapezoid.

(b) Note that the trough is open at the top.

$$AB + BC + CD = 15 + 20 + 15$$
$$= 50 \text{ cm}$$

∴ external surface area of the trough
$$= 50 \times 28 + 2 \times 352.5$$
$$= 2{,}105 \text{ cm}^2$$

(c) The required cost of material $= \$0.04 \times 2{,}105$
$$= \$84.20$$

Try It! 8 The figure shows a sauce dish shaped like a trapezoidal prism in which $AB = 10$ cm, $BC = AD = 5$ cm, $CD = 16$ cm, $BF = 18$ cm, and the depth of the dish is 4 cm.

(a) Find the volume of the dish.

(b) Find the external surface area of the dish.

(c) If the material for the dish costs \$0.02 per cm^2, find the cost of material used in making the dish.

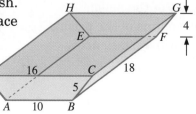

EXERCISE 13.2

BASIC PRACTICE

1. For each of the following,
   (i) draw a net of the prism,
   (ii) find the volume and the total surface area of the prism.

The unit of measurement is centimeter (cm).

(a)

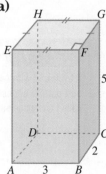

(b)

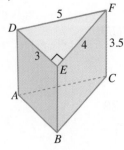

(c)

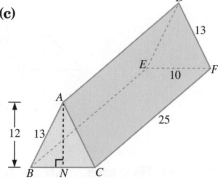

(d)

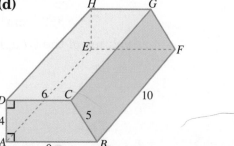

2. The figure shows a pentagonal prism in which the area of *ABCDE* is 150 cm², *AB* = 10 cm, *BC* = 6 cm, *CD* = 11 cm, *DE* = 13 cm, *EA* = 8 cm, and *CH* = 21 cm. Find

(a) the volume of the prism,

(b) the total surface area of the prism.

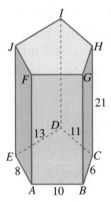

3. The figure shows a trapezoidal prism in which *AB* = *DC* = 5 in., *BC* = 4 in., *AD* = 10 in., and *BN* = 4 in. The volume of the prism is 210 in.³. Find

(a) the area of *ABCD*,

(b) the length of *DH*,

(c) the total surface area of the prism.

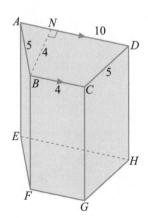

4. The figure shows a right triangular prism standing on a horizontal rectangular base *BCDE* and *AC* = *FD* = 25 cm.

(a) If the area of *BCDE* is 480 cm², *CD* = 32 cm, and *AB* = 20 cm, find

  (i) the length of *BC*,

  (ii) the total surface area and volume of the prism.

(b) If the area of △*ABC* is 84 cm², *CD* = 30 cm, and *BC* = 24 cm, find

  (i) the length of *AB*,

  (ii) the total surface area and volume of the prism.

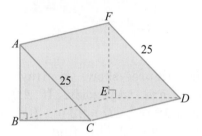

5. The figure shows a camping tent. The tent is closed at both ends and at the bottom. Given that *AB* = *AC* = 1.7 m, *BC* = 1.6 m, *AN* = 1.5 m, and *CF* = 2.1 m, find

(a) the space inside the tent,

(b) the surface area of the tent,

(c) the total cost of the material used in making the tent if the material of the tent costs $30 per square meter.

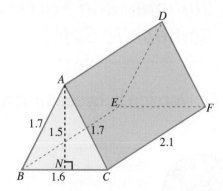

6. The figure shows a swimming pool with a rectangular surface $ABCD$ (not drawn to scale). $CD = 20$ m, $AE = 1.6$ m, $BF = 1$ m, and the area of $ABCD$ is 240 m². Find
(a) the length of AD,
(b) the volume of the pool.

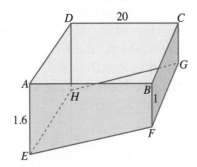

7. The figure shows a tray whose end faces are trapezoids. If $AB = 15$ in., $AN = 12$ in., $CD = 22$ in., $BF = 45$ in., and $BC = AD = 12.5$ in., find
(a) the area of $ABCD$,
(b) the volume of the tray,
(c) the external surface area of the tray.

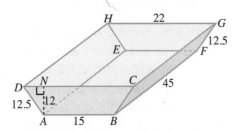

8. A manager wants to design a rectangular storage container of capacity 900 ft³. The container should have a square base of side a ft and a height of h ft, where a and h are integers greater than 1.
(a) Find two possible sets of dimensions for the container.
(b) Suggest a design that uses the least material to make the container.

13.3 Volumes and Surface Areas of Composite Solids

A Conversion between Different Units

The common metric units of volume are cm³ and m³.

The commom metric units of area are cm² and m².

Do you remember why we use "square units" and "cubic units" for areas and volumes respectively? Let us see the conversion between different units.

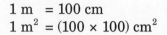

DISCUSS

1. How do you arrange 100 square pieces of area 1 cm² each to form a big square? What is the area of the big square in square meters (m²)?

2. How do you arrange 1,000 cubes of volume 1 cm³ each to form a big cube? What is the volume of the big cube in cube meters (m³)?

1 m = 100 cm
1 m² = (100 × 100) cm²

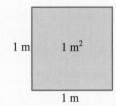

1 m³ = (100 × 100 × 100) cm³

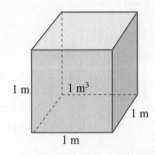
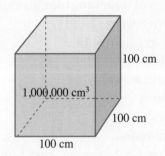

1 m² = 10,000 cm²
1 m³ = 1,000,000 cm³

Example 9

A cargo container is a cuboid that is 12.22 m long, 2.44 m wide, and 2.59 m high. Find
(a) its total surface area
   (i) in square meters,
   (ii) in square centimeters,
(b) its volume
   (i) in cubic meters,
   (ii) in cubic centimeters.
Round your answers correct to the nearest ten.

Solution

(a) (i) Total surface area of the container
$$= 2 \times (12.22 \times 2.44 + 12.22 \times 2.59 + 2.44 \times 2.59)$$
$$= 135.5724 \text{ m}^2$$
$$= 140 \text{ m}^2 \quad \text{(correct to the nearest ten)}$$

(ii) Total surface area of the container
$$= 135.5724 \times 10,000 \qquad 1 \text{ m}^2 = 10,000 \text{ cm}^2$$
$$= 1,355,724 \text{ cm}^2$$
$$= 1,355,720 \text{ cm}^2 \quad \text{(correct to the nearest ten)}$$

(b) (i) Volume of the container
$$= 12.22 \times 2.44 \times 2.59$$
$$= 77.225512 \text{ m}^3$$
$$= 80 \text{ m}^3 \quad \text{(correct to the nearest ten)}$$

(ii) Volume of the container
$$= 77.225512 \times 1{,}000{,}000 \quad 1 \text{ m}^3 = 1{,}000{,}000 \text{ cm}^2$$
$$= 77{,}225{,}512 \text{ cm}^3$$
$$= 77{,}225{,}510 \text{ cm}^3 \quad \text{(correct to the nearest ten)}$$

Try It! **9**

The internal dimensions of a rectangular storage container are 7.20 m by 4.88 m by 5.67 m. Find
(a) its total internal surface area
  (i) in square meters,
  (ii) in square centimeters,
(b) its internal volume
  (i) in cubic meters,
  (ii) in cubic centimeters.
Round your answers correct to the nearest hundred.

Example **10**

The figure shows the cross-section of a solid triangular prism in which $PQ = PR = 3$ cm, $QN = NR = 1.8$ cm, and $PN = 2.4$ cm. The length of the solid prism is 2.9 m. Find
(a) its total surface area
  (i) in square centimeters,
  (ii) in square meters,
(b) its volume
  (i) in cubic centimeters,
  (ii) in cubic meters.
Round your answers correct to 4 decimal places where appropriate.

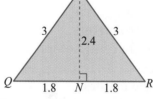

Solution

(a) (i) 2.9 m = 290 cm
Total surface area
= Perimeter of the cross-section × Length
  + 2 × Cross-section area
$$= (3 + 3 + 1.8 + 1.8) \times 290 + 2 \times \left(\frac{1}{2} \times 3.6 \times 2.4 \right)$$
$$= 2{,}792.64 \text{ cm}^2$$

(ii) Total surface area

$$= 2{,}792{,}64 \times \frac{1}{10{,}000}$$
$$= 0.279264$$
$$= 0.2793 \text{ m}^2 \quad \text{(correct to 4 d.p.)}$$

(b) (i) Volume = Area of cross-section × Length

$$= \left(\frac{1}{2} \times 3.6 \times 2.4 \right) \times 290$$
$$= 1252.8 \text{ cm}^3$$

(ii) Volume $= 1252.8 \times \dfrac{1}{1{,}000{,}000}$

$$= 0.0012528$$
$$= 0.0013 \text{ m}^3 \quad \text{(correct to 4 d.p.)}$$

Try It! 10

A solid metal bar has a uniform cross-section as shown. Given that $PQ = 2.1$ cm, $QR = 2.8$ cm, $PR = 3.5$ cm, and the length of the metal bar is 3.9 m, find
(a) its total surface area
 (i) in square centimeters,
 (ii) in square meters,
(b) its volume
 (i) in cubic centimeters,
 (ii) in cubic meters.
Round your answers correct to 4 decimal places where appropriate.

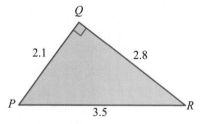

B Composite Solids

A solid can be made up of two or more basic solids. We can dissect such a composite solid into some parts to find its volume and total surface area.

Example 11

The figure shows a cross-section of a tunnel. *CDEF* is a trapezoid surmounted on a rectangle *ABCF*, where *AB* = 5 m, *BC* = 2.6 m, *DC* = *EF* = 2.5 m, and *DE* = 3.6 m. The distance between *CF* and *DE* is 2.4 m. The length of the tunnel is 130 m. Find

(a) the perimeter of the cross-section,
(b) the area of the cross-section,
(c) the lateral surface area of the tunnel,
(d) the volume of the tunnel.

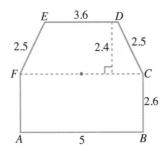

Solution

(a) Perimeter of the cross-section
$= AB + BC + CD + DE + EF + FA$
$= 5 + 2.6 + 2.5 + 3.6 + 2.5 + 2.6$
$= 18.8$ m

(b) Area of the cross-section
$=$ Area of *ABCF* + Area of *CDEF*
$= 5 \times 2.6 + \dfrac{1}{2} \times (5 + 3.6) \times 2.4$
$= 13 + 10.32$
$= 23.32$ m^2

(c) Lateral surface area of the tunnel
$=$ Perimeter of the cross-section $\times$ Length of the tunnel
$= 18.8 \times 130$
$= 2{,}444$ m^2

(d) Volume of the tunnel
$=$ Area of the cross-section $\times$ Length of the tunnel
$= 23.32 \times 130$
$= 3{,}031.6$ m^3

Try It! **11** The figure shows a right pentagonal prism in which $AB = 8$ in., $BC = 15$ in., $AF = 6$ in., $IJ = 17$ in., and $AJ = CI = 25$ in. Find

(a) the perimeter of the face $ABCIJ$,

(b) the area of the face $ABCIJ$,

(c) the total surface area of the prism,

(d) the volume of the prism.

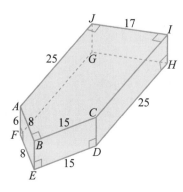

Example **12** The figure shows a prism whose cross-section is formed by cutting out the trapezoid $DCGE$ from the parallelogram $ABGF$. $AB = 15$ cm, $CD = 5$ cm, $EF = 6$ cm, and $BH = 12$ cm. The distance between DC and EG is 5 cm and the distance between DC and AB is 5 cm. Find the volume of the prism.

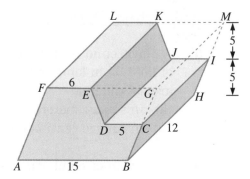

Solution

Area of parallelogram $ABGF = 15 \times (5 + 5)$

$= 150$ cm^2

$EG = 15 - 6$

$= 9$ cm

Area of trapezoid $DCGE = \dfrac{1}{2} \times (5 + 9) \times 5$

$= 35$ cm^2

Volume of the prism $= (150 - 35) \times 12$

$= 1{,}380$ cm^3

RECALL

Area of parallelogram
= Base × Height

Area of trapezoid
$= \dfrac{1}{2} \times$ Sum of parallel sides
× Height

The figure shows a prism whose cross-section is formed by cutting out △CDF from the parallelogram ABFE. AB = 25 cm, DE = 15 cm, and BH = 30 cm. The heights from C to EF and AB are 8 cm and 10 cm respectively. Find the volume of the prism.

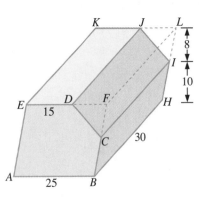

EXERCISE 13.3

BASIC PRACTICE

1. Express the following areas in cm^2.
   (a) 3 m^2 (b) 13.6 m^2

2. Express the following areas in m^2.
   (a) 4,000 cm^2 (b) 25,600 cm^2

3. Express the following volumes in cm^3.
   (a) 2 m^3 (b) 39.7 m^3

4. Express the following volumes in m^3.
   (a) 63,000 cm^3 (b) 9,280,000 cm^3

FURTHER PRACTICE

5. A playground is built on a rectangular plot of land 35 m long and 24 m wide. Find the area of the land
   (a) in square meters,
   (b) in square centimeters.

6. Jane drinks eight cups of water a day. If each cup contains 250 cm^3 of water, find the total amount of water she drinks per day in
   (a) cubic centimeters,
   (b) cubic meters.

7. Find the total surface area and volume of each prism, where the unit of length is centimeter (cm).

(a)

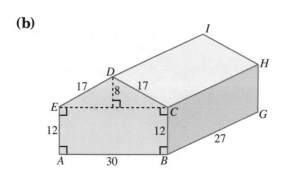

(b)

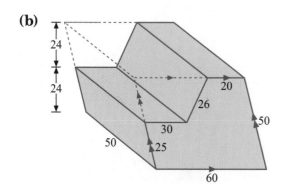

8. Find the total surface area and volume of each prism, where the unit of length is centimeter (cm).

(a)

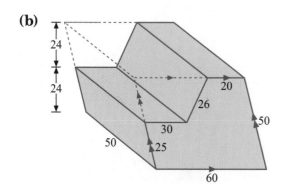

(b)

9. A cuboid measuring 10 in. by 7 in. by 12 in. has a square hole with side 2 in. drilled through it from the face *EFGH* to the face *ABCD*. Find
(a) the volume,
(b) the total surface area
of the solid.

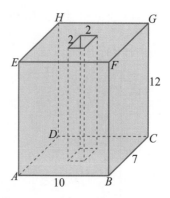

10. The figure shows the uniform cross-section of a solid. *ABCD* and *EFGH* are trapezoids with dimensions given in centimeters. If the length of the solid is 10 cm, find
(a) the volume,
(b) the total surface area
of the solid.

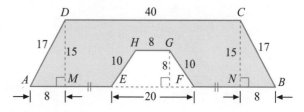

MATH@WORK

11. A rectangular gasoline tank measures 0.7 m by 0.8 m by 2.0 m. The gasoline in it is used to fill up small cubical cans of sides 25 cm each.
(a) Find the volume of the tank
  (i) in cubic meters,
  (ii) in cubic centimeters.
(b) Find the volume of a can
  (i) in cubic centimeters,
  (ii) in cubic meters.
(c) How many complete cans can be filled if the tank is completely filled with gasoline initially?

12. The figure shows the uniform cross-section of a sofa chair. Given that the dimensions are in centimeters and the length of the sofa is 1.8 m, find
   (a) the perimeter of the cross-section,
   (b) the area of the cross-section,
   (c) the total surface area of the sofa in square meters,
   (d) the volume of the sofa in cubic meters.

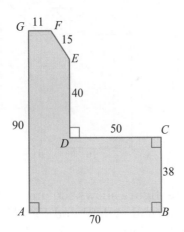

13. The figure shows a metal girder of uniform cross-section. *ABCD* is a trapezoid and *EFGH* is a square. Given that their dimensions are in feet, find
   (a) the volume of the girder,
   (b) the total surface area of the girder,
   (c) the number of such girders that can be casted using 14,000 ft³ of molten metal,
   (d) the number of cans of paint needed to coat six such girders if each can of paint can coat an area of 800 ft².

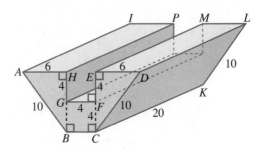

14. (a) Describe and draw two items in your home that are made up of basic solids.
   (b) Measure their dimensions and calculate their volumes and total surface areas.

Net

A net of a solid is a plane figure that can be folded up to form the solid.

Cube

A cube has six equal square faces.

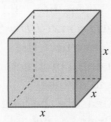

Volume = x^3

Total surface area = $6x^2$

where x is the length of a side of the cube.

Cuboid

A cuboid has six rectangular faces.

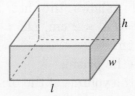

Volume = lwh

Total surface area = $2(lw + lh + wh)$

where $l, w,$ and h are the length, width, and height of the cuboid respectively.

Prism

A prism is a solid with two parallel polygonal bases and a uniform cross-section.

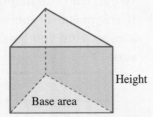

Volume = Base area × Height

Total surface area
= Perimeter of the base × Height
+ 2 × Base area

Unit Conversion

1 m^2 = 10,000 cm^2

1 m^3 = 1,000,000 cm^3

1. A cuboid is 3.5 cm long, 2 cm wide, and 1.5 cm high.
   (a) Draw a net of the cuboid.
   (b) Find the volume of the cuboid.
   (c) Find its total surface area.

2. The face of a cube has an area of 196 in.^{2} Find
   (a) the length of a side of the cube,
   (b) its total surface area,
   (c) its volume.

3. The figure shows the net of a prism. $BC = PB = PC = 2$ cm, $DE = 2.5$ cm, and $PN = \sqrt{3}$ cm.
   (a) Name the prism.
   (b) Find the volume of the prism.
   (c) Find its total surface area.

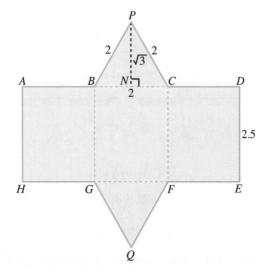

4. Find the volume and surface area of each prism, where the unit of length is cm.
   (a)

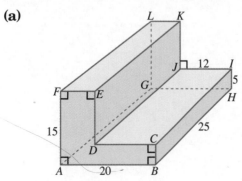

(b)

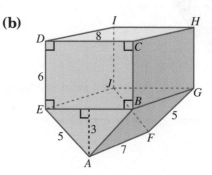

5. The figure shows the cross-section $ABCD$ of a prism of height 5.0 cm. $AB = 3.6$ cm, $BC = 3.2$ cm, $BD = 6.0$ cm, and $m\angle BAD = m\angle CBD = 90°$.
   (a) Construct the quadrilateral $ABCD$ using a protractor, a pair of compasses, and a ruler.
   (b) Measure the lengths of AD and CD.
   (c) Draw a net of the prism.
   (d) Find the volume of the prism.
   (e) Find its total surface area.

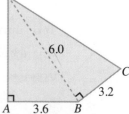

6. The figure shows the cross-section of a solid metal prism of height 20 cm.
   (a) Find the volume of the prism.
   (b) If the prism is melted and recast into a cuboid of length 30 cm and width 16 cm, find the height of the cuboid.
   (c) If the prism is melted and recast into a cube, find the length of a side of the cube.

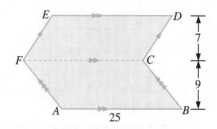

7. The figure shows a cabinet whose uniform cross-section is a triangle CDE on a rectangle $ABCE$. $AB = 60$ cm, $AE = 90$ cm, $DN = 40$ cm, $DC = DE = 50$ cm, and $BG = 40$ cm. Find

  (a) the perimeter of the cross-section,
  (b) the area of the cross-section,
  (c) the surface area of the cabinet, not including the bottom area in contact with the floor,
     (i) in square centimeters,
     (ii) in square meters,
  (d) the volume of the cabinet
     (i) in cubic centimeters,
     (ii) in cubic meters.

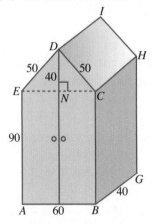

8. In the figure, a triangular prism $CMNGPQ$ is cut off from a cuboid $ABCDEFGH$. $AB = 6$ cm, $AD = 8$ cm, $BF = 10$ cm, M and N are the midpoints of BC and CD respectively.

  (a) Find the volume of the cuboid.
  (b) Find the volume of the triangular prism.
  (c) Find the volume of the remaining prism.
  (d) Find the percentage decrease in the volume of the cuboid due to the removal of the triangular prism.
  (e) Is the total surface area of the remaining prism greater than that of the cuboid? Explain briefly.

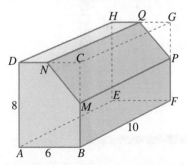

9. The figure shows an open wooden box. Its external length, width, and height are 25 cm, 22 cm, and 20 cm respectively. The thickness of the wood is 2 cm. Find

  (a) the volume of wood used in making the box,
  (b) the total surface area of the box.

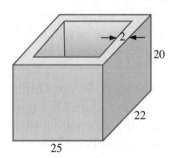

10. The figure shows an open water container whose uniform cross-section is a rectangle $ABDE$ on a triangle BCD. The length of the container is 13 cm.

  (a) Draw a net of the prism.
  (b) Find the total outer surface area and the volume of the container.
  (c) If water flows at a rate of 14 cm^3/s into the empty water container, how many minutes will it take to fill the container completely?

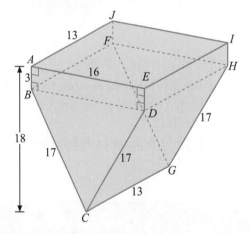

Slicing Solids

A cross-section is the face you get when you make one slice through an object. The figure on the right is a sample slice through a cube, showing one of the cross sections you can get.

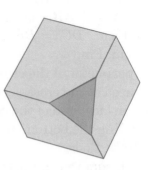

The polygon formed by the slice is the cross-section. The cross-section cannot contain any piece of the original face; it all comes from "inside" the solid. In this figure, only the shaded shape is a cross-section.

1. What shapes do you think you can get if you slice the solid cube at different angles other than slicing parallel to the end face? Record which of the shapes you are able to create and explain how you can make the following cross-sections by slicing a cube:
    (a) a rectangle,   **(b)** a parallelogram,
    (c) a triangle that is not equilateral.

One example is shown above. An equilateral triangle cross-section can be obtained by cutting a cube through the midpoints of the 3 edges originating from any one vertex.

2. Sketch the two-dimensional shape you would get if you slice the following solids as indicated.
    (a)   **(b)**

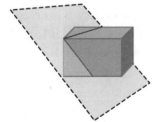   

You can find out more about slicing solids on the following websites:
*   http://www.learner.org/courses/learningmath/geometry/session9/part_c/index.html#c2
*   http://nlvm.usu.edu/en/nav/frames_asid_126_g_3_t_3.html?open=instructions

WRITE IN YOUR JOURNAL

Applying your knowledge of volumes and surface areas of solids, write a proposal on how you would design a product packaging for 300 cm³ of juice or food. You should include the following in your proposal:
*   a sketch of the packaging and its net
*   the dimensions and surface area of the packaging
*   the benefits/plus points of using the design

14 PROPORTIONS

Playing

LET'S LEARN TO...

① understand the scale factor of a scale drawing
② draw a simple scale drawing
③ understand the scale of a map
④ calculate the actual distance between two points and the area of a region from a scale drawing
⑤ use ratio to solve problems involving scales
⑥ understand the ideas of direct proportion and inverse proportion
⑦ determine whether two quantities are in direct proportion or inverse proportion

The map above has a scale. Do you know what this scale is? Why is it important for a map to have a scale? How would you calculate the actual distance between two locations such as Portland and Bend on the map?

14.1 Scale Drawings

A **scale drawing** is reduced or enlarged drawing of an actual object. It is often used in science, engineering, construction, and architecture to show how various parts of an object should be made and assembled together. A scale map is a special type of scale drawing. We will deal with scale maps in greater detail in the next section.

The **scale factor** of a scale drawing is the ratio of a length in the drawing to the corresponding length of the actual object. If a length PQ in the scale drawing represents on actual length AB, the scale factor of the drawing $= \dfrac{PQ}{AB}$. The scale drawing is a reduced drawing of an actual object if the scale factor < 1 and is an enlarged drawing if the scale factor > 1.

The scale factor of a drawing is also known as its **scale**. A scale is usually expressed as a ratio **1 : n** or a fraction $\dfrac{1}{n}$ where 1 unit length on the drawing represents an actual length of n units.

Suppose a length of 10 cm on a scale drawing represents an actual length of 5 cm.

The scale factor of the drawing is $\dfrac{10 \text{ cm}}{5 \text{ cm}} = \dfrac{2}{1} = 2$.

The scale of the drawing is 10 cm : 5 cm $= 1 : \dfrac{5}{10} = 1 : \dfrac{1}{2}$.

Note: • In ratios, the units of measurement for both lengths must be the same. Ratios bear no unit.

• The scale $1 : \dfrac{1}{2}$ means that a length of 1 cm on the drawing represents an actual length of $\dfrac{1}{2}$ cm and this is equivalent to the scale factor 2 which means that a length of 2 cm on the drawing represents an actual length of 1 cm.

Example 1 Express each of the following scales in the form $1 : n$.
(a) 1 in. : 200 ft   (b) 1 cm : 50 m   (c) 3 ft : 4 in.

Solution   (a) 1 in. : 200 ft
= 1 in. : 200 × 12 in.   Convert ft into in.; 1 ft = 12 in.
= 1 in. : 2,400 in.   Both sides of the ratio have the same units.
= 1 : 2,400

(b) 1 cm : 50 m
= 1 cm : 50 × 100 cm   Convert m into cm; 1 m = 100 cm.
= 1 cm : 5,000 cm
= 1 : 5,000

(c) 3 ft : 4 in.

$$= 3 \times 12 \text{ in.} : 4 \text{ in.}$$
$$= 36 : 4$$
$$= \frac{36}{36} : \frac{4}{36}$$
$$= 1 : \frac{1}{9}$$

Note: • As seen from the scales 1 in. : 200 ft and 1 cm : 50 m given in parts **(a)** and **(b)** respectively, these are scales for reduced drawings of actual dimensions. The value of n in the scale $1 : n$ is greater than 1 for these cases.
• The scale 3 ft : 4 in. given in **(c)** represents an enlargement and the value of n in the scale $1 : n$ is smaller than 1.

 Try It! **1** Express each of the following scales in the form $1 : n$.
(a) 1 in. : 50 yd
(b) 2 cm : 70 m
(c) 1 ft : 3 in.

Example 2 A soccer field is 300 ft long and 240 ft wide. It is represented by a rectangle with length 6 in. on a plan. Find
(a) the scale of the plan,
(b) the width of the rectangle on the plan.

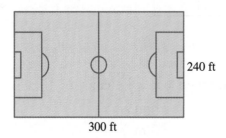

300 ft

240 ft

Solution **(a)** Scale of the plan = 6 in. : 300 ft
$$= 6 \text{ in.} : 300 \times 12 \text{ in.}$$
$$= 6 \text{ in.} : 3{,}600 \text{ in.}$$
$$= 1 : 600$$

(b) Width of the rectangle on the plan

$$= 240 \times \frac{1}{600} \text{ ft} \qquad \text{Using the scale 1 : 600 from (a)}$$

$$= 240 \times \frac{1}{600} \times 12 \text{ in.}$$

$$= 4.8 \text{ in.}$$

Try It! **2** A tennis court measures 24 m by 11 m. It is represented by a rectangle 22 cm wide on a plan. Find
(a) the scale of the plan,
(b) the length of the rectangle on the plan.

Example **3** The diagram shows a floor plan of a kitchen which is drawn to a scale of 1 : 50. The dimensions of the kitchen in the plan are 6 cm by 4.5 cm. Find the actual
(a) dimensions of the kitchen in m,
(b) area of the kitchen in m^2.

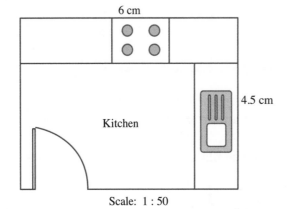

Scale: 1 : 50

Solution **(a)** Actual length of the kitchen $= 6 \times \dfrac{50}{1}$ cm

$$= 300 \text{ cm}$$

$$= 3 \text{ m}$$

Actual width of the kitchen $= 4.5 \times \dfrac{50}{1}$ cm

$$= 225 \text{ cm}$$

$$= 2.25 \text{ m}$$

(b) Actual area of the kitchen $= 3 \times 2.25$

$$= 6.75 \text{ m}^2$$

DISCUSS

In **(b)**, can we first find the area in cm^2, then multiply it by 50, and finally convert it to m^2? Explain your answers.

The diagram shows a floor plan of a bathroom which is drawn to a scale of 1 : 40. The dimensions of the bathroom in the plan are 6 cm by 5 cm. Find the actual

(a) dimensions of the bathroom in m,
(b) area of the bathroom in m².

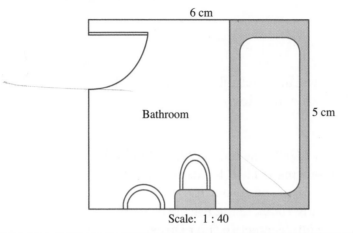

6 cm

Bathroom

5 cm

Scale: 1 : 40

Example 4

A rectangular school hall *ABCD* is 28 m long and 18 m wide. The diagonals *AC* and *BD* intersect at *M*.

(a) Draw a plan of the hall, using a scale of 1 : 400.
(b) Measure *AM* on the plan, correct to the nearest 0.1 cm.
(c) Hence, estimate the actual distance from *A* to *M*, correct to the nearest meter.

Solution

(a) Length of the hall on the plan $= 28 \times \dfrac{1}{400}$ m

$$= 0.07 \text{ m}$$
$$= 7 \text{ cm}$$

Width of the hall on the plan $= 18 \times \dfrac{1}{400}$ m

$$= 0.045 \text{ m}$$
$$= 4.5 \text{ cm}$$

Hence, the plan of the school hall can be drawn as shown below.

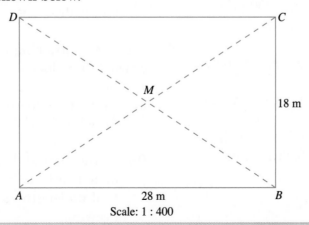

18 m

28 m

Scale: 1 : 400

(b) By measurement,
   AM on the plan = 4.2 cm (correct to 0.1 cm)

(c) Actual distance from A to M
   $\approx$ 4.2 × 400 cm
   = 1,680 cm
   = 16.8 m
   = 17 m (correct to the nearest meter)

Note: This example shows how actual distance can be estimated from a scale drawing.

 Try It! 4

A rectangular living room $PQRS$ has length $PQ = 9$ m and width $QR = 7.5$ m. A cable runs from P to the midpoint M of PQ, and then runs from M to the corner R.
(a) Draw a plan of the living room, using a scale of 1 : 150.
(b) Measure MR on the plan, correct to the nearest 0.1 cm.
(c) Hence, estimate the length of the cable, correct to the nearest meter.

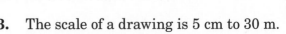

EXERCISE 14.1

⚙ BASIC PRACTICE

1. Express each of the following scales in the form 1 : n.
   (a) 1 in. : 20 ft   **(b)** 1 cm : 200 m
   (c) 1 ft : 2 in.   **(d)** 5 cm : 20 m

2. On a scale drawing, 100 ft is represented by 3 in.
   (a) Find the scale of the drawing in the form 1 : n.
   (b) What is the actual length of a wall if its length is 1.8 in. on the drawing?

3. The scale of a drawing is 5 cm to 30 m.
   (a) Find the scale of the drawing in the form 1 : n.
   (b) If a building is 75 m tall, find its height on the drawing.

4. On a scale drawing of insects, a beetle is drawn 7.5 cm long when its actual length is 1.5 cm.
   (a) Find the scale of the drawing in the form 1 : n.
   (b) If the actual length of a beetle is 5 cm, find its length on the drawing.

5. The scale used for drawing a plant is 2 : 1.

(a) The diameter of a flower is 3 inches. What is its diameter on the drawing?

(b) The length of a leaf on the same drawing is 7 inches. What is the actual length of the leaf?

6. The scale of a car drawing is 1 : 20. The actual length and width of the car are 4.5 m and 1.75 m respectively. Find the length and width of the car on the drawing, in centimeters.

7. The length of a room on a drawing with scale 1 : 50 is 9.2 cm. If the scale is changed to 1 : 40, what is the length of the room on the new drawing?

MATH @ WORK

8. The Fountain of Wealth in Suntec City, Singapore, is supposedly the world's largest fountain that is made of bronze as recorded in the 1998 edition of the Guinness Book of Records. Four 13.8 m bronze legs support a huge bronze ring measuring 21 m in diameter. On a design drawing, each leg is 27.6 cm high. Find

(a) the scale of the drawing in the form 1 : n,

(b) the diameter of the ring on the drawing.

9. The diameter of the face of a watch is 36 mm and the length of its minute-hand is 11 mm. On a scale drawing, the diameter of the watch is 180 mm. Find

(a) the scale of the drawing in the form 1 : n,

(b) the length of the minute-hand on the drawing.

10. The diagram shows a floor plan of an apartment. The scale of the plan is 1 : 200.

(a) Find the actual dimensions, in meters, of

(i) Bedroom 1,

(ii) the kitchen.

(b) Find the actual area, in square meters, of

(i) the apartment,

(ii) the living room.

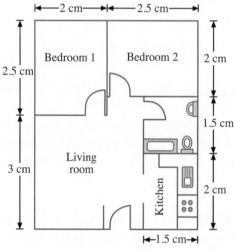

Scale: 1 : 200

BRAIN WORKS

11. (a) Measure the dimensions of your classroom and of the structures like the doors and windows in the room.

(b) Choose a suitable scale such that the floor plan of your classroom can be drawn to fit on an entire sheet of letter-size paper.

(c) Draw the floor plan of your classroom on the sheet of paper.

14.2 Map Scale and Calculation of Area

A Map Scale

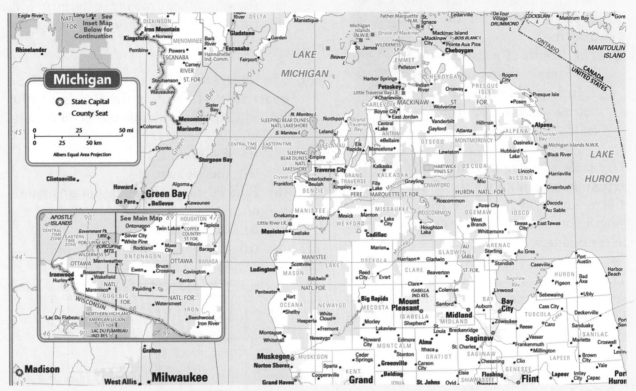

A map is a scale drawing of actual land. The **map scale** is the ratio of a distance on the map to the corresponding actual horizontal distance on the ground. It is usually located at a corner of the map. The scale of a map can be presented in several ways.

A **bar scale** or a **linear scale** is drawn to assist the measurement of distance on the map. The bar scale below shows the scale of 1 : 316,800 which means that 1 inch on the map represents 316,800 inches (or 5 miles) on the real land.

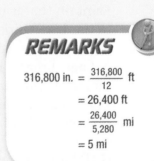

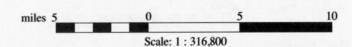

miles 5   0   5   10

Scale: 1 : 316,800

To the right of zero on the bar scale, the scale is graduated in primary divisions of 5 mi. To the left of zero, the scale is graduated in secondary divisions of 1 mi each and are used to estimate smaller distances.

A **ratio** or a **representative fraction (RF)** indicates how many units on the Earth's surface is equal to one unit on the map. Map scale can be expressed as a ratio, for example 1 : 100,000, or as a fraction, $\dfrac{1}{100,000}$. In this RF, 1 cm on the map equals 100,000 cm (or 1 km) on the land. It can also mean that 1 in. on the map equals to 100,000 in. (or about 1.6 mi) on the land.

Common map scales used in the United States are

      1 : 24,000 (1 in. to 2,000 ft), 1 : 63,360 (1 in. to 1 mi),

      1 : 316,800 (1 in. to 5 mi), 1 : 50,000 (1 cm to 0.5 km),

and   1 : 1,000,000 (1 cm to 10 km).

DISCUSS

1. Do you know why the numerator of a scale is usually 1?

2. If 1 cm on the map represents 20,000 cm on the ground, how many meters on the ground would 1 mm on the map represent?

Example 5

A distance of 3 cm on a map represents an actual distance of 1.5 km.

(a) Express the scale of the map in the form $\frac{1}{r}$.

(b) If the distance between two schools on the map is 7 cm, find the actual distance between the two schools.

(c) If the actual distance between two stores is 6 km, find the distance on the map.

Solution

(a) Map scale = 3 cm : 1.5 km

          = 3 cm : 1.5 × 1,000 × 100 cm

          = 3 cm : 150,000 cm

          = 1 : 50,000

The scale of the map is $\frac{1}{50,000}$.

RECALL

1 m = 100 cm

1 km = 1,000 m
      = 100,000 cm

(b) The map scale shows that 1 cm on the map represents 50,000 cm on the ground.

  ∴ the actual distance between the two schools

    = 7 × 50,000 cm

    = 350,000 cm

    = 3.5 km

(c) Distance on the map = $6 \times \dfrac{1}{50,000}$ km

                 = $6 \times \dfrac{1}{50,000} \times 1{,}000 \times 100$ cm

                 = 12 cm

Note: Alternatively, we can use the given scale 3 cm : 1.5 km to find the distance on the map when the actual distance is 6 km as $\dfrac{6}{1.5} \times 3 = 12$ cm.

Try It! 5

A distance of 4 in. on a map represents an actual distance of 5 mi.

(a) Express the scale of the map in the form $\frac{1}{r}$.

(b) If the distance between two cafes on the map is 6 in., find the actual distance between the two cafes.

(c) What is the distance between two supermarkets on the map when their actual distance apart is 6 mi?

RECALL

1 mi = 5,280 ft

1 ft = 12 in.

B Calculation of Area

When the scale of a map is $1 : r$, a square of side 1 cm on the map represents an actual square of side r cm. Hence, area on the map : actual area = $1 \text{ cm}^2 : r^2 \text{ cm}^2$
$$= 1 : r^2$$

 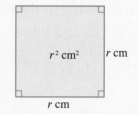

If the scale on a map is given by $1 : r$, then the ratio of the area measured on the map to the actual area is $1 : r^2$.

Example 6

The scale of a map is 1 : 30,000. A rectangular piece of land is 4 cm by 2.5 cm on the map.
(a) Find the actual area of the land in square kilometers.
(b) If the actual area of a town is 0.63 km², find its area on the map in square centimeters.

MATH WEB
You can learn more about the scales of maps at the websites *http://www.mapblast.com* and *http://www.maps.google.com*.

Solution **(a)**

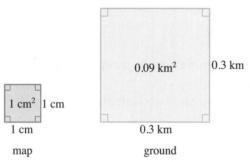

map   ground

As illustrated in the figure,
scale of the map = 1 : 30,000
$$= 1 \text{ cm} : 0.3 \text{ km}$$
Hence, area on the map : actual area
$$= 1 \text{ cm}^2 : 0.3 \times 0.3 \text{ km}^2$$
$$= 1 \text{ cm}^2 : 0.09 \text{ km}^2$$

Area of the land on the map $= 4 \times 2.5 \text{ cm}^2 = 10 \text{ cm}^2$
$\therefore$ actual area of the land $= 10 \times 0.09 \text{ km}^2 = 0.9 \text{ km}^2$

(b) Area of the town on the map = $0.63 \div 0.09 \text{ cm}^2$
$$= 7 \text{ cm}^2$$

Try It! 6

The scale of a map is 1 : 40,000. A rectangular field is 3 cm by 2 cm on the map.
(a) Find the actual area of the field in km².
(b) If the actual area of the region that is covered with bush is 2 km², find its area on the map in cm².

EXERCISE 14.2

BASIC PRACTICE

1. Express each map scale in the form $1 : r$.
 (a) 1 in. : 5,000 yd   **(b)** 0.5 in. : 3 mi
 (c) 3 cm : 900 m   **(d)** 5 cm : 20 km

2. Express each map scale in the form $\dfrac{1}{r}$.
 (a) 1 in. : 1 mi   **(b)** 2 in. : 5 mi
 (c) 4 cm : 1 km   **(d)** 7 cm : 28 km

3. Study the map of Ubin Island below.

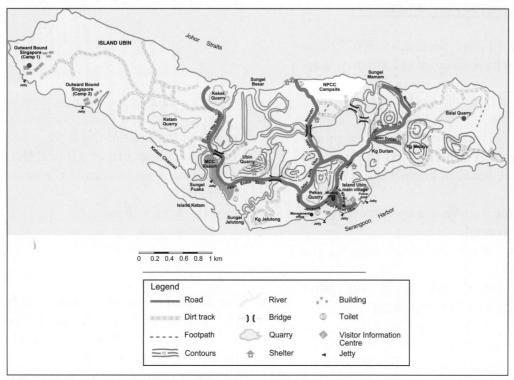

(a) Express the scale of the map in the form $\dfrac{1}{r}$.

(b) What is the actual direct distance between Outward Bound Singapore (Camp 1) and Balai Quarry?

4. **(a)** The scale of a road map is 1 : 5,000. How many meters is a distance 7 cm on the map?

 (b) Another road map has a scale of 1 : 63,360. How many miles is a distance of 7 in. on this map?

5. The scale of a district map is $\dfrac{1}{10,000}$. Find the distance on the map, in centimeters, for each of the following actual distances.
 (a) 800 m   **(b)** 5 km

6. The scale of a detailed map is 1 : 2,000. Find the actual area, in m^2, for each of the following areas on the map.
   (a) $1 \, cm^2$ **(b)** $5 \, cm^2$

7. The scale of a city map is 1 : 50,000. Find the area on the map, in cm^2, for each of the following actual areas.
   (a) $1 \, km^2$ **(b)** $15 \, km^2$

FURTHER PRACTICE

8. An actual ground distance of 6 km is represented by a distance of 2 cm on a map.
   (a) Express the scale of the map in the form $\dfrac{1}{r}$.
   (b) If the distance between two banks on the map is 5 cm, find their actual distance apart in kilometers.

9. Suppose that 3 cm on a map represents 1.2 km on the ground.
   (a) Express the scale of the map in the form 1 : r.
   (b) If the area of a lake is $0.32 \, km^2$, what is its area on the map in cm^2?

10. A map is drawn to a scale of 1 : 316,800.
   (a) How many miles is a distance of 5 in. on this map?
   (b) What area, in square inches, on the map would represent a nature reserve of area 50 square miles?

11. A street 250 yd long is represented by a distance of 6 in. on a map.
   (a) Express the scale of the map in the form 1 : r.
   (b) What is the distance on the map that represents another street which is 400 yd long?
   (c) Find the actual area of a park, in square feet, if its area on the map is $0.6 \, in^2$.

MATH@WORK

12. An actual region of area $18 \, km^2$ is represented by an area of $2 \, cm^2$ on a map.
   (a) Express the scale of the map in the form $\dfrac{1}{r}$.
   (b) If the area of a farm is $0.25 \, cm^2$ on the map, find its ground area in km^2.

13. The figure shows a piece of land in which $AB = 45$ m, $BC = 24$ m, and $AD = 16$ m.

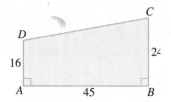

   (a) Find the area of the land.
   (b) Find the length of AB and the area of the land on a map if the scale of the map is
   (i) 1 cm to 5 m,
   (ii) 1 : 200,
   (iii) $\dfrac{1}{2,500}$.

14. The scale of a map of Asia is 1 : 25,000,000. The actual distance between Singapore and Beijing is 4,457 km. The total area of Taiwan is $36,000 \, km^2$. Find
   (a) the distance between Singapore and Beijing on the map,
   (b) the total area of Taiwan on the map.
   Give your answers correct to 2 decimal places.

15. The actual distance between New York City and Los Angeles is 3,935 km. The total area of Alaska is $1,717,850 \, km^2$. A map is drawn to the scale of 1 : 15,000,000. Determine, correct to 1 decimal place,
   (a) the distance between New York City and Los Angeles on the map,
   (b) the total area of Alaska on the map,
   (c) the actual distance between Dallas and Detroit if their distance apart on this map is 10.7 cm.

16. California, the third largest state in the United States, has an east-west dimension of 480 km.

(a) A map of California, drawn with a scale of 1 : 1,500,000, fits exactly from north to south inside a rectangle of length 84 cm. What is the north-south dimension of California?

(b) If you sketch a map of California on a piece of paper 21 cm by 28 cm, what is an appropriate scale you would choose such that the map fits inside a rectangle with a uniform border of 1 cm around the sides of the paper?

14.3 *Direct Proportion*

When two quantities are related to each other, their changes may follow a certain pattern. For instance, if a sandwich costs $1 at your school cafeteria, you will have to pay $2 for two sandwiches, $3 for three sandwiches, and so on. Thus, the amount you pay is related to the number of sandwiches ordered.

We shall explore this special relationship further in the following class activity.

Objective: To understand the idea of direct proportion.

Questions

The following table shows the relationship between the number of books bought (x) and the total cost of the books (y).

Number of books (x)	1	2	3	4	5	6
Total cost (y)	5	10	15	20	25	30

(a) Copy and complete the following table.

x	1	2	3	4	5	6
y	5	10	15	20	25	30
$\frac{y}{x}$						

(b) On a sheet of graph paper, plot the corresponding points (x, y) in **(a)** using the scale for both axes as shown.

(c) What can you say about the points you have plotted in **(b)**?

(d) Write down an equation connecting x and y.

(e) What is the value of y when $x = 8$?

(f) Does the graph of the equation in **(d)** pass through the origin $(0, 0)$?

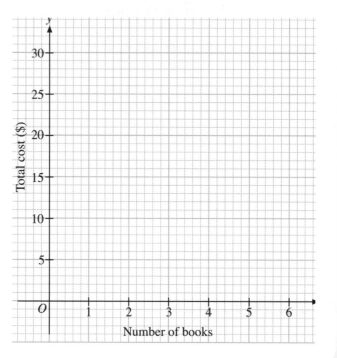

When two quantities, x and y, vary in such a way that $\frac{y}{x}$ is a constant, they are said to be in **direct proportion**, or y is said to be **directly proportional** to x.

REMARKS
Do you know that a distance on a map and its actual distance are in direct proportion?

In Class Activity 1, we have

$$\frac{y}{x} = \frac{5}{1} = \frac{10}{2} = \ldots = \frac{30}{6} = 5,$$

which is a constant.

Hence, the number of books bought (x), and the total cost $(\$y)$ are in direct proportion. Also, we see that the points (x, y) lie on a straight line passing through the origin. The equation of the straight line is $y = 5x$.

When two quantities, x and y, are in direct proportion, we have

$\frac{y}{x} = k$, where k is a constant.

that is $y = kx$

In Class Activity 1, the constant $k = 5$. Thus, $y = 5x$.

In general, we have the following properties:

When two quantities, x and y, are in direct proportion:
- $y = kx$, where k is a constant
- the graph of $y = kx$ is a straight line passing through the origin

DISCUSS

In the graph in Class Activity 1,
(a) what is the gradient of the straight line?
(b) what does the gradient represent?

Example 7

The following table shows the traveling time (t hr) and the distance covered (y mi) by a car.

Traveling time (t hr)	0.5	1.0	1.5	2.0	2.5
Distance covered (y mi)	30	60	90	120	150

(a) Show that t and y are in direct proportion.
(b) Draw the graph of y against t.
(c) Find the equation connecting t and y.
(d) Find the value of y when $t = 1.25$.
(e) Find the value of t when $y = 72$.

Solution   (a)

t	0.5	1.0	1.5	2.0	2.5
y	30	60	90	120	150
$\frac{y}{t}$	60	60	60	60	60

Since $\frac{y}{t}$ is a constant, t and y are in direct proportion.

(b) The graph of y against t is shown below.

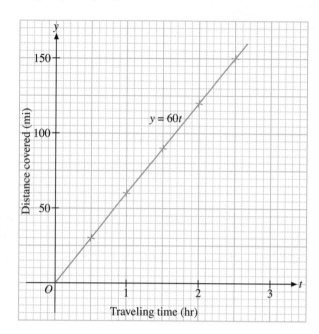

(c) Since $\dfrac{y}{t} = 60$, the equation connecting t and y is $y = 60t$.

(d) When $t = 1.25$, $y = 60 \times 1.25$ Substitute $t = 1.25$ into the
                             $= 75$.   equation in **(c)**.

(e) When $y = 72$, $72 = 60t$ Substitute $y = 72$ into the equation in **(c)**.

$$t = \frac{72}{60}$$

$$= 1.2$$

Try It! **7**

The following table shows the number of hours (t) worked and the corresponding wages ($\$w$) of a worker.

Number of hours worked (t)	10	20	30	40	50
Wages ($\$w$)	150	300	450	600	750

(a) Show that t and w are in direct proportion.
(b) Draw the graph of w against t.
(c) Find the equation connecting t and w.
(d) If the worker worked 35 hours, find his wages.
(e) If the wages of a worker were $675, find the number of hours he worked.

When two quantities, x and y, are in direct proportion,

$$y = kx, \text{ where } k \text{ is a constant.}$$

Suppose (x_1, y_1) and (x_2, y_2) are any two pairs of values of x and y, where $x_2 \neq 0$ and $y_2 \neq 0$,

then $\qquad\qquad y_1 = kx_1$ and $y_2 = kx_2$.

Hence, $\qquad\qquad \dfrac{y_1}{y_2} = \dfrac{kx_1}{kx_2}$

that is $\qquad\qquad \dfrac{y_1}{y_2} = \dfrac{x_1}{x_2}$.

> When two quantities, x and y, are in direct proportion, given any two pairs of values of x and y, (x_1, y_1) and (x_2, y_2), we have $\dfrac{y_1}{y_2} = \dfrac{x_1}{x_2}$, where $x_2 \neq 0$ and $y_2 \neq 0$.

The equality of two ratios is called a **proportion**. We say that $y_1, y_2, x_1,$ and x_2 are **in proportion**.

Example 8

The height, H cm, of a pile of books is directly proportional to the number of books, n, in the pile. The height of a pile of 10 books is 15 cm. What is the height of a pile of 24 books?

Solution

Method 1

Since n and H are in direct proportion, $H = kn$, where k is a constant.

When $n = 10$, $H = 15$.

$\therefore \qquad\qquad 15 = k \times 10$

$\qquad\qquad\quad k = \dfrac{15}{10}$

$\qquad\qquad\qquad = 1.5$

Hence, $\qquad H = 1.5n$

When $n = 24$, $H = 1.5 \times 24$

$\qquad\qquad\qquad = 36$

The height of a pile of 24 books is 36 cm.

REMARKS

The value of k is actually the thickness of each book in centimeters.

Estimate: Is the answer reasonable?

24 books are slightly more than twice of 10 books. Is the answer '36 cm' slightly more than twice of '15 cm'?

Method 2

Since n and H are in direct proportion,

$$\frac{H_1}{H_2} = \frac{n_1}{n_2}$$

Let $n_1 = 10$, $H_1 = 15$, and $n_2 = 24$.

Substituting these values into the proportion, we have:

$$\frac{15}{H_2} = \frac{10}{24}$$

$$H_2 = 15 \times \frac{24}{10}$$

$$= 36$$

Hence, the height of a pile of 24 books is 36 cm.

Try It! 8

The number of pieces, n, of chocolate and their total mass, M grams, are in direct proportion. The mass of 15 pieces of chocolate is 180 g. Find the mass in grams of 20 pieces of chocolate.

In real life, two quantities, x and y, may not be in direct proportion but x^n and y^m, where n and m are rational numbers, may be in direct proportion. The following example illustrates such a situation.

Example 9

The weight of a solid metal sphere and the cube of its radius are in direct proportion. When the radius of the sphere is 2 in., its weight is 192 oz. Find the weight in ounces of a sphere of radius of 1.5 in.

Solution

Let the weight of a sphere of radius r in. be m oz.
Then, we have $m = kr^3$, where k is a constant.

When $r = 2$, $m = 192$.

$$\therefore \ 192 = k \times 2^3$$

$$k = \frac{192}{8}$$

$$= 24$$

$$\therefore \ m = 24r^3$$

When $r = 1.5$, $m = 24 \times 1.5^3$

$$= 81$$

The weight of a sphere of radius 1.5 in. is 81 oz.

Try It! 9

The mass of a square piece of glass panel is directly proportional to the square of the length of its side. When its side is 20 cm, the mass is 1,000 g. Find the mass in grams of a glass panel of side 30 cm.

BASIC PRACTICE

1. In each of the following tables, determine whether x and y are in direct proportion.

(a)
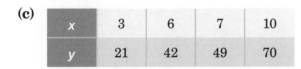

x	1	2	3	4
y	3	6	9	12

(b)
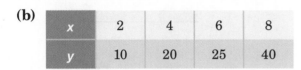

x	2	4	6	8
y	10	20	25	40

(c)
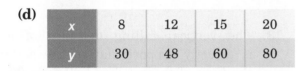

x	3	6	7	10
y	21	42	49	70

(d)

x	8	12	15	20
y	30	48	60	80

2. In each of the following graphs, determine whether x and y are in direct proportion.

(a)
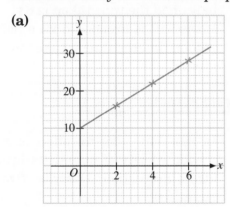

(b)
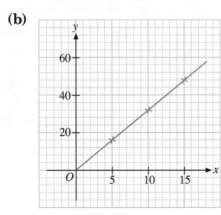

3. In each of the following equations, determine whether x and y are in direct proportion.

(a) $y = 4x$ (b) $y = x + 2$

(c) $y = x^2$ (d) $y = \dfrac{1}{2}x$

4. If two quantities, x and y, are in direct proportion, find the values of p and q in the following table.

x	12	18	q
y	8	p	24

5. It is given that w is directly proportional to t. When $t = 4$, $w = 20$. Find

(a) the value of w when $t = 6$,

(b) the value of t when $w = 45$.

6. It is given that A is directly proportional to r^2 and $r > 0$. When $r = 5$, $A = 75$. Find

(a) the value of A when $r = 4$,

(b) the value of r when $A = 147$.

FURTHER PRACTICE

7. The following table shows the total price ($\$P$) for x copies of books.

Copies of books (x)	1	2	3	4	5
Total price ($\$P$)	15	30	45	60	75

(a) Show that x and P are in direct proportion.

(b) Draw the graph of P against x.

(c) Describe the graph in **(b)**.

(d) Find the equation connecting x and P.

(e) Hence, find the total price for 8 copies of books.

8. The following table shows the mass (m g) of a pinewood cube of side x cm.

Length of a side (x cm)	2	4	5	8	10
Mass (m g)	5.2	41.6	81.25	332.8	650

(a) Is m proportional to x?
(b) Is m proportional to x^3?
(c) Find an equation connecting m and x.
(d) Hence, find the mass in grams of a pinewood cube of side 9 cm.

 **MATH@WORK**

9. The cost of renting a car is directly proportional to the number of days the car is being rented for. The cost of renting a car for 4 days is $240. Find the cost of renting a car for 7 days.

10. The mass of a metal plate is directly proportional to its volume. When its volume is 20 cm^3, its mass is 210 g. If the volume of the metal plate is 50 cm^3, what is its mass?

11. When a car is traveling steadily along a highway, its consumption of gasoline is directly proportional to the distance traveled. A car travels 100 mi on 2.7 gal of gasoline. Find, giving your answer correct to 1 decimal place,
(a) the gasoline consumption of the car for a distance of 74 mi,
(b) the maximum distance that the car can travel with 1 gal of gasoline.

12. The period (the time taken for one complete oscillation) of a simple pendulum is directly proportional to the square root of its length. When its length is 1.02 m, its period is 2.01 seconds. Find
(a) the period of the pendulum when its length is 0.8 m,
(b) the length of the pendulum when its period is 1.0 second.
Give your answers correct to 2 decimal places.

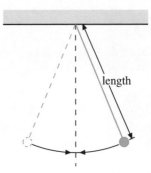

length

13. The vertical falling distance of a ball is directly proportional to the square of the time of falling. The ball falls 80 m in 4 s.
(a) Find the vertical falling distance of the ball when the time taken is 6 s.
(b) If the ball is dropped from a height of 245 m, find the time it takes to hit the ground.

BRAINWORKS

14. (a) In our daily life, we often encounter a wide variety of quantities involving direct proportion. Describe two such quantities.
(b) Draw a graph to show their relationship.
(c) Find an equation connecting the quantities.

15. Jordan's height and weight increase as he grows bigger. Do you think his height and weight are in direct proportion? Give reasons for your answer.

14.4 Inverse Proportion

We have learned that when two quantities x and y are in direct proportion, both x and y increase (or decrease) at the same rate. However, in our daily life, we do come across situations where an increase in one quantity results in a corresponding decrease in another related quantity or vice versa. For instance, when a motorist travels at a higher speed, the time taken to cover a certain distance is reduced.

 CLASS ACTIVITY 2

Objective: To understand the idea of inverse proportion between two quantities.

Questions

A fixed amount of water is poured into individual containers of various uniform cross-sections. The following table shows the correspondence between the cross-sectional area (x cm^2) of each container and the depth of water (y cm) in it.

Cross-sectional area (x cm^2)	10	20	30	40	50	60
Depth of water (y cm)	36	18	12	9	7.2	6

(a) Copy and complete the following table. Give the values of $\frac{1}{x}$ correct to 3 decimal places.

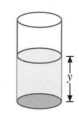

x	10	20	30	40	50	60
y	36	18	12	9	7.2	6
$\frac{1}{x}$						
xy						

(b) On a sheet of graph paper, plot the corresponding points (x, y) in (a) using the scales for both axes as shown below.

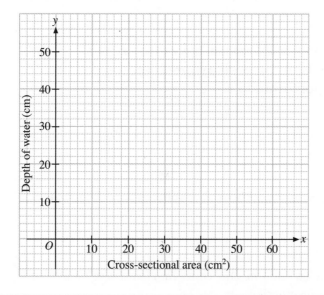

(c) What can you say about the points you have plotted in **(b)**?

(d) What happens to the depth of the water as the cross-sectional area of a container increases?

(e) On a sheet of graph paper, plot the corresponding points $\left(\dfrac{1}{x}, y\right)$ in **(a)** using the scales for both axes as shown below.

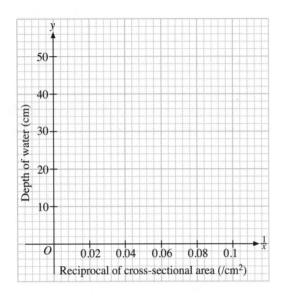

(f) What can you say about the points you have plotted in **(e)**?

(g) Suggest an equation connecting x and y.

(h) What is the value of y when $x = 80$?

When two quantities, x and y, vary in such a way that xy is a constant, they are said to be in **inverse proportion**, or y is said to be **inversely proportional** to x.

In Class Activity 2, we have

$$xy = 10 \times 36 = 20 \times 18 = \ldots = 60 \times 6 = 360,$$

which is a constant.

Hence, the cross-sectional area (x cm^2) of the container and the depth of water (y cm) in it are in inverse proportion.

In (b) and (e) of Class Activity 2, when the plotted points on each graph are joined with a smooth curve, the graphs look like Fig. 1 and Fig. 2 respectively.

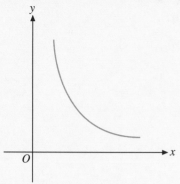

Fig. 1

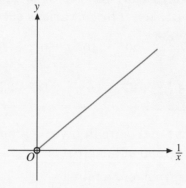

Fig. 2

The graph of y against x is a curve which approaches the y-axis when x is small, and it tends to the x-axis as x increases. The curve is part of a curve, called a **hyperbola**.

The graph of y against $\frac{1}{x}$ is part of a straight line which passes through the origin. Since $\frac{1}{x}$ is never zero, the origin is NOT on the graph.

From **(a)**, the equation connecting x and y is:

$$xy = 360$$

that is

$$y = 360 \times \frac{1}{x}$$

$$y = 360\left(\frac{1}{x}\right)$$

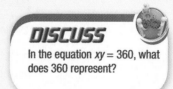

DISCUSS

In the equation $xy = 360$, what does 360 represent?

When two quantities, x and y, are in inverse proportion, we have

$$xy = k, \text{ where } k \text{ is a constant.}$$

Since $xy = k$,

$$\therefore \qquad y = k\left(\frac{1}{x}\right)$$

In Class Activity 2, $k = 360$. Thus, $y = 360\left(\frac{1}{x}\right)$ or $y = \frac{360}{x}$.

In general, we have the following properties:

> When two quantities, x and y, are in inverse proportion:
> - $xy = k$, where k is a constant
> - the graph of y against $\frac{1}{x}$ is part of a straight line which passes through the origin

Example 10

A car travels uniformly from A to B. The following table shows the time taken (t hr) at various speeds (v km/hr).

Speed (v km/hr)	20	40	50	80	100	120
Time taken (t hr)	10	5	4	2.5	2	$1\frac{2}{3}$

(a) Show that t and v are in inverse proportion.

(b) Draw the graph of t against v.

(c) Draw the graph of t against $\dfrac{1}{v}$.

(d) Find the equation connecting t and v.

(e) Find the time taken when the speed is 90 km/hr.

Solution

(a)

v	20	40	50	80	100	120
t	10	5	4	2.5	2	$1\frac{2}{3}$
vt	200	200	200	200	200	200
$\dfrac{1}{v}$	0.05	0.025	0.02	0.013	0.01	0.008

Since $vt = 200$ is a constant, t and v are in inverse proportion.

(b) The graph of t against v is shown below.

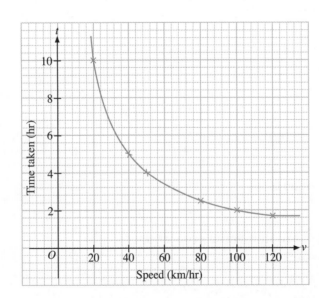

(c) The graph of t against $\dfrac{1}{v}$ is shown below.

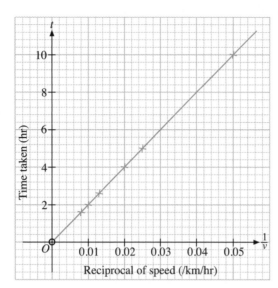

The small circle at the origin O indicates that the point $(0, 0)$ is not included on the straight line graph.

(d) From **(a)**, the equation connecting t and v is
$$vt = 200 \text{ or } t = \frac{200}{v}.$$

(e) When $v = 90$,
$$90 \times t = 200 \qquad \text{Substitution}$$
$$t = \frac{200}{90}$$
$$= 2\frac{2}{9}$$

When the speed is 90 km/hr, the time taken is $2\dfrac{2}{9}$ hours.

Note: In the equation $vt = 200$, the value 200 represents the distance between A and B in kilometers.

Try It! 10 The following table shows the corresponding volume (V cm^3) of air inside a syringe when the air pressure is P units.

Pressure (*P* units)	1	2	3	4	5	6
Volume (*V* cm³)	120	60	40	30	24	20

(a) Show that P and V are in inverse proportion.

(b) Draw the graph of V against P.

(c) Draw the graph of V against $\dfrac{1}{P}$.

(d) Find the equation connecting P and V.

(e) Find the volume of air when the air pressure is 8 units.

When two quantities, x and y, are in inverse proportion,

$$xy = k, \text{ where } k \text{ is a constant.}$$

Suppose (x_1, y_1) and (x_2, y_2) are any two pairs of values of x and y, then $x_1 y_1 = k$ and $x_2 y_2 = k$.

$\therefore \qquad x_1 y_1 = x_2 y_2$

When two quantities, x and y, are in inverse proportion, we have $x_1 y_1 = x_2 y_2$, where (x_1, y_1) and (x_2, y_2) are any two pairs of values of x and y.

REMARKS

By dividing both sides by $x_1 y_2$, we can also write $x_1 y_1 = x_2 y_2$ as $\dfrac{y_1}{y_2} = \dfrac{x_2}{x_1}$.

Example 11

The time taken, t hours, to do a paint job is inversely proportional to the number of workers, N. Given that 9 workers take 20 hours to complete a job, find the time taken by 6 workers to complete the same job.

Solution

Method 1

Since t and N are in inverse proportion,
$tN = k$, where k is a constant.

When $N = 9$, $t = 20$.
$\therefore \qquad 20 \times 9 = k$
$\qquad\qquad\quad k = 180$
$\qquad\qquad\quad tN = 180$

When $N = 6$, $t \times 6 = 180$
$\qquad\qquad\qquad\quad t = 30$

The time taken by 6 workers to complete the job is 30 hours.

Method 2

Since t and N are in inverse proportion,
$$t_1 N_1 = t_2 N_2 \quad .... \text{(1)}$$
Let $t_1 = 20$, $N_1 = 9$, and $N_2 = 6$.

Substituting these values into (1), we have:
$$20 \times 9 = t_2 \times 6$$
$$t_2 = \frac{20 \times 9}{6}$$
$$= 30$$

The time taken by 6 workers to complete the job is 30 hours.

Try It! 11

A big bottle of orange juice is shared equally among n boys. Each boy drinks V cm^3 of the juice. It is known that n and V are in inverse proportion. If there are 6 boys sharing the drink, each boy has 250 cm^3 of it. How much can each boy drink when there are 10 boys?

Example 12

The intensity of illumination from a desk lamp on a book is inversely proportional to the square of the distance of the book from the lamp. When the book is 15 in. from the lamp, the intensity of illumination is 6 units. Find the intensity of illumination when the book is 10 in. from the lamp.

Solution

Let the intensity of illumination be I units when the book is d in. from the lamp.

Since I and d^2 are in inverse proportion,
$$Id^2 = k, \text{ where } k \text{ is a constant.}$$

When $d = 15$, $I = 6$.
$$\therefore \quad 6 \times 15^2 = k$$
$$k = 1,350$$
$$Id^2 = 1,350$$

When $d = 10$, $I \times 10^2 = 1,350$
$$I = \frac{1,350}{100}$$
$$= 13.5$$

The intensity of illumination when the book is 10 in. from the lamp is 13.5 units.

DISCUSS

Do you expect the intensity to be greater when the distance is lesser? Check to see if the answer is reasonable.

REMARKS

We can also use Method 2 as shown in Example 11 to answer the question.

Try It! 12

When a fixed amount of water is poured into a cylinder, the depth of water is inversely proportional to the square of the base radius of the cylinder. When the radius is 3 in., the depth of water is 24 in. Find the depth when the radius is 6 in.

EXERCISE 14.4

BASIC PRACTICE

1. In each of the following tables of values, determine whether x and y are in inverse proportion.

(a)

x	1	2	3	4
y	12	10	8	6

(b)

x	2	4	6	8
y	12	6	4	3

(c)

x	10	20	25	40
y	60	30	24	15

(d)

x	12	15	18	24
y	30	24	18	15

2. In each of the following graphs, determine whether x and y are in inverse proportion.

(a)

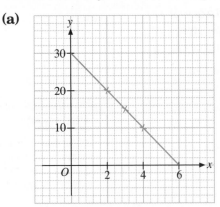

(b)

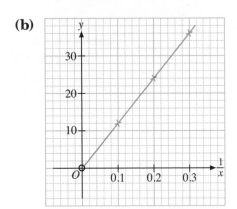

3. In each of the following equations, determine whether x and y are in inverse proportion.
   (a) $xy = 20$
   (b) $x - y = 20$
   (c) $y = \dfrac{18}{x}$
   (d) $y = \dfrac{1}{x} + 1$

4. If two quantities, x and y, are in inverse proportion, find the values of p and q in the following table.

x	32	20	q
y	5	p	16

5. It is given that z is inversely proportional to t. When $t = 9$, $z = 28$. Find
   (a) the value of z when $t = 12$,
   (b) the value of t when $z = 36$.

6. It is given that D is inversely proportional to $\sqrt{m}$. When $m = 9$, $D = 64$. Find
   (a) the value of D when $m = 4$,
   (b) the value of m when $D = 32$.

7. The diagram shows a lever system with a load that is balanced by a weight m grams at a distance d cm from the fulcrum.

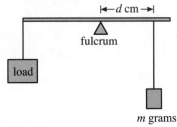

The following table shows various pairs of values of d and m.

d (cm)	10	20	30	40	50
m (g)	60	30	20	15	12

   (a) Show that d and m are in inverse proportion.
   (b) Draw the graph of m against d.
   (c) Draw the graph of m against $\dfrac{1}{d}$.
   (d) Find the equation connecting d and m.
   (e) Find the value of m when $d = 25$.

8. The following table shows the number of trees (y) required to be planted on a hillside when the distance between two adjacent trees is x meters.

x	1	2	3	5	6
y	900	225	100	36	25

   (a) Is y inversely proportional to x?
   (b) Is y inversely proportional to x^2?
   (c) Find an equation connecting x and y.
   (d) Find the number of trees required when $x = 1.5$.

9. Given that y is inversely proportional to the cube of x, and $y = 30$ when $x = 2$. Find
   (a) the value of y when $x = 5$,
   (b) the value of x when $y = 3.75$.

10. It is given that S is inversely proportional to t^n for the values given in the following table.

t	1	3	5	
S	90	10		0.9

   (a) Find the value of n.
   (b) Copy and complete the given table.

MATH@WORK

11. The time taken, t minutes, to download a file from a computer is inversely proportional to the Internet connection speed, v kB/s. When the speed is 64 kB/s, the time taken is 12 minutes. Find the time taken when the speed is 512 kB/s.

12. The rate of water delivered and the time taken to fill up a pool are in inverse proportion. If the rate is 16 gal/min, the time taken is 20 minutes. What is the time taken when the rate is 40 gal/min?

13. The frequency of sound produced by a string is inversely proportional to the length of the string. When the string is 50 cm long, the frequency of sound is 256 Hz. Find
   (a) the frequency of sound when the string is 40 cm long,
   (b) the length of the string when the frequency of sound is 400 Hz.

14. The force of attraction between two magnets is inversely proportional to the square of the distance between them. When their distance apart is 3 in., the force of attraction is 56 units. Find
   (a) the force of attraction when the distance apart is 2 in.,
   (b) the distance apart when the force of attraction is 14 units.

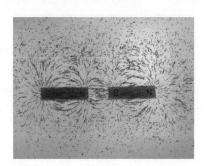

15. The speed of a bullet fired from a gun is inversely proportional to the square root of its mass. When the mass is 49 g, the speed is 640 m/s. Find
   (a) the speed when its mass is 36 g,
   (b) the mass when its speed is 560 m/s.

BRAINWORKS

16. In your science laboratory studies, you would have come across two quantities that are in inverse proportion. Show how these quantities are related, using a graph.

17. If 12 workers take 100 days to build a house, is it true that 1,200 workers will take one day to build the house? Explain briefly.

Scale Drawings

Scale drawings are reduced or enlarged drawings of actual objects.

Scale of a Drawing

The scale of a drawing can be expressed as a ratio $1 : n$ where 1 unit length on the drawing represents an actual length of n units.

Map Scale

- Scale = Map length : Actual length

$$= 1 : r \left(\text{or } \frac{1}{r} \right)$$

- Area on a map : Actual area = $1 : r^2$

Direct Proportion

When two quantities, x and y, are in direct proportion:

- $y = kx \left(\text{or } \dfrac{y}{x} = k, x \neq 0 \right)$, where k is a constant

- the graph of y against x is a straight line passing through the origin

- $\dfrac{y_1}{y_2} = \dfrac{x_1}{x_2}$, where (x_1, y_1) and (x_2, y_2) are any two pairs of values of x

  and y, $x_2 \neq 0$ and $y_2 \neq 0$

Inverse Proportion

When two quantities, x and y, are in inverse proportion:

- $xy = k$, where k is a constant

- the graph of y against x is part of a curve called a hyperbola

- the graph of y against $\dfrac{1}{x}$ is part of a straight line passing through the origin but $(0, 0)$ is not inclusive on the graph

- $x_1 y_1 = x_2 y_2$, where (x_1, y_1) and (x_2, y_2) are any two pairs of values of x and y

1. The shaft of a gardening tool has a length of 25 cm and a diameter of 3.8 cm. It is drawn 5 cm long in a mechanical drawing. Find
    (a) the scale of the drawing,
    (b) the diameter of the shaft in the drawing.

2. The diagram shows a part of the floor plan of an apartment. The actual length of the wall, AB, of the living room is 8 m.

    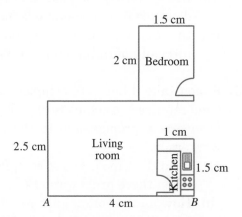

    (a) the scale of the floor plan,
    (b) the actual width of the living room,
    (c) the actual dimensions of the bedroom.

3. The scale of a floor plan is 1 in. to $16\frac{2}{3}$ ft.
    Find
    (a) the scale of the plan,
    (b) the length of a hallway on the plan if its actual length is 50 ft,
    (c) the actual area of a rectangular garden if its dimensions on the plan are 3 in. by $1\frac{1}{2}$ in.

4. A map is drawn to the scale 1 : 4,000.
    (a) The length of a road on the map is 3.5 cm. Find its actual length in meters.
    (b) The area of a garden is 20,000 m². Find the area of the garden on the map in square centimeters.

5. The scale of map A is 1 : 5,000 and the scale of map B is 1 : 3,000.
    (a) The distance between two schools on map A is 6 cm. Find their distance apart on map B.
    (b) The area of a lake on map B is 18 cm². Find
        (i)   the actual area of the lake in m²,
        (ii) the area of the lake on map A.

6. A carat is a measure of mass used for gemstones. The following table shows the conversion between carats and grams.

Gram (x)	2	4	6	8	10
Carat (y)	10	20	30	40	50

    (a) Show that x and y are in direct proportion.
    (b) Draw the graph of y against x.
    (c) Find the equation connecting x and y.
    (d) The mass of a piece of diamond is 7 g. How many carats is this?

7. The cost $\$C$ of a metal wire is directly proportional to its length x in. When the length is 3 in., its cost is \$0.20.
    (a) Find the length of the wire if its cost is \$15.
    (b) Metal wire is used to make the frame of a rectangular prism that measures 25 in. by 20 in. by 15 in. Find the total cost of the wire used.

    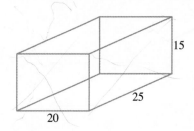

8. The mass of a model car is directly proportional to the cube of its length. When the length is 6 cm, its mass is 96 g.
    (a) Find the length of the model car when its mass is 324 g.
    (b) The model car is made using a scale of 1 : 50. The length of the real car is 4 m. Find
        (i) the length of the model car in centimeters,
        (ii) the mass of the model car, correct to the nearest gram.

9. The following table shows some corresponding values of two quantities, x and y.

x	0	1	2	3	4
y	0	2	8	18	32

    (a) Draw the graph of y against x.
    (b) Draw the graph of y against x^2.
    (c) State the relationship between x and y.
    (d) Write down an equation connecting x and y.
    (e) Find the value of y when $x = 2.5$.

10. Suppose the amount of food served to each person at a party is inversely proportional to the number of people who attend the party. When there are 25 people at the party, each person will have 1.2 kg of food.
    (a) If there are 60 people, find the amount of food each person is served.
    (b) How many people are there at the party if each person is served 0.4 kg of food?

11. The dimensions of a rectangle are x in. by y in. It is known that x and y are in inverse proportion. When $x = 36$, $y = 20$.
    (a) Find the equation connecting x and y.
    (b) Find the value of y when $x = 24$.
    (c) Find the value of x when $y = 15$.
    (d) What can you say about the area of the rectangle?

12. The intensity of radiation is inversely proportional to the square of the distance from a radioactive source. When the distance is 4 m, the intensity of radiation is 900 units. Find
    (a) the intensity of radiation when the distance from its source is 5 m,
    (b) the distance from the source if its intensity of radiation is 1,600 units.

13. 6 men take 6 hours to complete a job. The time required to complete the job, T hours, is inversely proportional to the number of workers, x.
    (a) Find the time taken to complete the job when there are 9 workers.
    (b) How many workers are required if the job has to be completed in 45 minutes?

14. In kick boxing, it is found that the force needed to break a board is inversely proportional to the length of the board. If it takes 6 lb of pressure to break a board 2 ft long, how many pounds of pressure will it take to break a board that is 5 ft long?

EXTEND YOUR LEARNING CURVE

Time Taken By A Planet To Revolve Around The Sun

In our solar system, planets revolve around the Sun in orbits. The shape of each orbit is an ellipse. This means the distance between a planet and the Sun is not a constant. The mean distance of a planet from the Sun is an average distance. The period of a planet is the time it takes to complete one orbit.

The following table gives the mean distance ($d \times 10^6$ km) and the period (p years) of the eight planets.

Planet	Mercury	Venus	Earth	Mars	Jupiter	Saturn	Uranus	Neptune
Mean distance ($d \times 10^6$ km)	57.91	108.21	149.60	227.94	778.41	1426.73	2870.97	4498.25
Period (p years)	0.241	0.615	1.0	1.88	11.86	29.46	84.01	164.79

An astronomer found that d^m and p^n, where m and n are certain positive integers, have a proportional relationship. What is this relationship?

WRITE IN YOUR JOURNAL

1. **(a)** Discuss why it is important that maps should be drawn to scale.
    (b) What are the differences when you choose a scale of 1 : 25,000 and 1 : 500,000 to draw the map of your town?

2. Describe how you can tell if two quantities are in direct proportion or inverse proportion.

15 DATA HANDLING

Playing

LET'S LEARN TO...

1. use different data-collection methods
2. use dot plots to organize and analyze data
3. understand measures of center
4. use measures of center to analyze and compare data

It is important for countries to have an accurate population figure. This helps governments to plan future health and education services, future housing needs, and so on. Most countries use a census to determine their population figures. It is estimated that there are more than seven billion people on the planet currently. Global population is projected to reach nine billion by the year 2045. Can the planet take the strain?

15.1 Collection of Data

Statistics is a branch of mathematics that involves collecting, organizing, interpreting, presenting, and analyzing data. Based on studies of data obtained, people are able to draw conclusions, make decisions, and plan wisely.

When the group we want to collect data from is large, we often randomly select a smaller group as a representative of the entire group. This method of data collection is called **random sampling**. Random sampling makes data collection faster, less costly, and easier to analyze since the data population is smaller.

> Generalizations about a population from a sample are valid only if the sample is representative of that population.

• Taking Measurements in Experiments

In biology and engineering, we can set up control experiments to take measurements from random samples of particular objects of interest.

(a) The yield of cross-fertilization of different types of rice can be measured by using samples from a patch of rice field.

(b) The life time of a certain battery can be tested in a quality-control laboratory by using a small random sample of batteries.

• Observing Outcomes of Events

Some data, such as air pollution levels and bird migration paths, are observed through real-life situations.

(a) Air pollution levels are observed by taking random air samples.

(b) Bird migration paths are traced by tagging a sample population of birds with identification numbers.

> It would be impossible to test all of the air, wouldn't it?

• Conducting Surveys

We usually conduct a survey to gather personal data and public opinion by requesting sample populations of target groups to complete a questionnaire. The survey may be conducted through face-to-face interviews, telephone interviews, postal surveys, or Internet surveys.

(a) The United States Census is a 100% population survey that is conducted once every 10 years.

(b) Customer satisfaction surveys taken by random samples of customers are very common in the service sector.

DISCUSS

Do you know the purpose of conducting a population census?

The first census taken after the American Revolution was conducted in 1790.

Food Survey

	Good	Bad
Food		
Price		
Presentation		

• Reading Statistical Publications

Some data such as economic conditions and the population of a country are obtained by conducting large-scale surveys that cannot be done by individuals or small companies. We can obtain these types of data from official statistics published by government organizations.

(a) *www.fedstats.gov* is a useful website for the United States statistics.

(b) The *United Nations Statistical Yearbook* contains a wide range of international economic, social, and environmental data.

EXERCISE 15.1

 BASIC PRACTICE

1. Suggest a way (taking measurements, observing outcomes, conducting surveys, reading publications) to collect a random sample of each set of data below.

   (a) Favorite sports of seventh grade students in your school

   (b) Total number of seventh grade students in the United States in a given year

   (c) Actual volume of each carton of orange juice in a sample of 20 cartons

   (d) Body temperatures of patients in a hospital

   (e) Popularity of a pop singer

   (f) Customers' opinions about a bank's services

   (g) Number of incoming calls in a doctor's office from 9:00 A.M. to 10:00 A.M.

   (h) Birth weight of babies in a hospital

   (i) Effectiveness of a new medicine

   (j) Population of the United States, Canada, and Mexico

2. Professor Smith wanted to test the air quality in a certain city. He collected samples from some areas of the city with the busiest traffic during rush hour.
   (a) What kind of data-collection method did he use?
   (b) Do you think his results are representative of the general air quality of the city? Explain your answer.

3. The principal wants to find out the favorite sports of students in the middle school. He collects the data in the following ways.
   (i) Checking the school database of students who play sports in the school and tabulating how many play each sport
   (ii) Asking five students from each class to fill out a survey about their favorite sports
   (iii) Designing a form for students to fill in their favorite sports and return the forms to him
   (a) Name the data-collection method used in each case.
   (b) Which method(s) do you think will produce the most accurate results? Why?

MATH@WORK

4. A restaurant manager requests a random sample of 100 customers to fill in the following questionnaire.

   ABC Restaurant
   Customer Satisfaction Survey

   1. How would you rate our food?
      ☐ very good ☐ good ☐ OK
      ☐ poor ☐ very poor

   2. Is the service of our staff up to your expectation? _____

   (a) What kind of data-collection method does the manager use?
   (b) Which question in the survey is better? Why?
   (c) Is it a good idea to ask customers to fill in the date of visit in the form? Why?

BRAIN WORKS

5. Design a questionnaire and collect data by using random sampling. Then, answer the following questions based on it.
   (a) What is the objective of the survey?
   (b) What types of questions will you use?
   (c) What are some of the good features of your survey?
   (d) How can you make sure that the people who participate in the survey are representative of the entire population?
   (e) Suggest some ways to improve your survey.

15.2 Dot Plots

In earlier grades, we learned to display data in **dot plots**. In this section, we will use dot plots to organize and compare small sets of data.

To construct a dot plot, we first draw a horizontal number line that covers the range of the given data. Then we plot the individual items as dots above their values on the number line.

REMARKS

Dot plot in statistics is also called a line plot. In a dot plot, dots (·) or crosses (×) represent the values of a set of data.

Example 1

The noon temperatures in degrees Celsius in Miami during a two-week period were as follows:

Noon Temperatures

30	27	29	30	31	35	28
25	31	30	29	28	30	29

(a) Represent the data on a dot plot.
(b) Briefly describe the distribution of the data.

Solution

(a) Since the temperatures vary from 25 °C to 35 °C, we draw a number line that includes this range of values. We then read the data one by one and plot them as dots over their values on the line as shown below.

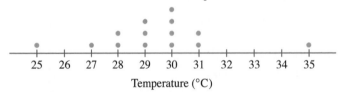

Dot Plot for Noon Temperatures

Temperature (°C)

(b) From the dot plot, we observe that
- the data vary from 25 °C to 35 °C
- the data cluster around 29 °C and 30 °C
- the extreme temperature 35°C deviates considerably from other temperatures observed

Try It! 1

The midnight temperatures in degrees Celsius in Miami during the same two-week period were as follows:

Midnight Temperatures

18	14	15	17	28	20	16
12	19	30	15	20	19	18

(a) Represent the data on a dot plot.
(b) Briefly describe the distribution of the data.
(c) Compare the distribution of the data for the noon temperatures and midnight temperatures. What conclusions can you draw?

Objective: To observe patterns of distributions revealed by dot plots.

Questions

1. The dot plot below displays the scores of the students from Class *A* in a math quiz. The maximum possible number of points of the quiz is 20.

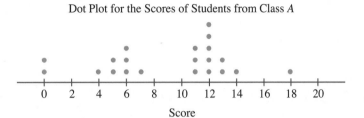

Dot Plot for the Scores of Students from Class *A*

Score

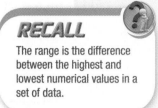

   (a) How many students are there?
   (b) What is the range of the data?
   (c) At which values do the scores cluster around?

2. The dot plot below displays the scores of the students from Class *B* in the same math quiz.

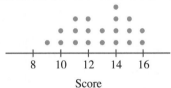

Dot Plot for the Scores of Students from Class *B*

Score

   (a) How many students are there?
   (b) Briefly describe the distribution of the scores.
   (c) Compare the dot plot for Class *A* with that for Class *B*. What do you notice? What conclusions can you draw?

3. (a) Record the pulse rates (beats per minute) of 10 classmates who are resting or sitting and plot the data on a dot plot.
   (b) Record the pulse rates of 10 classmates who are moving around and plot the data on another dot plot.
   (c) Analyze and compare the two distributions. What conclusions can you draw?

From Class Activity 1, we notice that the dot plot reveals the pattern of a distribution. We can observe that the data are either clustered around certain values or are spread out. Dot plots can help us visualize data patterns, draw inferences about populations, and make decisions. We can also detect unusual observations (like the data values that are too small or too large). If this happens, we may need further investigation to find out the cause of such observations.

BASIC PRACTICE

1. The following dot plot shows the number of text messages sent by a random sample of adults on a particular day.

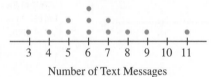

Dot Plot for the Number of Text Messages
Sent by Adults

Number of Text Messages

(a) How many adult responses were collected?
(b) What is the range of the number of text messages that were sent by the adults?
(c) Briefly describe the distribution of the number of text messages sent by the adults.

2. The following dot plot shows the number of text messages sent by a random sample of seventh grade students on the same day.

Dot Plot for the Number of Text Messages
Sent by Students

Number of Text Messages

(a) How many student responses were collected?
(b) What is the range of the number of text messages that were sent by the students?
(c) Compare the distributions of the data collected from the adults in Question 1 and the students in this question. What conclusions can you draw?

 FURTHER PRACTICE

3. The masses (in grams) of 12 randomly selected eggs each in Carton *A* and Carton *B* are presented in the following dot plots.

Dot Plot for the Masses of Eggs in Carton *A*

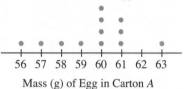

Mass (g) of Egg in Carton *A*

Dot Plot for the Masses of Eggs in Carton *B*

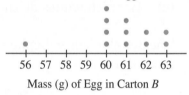

Mass (g) of Egg in Carton *B*

(a) Find the range of the masses of eggs in each carton.
(b) Briefly describe the distribution of the masses of eggs in each carton.
(c) Analyze and compare the two distributions. What conclusions can you draw?

MATH@WORK

4. Ronald made a six-faced die numbered 1 to 6. He rolled it 20 times and presented the scores in the dot plot below.

Dot Plot for the Scores Obtained in Rolling a Die

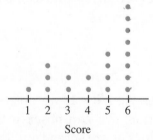

Score

(a) Find the percentage of times that the score is 6.
(b) Discuss the distribution of the scores obtained.

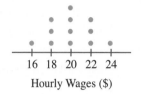

Dot Plot *B* for Hourly Wages of Workers

16 18 20 22 24
Hourly Wages ($)

5. The hourly wages (in dollars) of 12 workers in a company are presented in two different dot plots below.

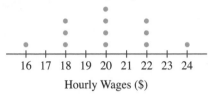

Dot Plot *A* for Hourly Wages of Workers

16 17 18 19 20 21 22 23 24
Hourly Wages ($)

(a) Do both dot plots give the same information?

(b) Compare the visual impressions between these two dot plots.

(c) What causes the difference between the visual impressions of these two dot plots?

15.3 *Measure of Center: Mean*

A Measures of Center

Consider the scores of eight randomly chosen students in a mathematics test.

$$67, \quad 64, \quad 37, \quad 46, \quad 82, \quad 98, \quad 71, \quad 56$$

We can draw a dot plot to see how the scores are distributed and whether there are any clusters. However, it is useful to describe the data set with some numerical values that reveal the characteristics of the data. We can do this by using a measure of center.

A **measure of center** is a single value that reflects the average value, or the approximate center, of a set of data. Two common measures of center are **mean** and **median**.

B Mean

The **mean** of a data set is the sum of all the data values divided by the total number of data.

If N items in a data set are $x_1, x_2, x_3, \ldots, x_N$, then its mean, usually denoted by $\bar{x}$ (read as x bar), is given by

$$\bar{x} = \frac{x_1 + x_2 + \ldots + x_N}{N}$$

Example 2

The scores of eight students in a test are
66, 64, 37, 46, 82, 98, 71, and 56.
Find their mean score.

Solution

Sum of the scores = 66 + 64 + 37 + 46 + 82 + 98 + 71 + 56
$$= 520$$

Mean score $= \dfrac{520}{8}$

$$= 65$$

REMARKS
The mean is often referred to as the average.

Try It! 2

The masses of five girls are 42 kg, 39 kg, 45 kg, 40 kg, and 44 kg. Find their mean mass.

Example 3

The mean of three numbers 32, y, and 56 is 47. Find the value of y.

Solution

$$\frac{32 + y + 56}{3} = 47$$
$$y + 88 = 141$$
$$\therefore \; y = 53$$

Try It! 3

The mean of four numbers 17, t, 23, and 29 is 20.5. Find the value of t.

Example 4

The mean height of four basketball players is 175 cm. The mean height of twelve soccer players is 171 cm. Find the mean height of all these players.

Solution

Mean height of the basketball players

$$= \frac{\text{Total height of the basketball players}}{\text{Total number of basketball players}}$$

Total height of the basketball players = 175 × 4 = 700 cm

Similarly, total height of the soccer players = 171 × 12
$$= 2{,}052 \text{ cm}$$

Mean height of all the players $= \dfrac{700 + 2{,}052}{4 + 12}$

$$= \frac{2{,}752}{16}$$

$$= 172 \text{ cm}$$

REMARKS
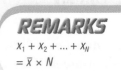
$$x_1 + x_2 + \ldots + x_N$$
$$= \bar{x} \times N$$

Try It! 4

The mean mass of four mathematics books is 1.4 kg. The mean mass of six English books is 0.9 kg. Find the mean mass of all the books, to the nearest tenth of a kg.

C Using Mean to Compare Two Populations

Example 5

In a study on plant reproduction, seven seeds are placed in each of 32 pots where 16 pots of seeds are grown under condition *A*, and the other 16 pots under condition *B*. The numbers of seeds that germinate in the pots under each condition are presented in the dot plots below.

Dot Plot for the Number of Seeds that
Germinate in each Pot

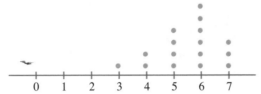

Number of Seeds that Germinate under Condition *A*

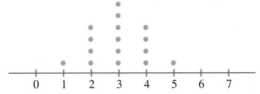

Number of Seeds that Germinate under Condition *B*

(a) Analyze and compare the two distributions. What conclusions can you draw?

(b) Find the mean number of seeds germinated in each pot of each set of data. What can you infer?

Solution

(a) The data values for condition *A* cluster around 6 and the number of seeds germinated in each pot varies from 3 to 7. The data values for condition *B* cluster around 3 and the number of seeds germinated varies from 1 to 5. That is, the data values for condition *A* are higher than those for condition *B*.

(b) Mean number of seeds germinated in each pot under condition *A*

$$= \frac{88}{16}$$

$$= 5.5$$

Mean number of seeds germinated in each pot under condition *B*

$$= \frac{48}{16}$$

$$= 3$$

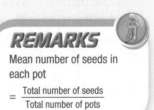

REMARKS

Mean number of seeds in each pot

$$= \frac{\text{Total number of seeds}}{\text{Total number of pots}}$$

The mean number of seeds that germinated in one pot under condition A is 2.5 seeds more than that under condition B. Hence, condition A is more suitable than condition B for the germination of the seeds.

Try It! **5** The dot plots below show the heights in inches of 10 basketball players and 10 soccer players chosen at random.

Dot Plots for the Heights of Players

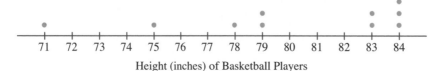

Height (inches) of Basketball Players

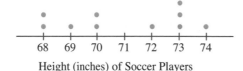

Height (inches) of Soccer Players

(a) Analyze and compare the two distributions. What conclusions can you draw?

(b) Find the mean height of each set of players. What can you infer?

D Variation from the Mean

Although mean reflects the average value of a set of data, the values within a set of data may vary considerably. One way to measure this variation is to look at how the data values deviate on average from the mean value.

> The **mean absolute deviation (MAD)** of a data set is the total distance of all data values from the mean value divided by the number of values.
>
> $$\text{MAD} = \frac{\text{Sum of absolute values of the deviations from the mean}}{\text{Number of data values}}$$

The absolute value of the deviation from the mean is called the **absolute deviation**.

Example **6**

Two students each surveyed 10 friends about the number of people in their households. Both surveys, A and B, found a mean household size of four people. The data values for each survey are presented in the dot plots below.

Dot Plot for Family Size from Survey A

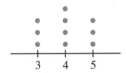

Number of People in Each Household

Dot Plot for Family Size from Survey B

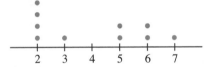

Number of People in Each Household

(a) Visually compare the two data distributions. What conclusions can you draw?

(b) Complete the table below for Survey B.

Survey A			Survey B		
Household Size			Household Size		
Data Value	Deviation from Mean	Absolute Deviation	Data Value	Deviation from Mean	Absolute Deviation
3	−1	1			
3	−1	1			
3	−1	1			
4	0	0			
4	0	0			
4	0	0			
4	0	0			
5	1	1			
5	1	1			
5	1	1			
	Sum = 0	Sum = 6			

(c) Find the mean absolute deviation (MAD) for each survey.

(d) Compare the MADs. What can you infer?

Solution

(a) The data values in Survey A are closer to the mean while the data values in Survey B are more spread out.

(b)

	Survey A			Survey B	
	Household Size			**Household Size**	
Data Value	Deviation from Mean	Absolute Deviation	Data Value	Deviation from Mean	Absolute Deviation
3	−1	1	2	−2	2
3	−1	1	2	−2	2
3	−1	1	2	−2	2
4	0	0	2	−2	2
4	0	0	3	−1	1
4	0	0	5	1	1
4	0	0	5	1	1
5	1	1	6	2	2
5	1	1	6	2	2
5	1	1	7	3	3
	Sum = 0	Sum = 6		Sum = 0	Sum = 18

(c) Mean absolute deviation (MAD)

$$= \frac{\text{Sum of absolute values of the deviations from the mean}}{\text{Number of data values}}$$

MAD for Survey $A = \dfrac{6}{10}$

$\qquad\qquad\qquad = 0.6$

MAD for Survey $B = \dfrac{18}{10}$

$\qquad\qquad\qquad = 1.8$

(d) On average, the data values from Survey A differ from the mean by 0.6 people while the data values from Survey B differ from the mean by 1.8 people.

Since $1.8 \div 0.6 = 3$, Survey B has 3 times as much variation from the mean as Survey A.

Note: The MAD tells us how much, on average, the values in a dot plot differ from the mean. If the MAD is small, it tells us that the values in the set are clustered closely around the mean. If it is large, there are at least some values that are quite far away from the mean.

Try It! 6

Jamie and Brenda each surveyed eight friends about the number of books they read in a week. Both surveys found a mean of five books read per week. The data values are presented in the dot plots below.

Jamie's Dot Plot for the Number of Books
Read per Week

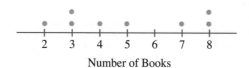

Number of Books

Brenda's Dot Plot for the Number of Books
Read per Week

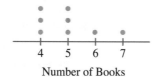

Number of Books

(a) Visually compare the two data distributions. What conclusions can you draw?

(b) Create a table showing the Data Value, Deviation from Mean, and Absolute Deviation for each set of data.

(c) Find the mean absolute deviation (MAD) for each set of data.

(d) Compare the MADs. What can you infer?

EXERCISE 15.3

⚙ BASIC PRACTICE

1. Find the mean of each of the following data sets.

    (a) 13, 16, 23

    (b) 3, 7, 15, 20

    (c) 2, 5, 8, 13, 24

    (d) 6, 8, 9, 11, 37, 40

2. The mean of five numbers is 29. Find the sum of these five numbers.

3. The mean of the numbers 52, t, and 68 is 61. What is the value of t?

4. Find the mean of each of the following data sets.

    (a)

34	31	40	28	33	29
30	37	28	35	32	36

    (b)

12	18	9	10	14	20	18	11	16	17
14	22	13	15	21	16	10	19	19	12

5. Plot the following sets of data on separate dot plots.

    Set A: 8, 2, 6, 3, 4, 6, 5, 8, 3

    Set B: 6, 5, 4, 5, 5, 4, 5, 5, 6

    Set C: 9, 1, 10, 1, 2, 10, 2, 1, 9

(a) Visually compare the three data distributions. Which set of data has the greatest variation?

(b) Duplicate the following table, one each for Sets *A*, *B*, and *C*, and hence, find the mean absolute deviation of each set of data.

Set _____		
Data Value	Deviation from Mean	Absolute Deviation
Sum =	Sum =	

(c) What can you say about the variation of the three sets of data?

FURTHER PRACTICE

6. The hourly wages of five workers are $15, $18, $20, $23, and $36. Find their mean hourly wage.

7. The daily minimum temperature was 20 °C, 26 °C, 21 °C, 25 °C, 26 °C, 23 °C, and 20 °C during a certain week. Find the mean daily minimum temperature.

8. The mean mass of four apples is 250 g. If two apples of mass 280 g each are added to the group, what is the mean mass of the six apples?

9. The mean age of 10 members in a committee is 42.5 years. If a member of age 74 years old retires, what is the mean age of the remaining nine members?

10. The mean of a, b, and c is 16. Find the mean of
(a) $a + 5$, $b + 5$, and $c + 5$,
(b) $a - 7$, $b + 11$, and $c + 17$,
(c) $3a - 1$, $3b - 1$, and $3c - 1$.

11. The number of children per family in a survey is as follows:

Number of children	0	1	2	3	4
Number of families	5	10	12	6	7

Find the mean number of children per family.

12. The dot plots below show the masses in kilograms of 10 boys from a sixth grade class and 10 boys from a seventh grade class.

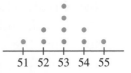

Dot Plot for the Masses of Boys from a Sixth Grade Class

Mass (kilograms) of boys

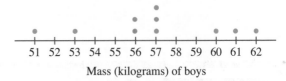

Dot Plot for the Masses of Boys from a Seventh Grade Class

Mass (kilograms) of boys

(a) Analyze and compare the two distributions. What conclusions can you draw?
(b) Find the mean mass of each group of boy.
(c) Compare the means. What can you infer?
(d) Create a table showing the Data Value, Deviation from Mean, and Absolute Deviation for each set of data. Find their respective mean absolute deviations (MAD).
(e) Compare the MADs. What conclusions can you draw?

13. The mean score of Jason in three tests is 46 points. How many points must he score in the fourth test so that the mean score of the four tests is 50 points?

14. The mean mass of 24 boys is 52 kg and the mean mass of 16 girls is 47 kg. Find the mean mass of all the boys and girls.

15. The scores that two gymnasts, Bryan and Josh, obtained in six events of parallel bars were as follows:

| Bryan | 8.1 | 9.6 | 9.2 | 7.5 | 9.4 | 9.0 |
| Josh | 9.3 | 9.5 | 8.0 | 9.1 | 7.8 | 8.5 |

  (a) Find the mean score of Bryan.
  (b) Find the mean score of Josh.
  (c) Whose performance was better?
  (d) Find the mean absolute deviation for each set of data, correct your answers to one decimal place.

16. The Lawrence family must drive an average of 250 mi per day to complete their seven-day vacation on time. During the first six days, they travel 220 mi, 300 mi, 210 mi, 255 mi, 240 mi, and 250 mi. How many miles must they travel on the seventh day in order to finish their vacation on time?

17. Measure the length of a room five times in centimeters with two different measuring devices, a ruler and a meter-stick.
  (a) Record the results and find the mean absolute deviation of each set of data.
  (b) Briefly explain any difference in variation from its mean.
  (c) Suggest a measuring device which will give less variation. Measure the length of the room again with the suggested device and verify if the mean absolute deviation has been reduced.

15.4 *Measure of Center: Median*

Suppose a company employs one manager and six clerks. Their monthly salaries are $6,400, $3,200, $3,100, $2,600, $2,500, $2,500, and $2,100 respectively. What is the mean monthly salary of the seven members of staff?

RECALL

A measure of center is a single value that reflects the average value of a data set.

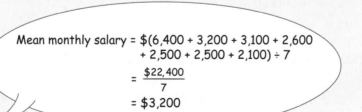

Mean monthly salary = $(6,400 + 3,200 + 3,100 + 2,600 + 2,500 + 2,500 + 2,100) ÷ 7

$$= \frac{\$22,400}{7}$$

$$= \$3,200$$

Does this mean value reflect the average monthly salary of the seven staff members accurately? Notice that the monthly salaries of five of the staff members are less than this mean value. Therefore, this mean value is not a good representation of the center of this distribution. It is more appropriate to use another measure of center, that is, the **median**.

> The **median** of a data set is the middle value when the data are arranged in order from the smallest to the largest.

For example, in the above case, the monthly salaries in ascending order are as follows:

$2,100 $2,500 $2,500 $2,600 $3,100 $3,200 $6,400

↑
median salary
(in the "middle" position)

The middle value is the 4th item.
∴ median salary = $2,600

Example 7

The prices of a computer game in six shops are
$78, $80, $56, $64, $72, and $69.

Find the median price of the computer game.

Solution

We arrange the prices in ascending order.

$56 $64 $69 $72 $78 $80

↑
middle position

Since there is an even number of items, the median is taken to be the mean (average) of the two middle items.

$$\therefore \text{ median price} = \frac{\$69 + \$72}{2}$$
$$= \$70.50$$

Try It! 7

The lengths (in centimeters) of eight fish caught by Billy are

28, 31, 20, 33, 17, 27, 25, and 30.

Find the median length of the fish.

In general, the calculation of the median of a data set with N items is as follows:

> 1. Arrange the N items in the data in ascending order.
> 2. (a) When N is odd, the median is the middle term of the ordered items.
>   (b) When N is even, the median is the mean of the two middle terms of the ordered items.

Consider the data set $A = \{18, 25, 56, 47, 39, 13, 38, 11, 43\}$.
The nine items in ascending order are

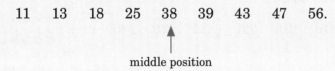

11   13   18   25   38   39   43   47   56.

middle position

Median of data set A = Middle item = 38
Consider the data set $B = \{52, 36, 71, 63, 32, 81, 41, 74, 61, 49\}$.
The 10 items in ascending order are

32   36   41   49   52   61   63   71   74   81.

middle position

Median of data set B = Mean of the two middle items
$$= \frac{1}{2} \times (52 + 61)$$
$$= 56.5$$

Example 8

The masses (in grams) of five apples in basket A are
209,   218,   193,   220,   and   205.

The masses (in grams) of four apples in basket B are
236,   216,   240,   and   224.

Find the median mass of
(a) the apples in basket A,
(b) the apples in basket B,
(c) all the apples in the two baskets.

Solution   (a) The masses (in grams) of the apples in basket A in ascending order are as follows:

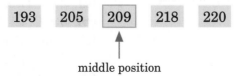

193   205   209   218   220

middle position

∴ median mass of apples in basket A = 209 g

(b) The mass (in grams) of the apples in basket B in ascending order are as follows:

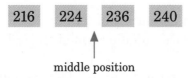

middle position

∴ median mass of apples in basket B = $\frac{1}{2}(224 + 236)$

= 230 g

DISCUSS

If we know the number of apples and the median masses for apples in basket A and basket B, can we derive the overall median mass?

(c) The masses (in grams) of all the apples arranged in ascending order are as follows:

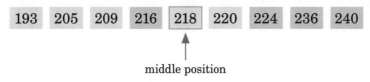

middle position

∴ median mass of all the apples = 218 g

REMARKS

• If the distribution of a set of data has no extreme large or small values, it is better to use the mean as a measure of center.

• If the distribution of the data has extreme large or small values, it is better to use the median as it is less sensitive to extreme values.

Try It! 8 The floor areas (in square meters) of six apartments in building A are as follows:

63, 94, 78, 80, 71, 62

The floor areas (in square meters) of five apartments in building B are as follows:

93, 104, 75, 88, 83

Find the median floor area of
(a) the apartments in building A,
(b) the apartments in building B,
(c) all the apartments.

EXERCISE 15.4

 BASIC PRACTICE

1. Find the median of each of the following data sets.
   (a) 9, 12, 17, 18, 25
   (b) 25, 36, 38, 41, 50, 52, 58
   (c) 137, 151, 167, 180
   (d) 9, 12, 24, 33, 47, 59

2. Find the median of each of the following data sets.
   (a) 24 s, 17 s, 32 s, 19 s
   (b) 36 °C, 21 °C, 17 °C, 28 °C, 24 °C
   (c) 9 m, 12 m, 11 m, 35 m, 42 m, 77 m, 29 m, 13 m
   (d) 2.7 g, 3.0 g, 5.8 g, 4.7 g, 1.6 g, 5.2 g, 4.5 g, 8.1 g, 3.9 g

3. The areas of the four bedrooms in a house are 12 m², 9 m², 17 m², and 10 m² respectively. Find
    (a) the mean area,
    (b) the median area
    of these rooms.

4. The grade point averages (GPA) of 10 seventh grade students are

    3.62, 3.31, 3.14, 2.17, 3.75, 2.63, 3.97, 3.58, 2.50, and 3.23.

    Find
    (a) the median grade point average,
    (b) the mean grade point average
    of these students.

5. (a) The median of the data set
           16, 5, 11, 19, x, 4
       is 9. Find the value of x.
    (b) Find the median of the data set
           23, 17, 14, 8, 6, 2, 25.
    (c) The data sets in (a) and (b) are pooled together. Find the median of the combined data set.
    (d) Can you derive the result in (c) using the results in (a) and (b)?

6. The dot plot below shows the heights (in centimeters) of some plants.

    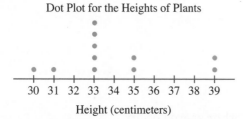

    Dot Plot for the Heights of Plants
    Height (centimeters)

    (a) Find the mean height of the plants.
    (b) Find the median height of the plants.
    (c) Which of the above two measures is a better representation of the center of the distribution?

7. The population growth rates in the United States from 2005 to 2011 are as follows:

Year	Population Growth Rate (%)
2005	0.92
2006	0.91
2007	0.89
2008	0.88
2009	0.98
2010	0.97
2011	0.96

    Source: www.indexmundi.com

    (a) Find the mean population growth rate from 2005 to 2011.
    (b) Find the median of these population growth rate figures.

8. The monthly household incomes of 15 families in a survey are as follows:

$6,380	$3,150	$5,890	$4,136	$4,259
$5,420	$4,780	$2,830	$3,459	$8,125
$3,630	$7,365	$4,630	$2,396	$4,950

    (a) Find the median income.
    (b) Find the mean income.
    (c) Determine whether the mean or median is a better representation of the measure of center in this survey.

 BRAIN WORKS

9. Construct a data set with five different items so that the median is 37.

10. Construct a data set with six different items so that the mean is 13 and the median is 10.

15.5 *Mode*

A Definition of Mode

Suppose the sizes of eight coats sold by a manager of a boutique are

$$7, \quad 8, \quad 8, \quad 8, \quad 9, \quad 10, \quad 12, \quad \text{and} \quad 16.$$

In this case,   the mean = 9.75
and   the median = 8.5.

These two measures of center are not very meaningful to the manufacturer of the coats and manager of the boutique. This is because they are not production size numbers. Instead they will be more interested to know the most popular size (**modal size**) so that they can cater to the customers' needs and stock up on this particular size.

The **mode** is sometimes used as a measure of center and it is defined as follows:

> The **mode** of a set of data is the value that occurs most often.

In this case, the modal size or the mode of the distribution is 8 as it is the size of coats that is most popular. When the mode is used for categorical data, as in this instance where we are finding the most popular coat size, it is not a measure of center.

RECALL

The mean and the median can be worked out as follows:

Mean

$$= \frac{7 + 8 + 8 + 8 + 9 + 10 + 12 + 16}{8}$$

$$= 9.75$$

Median

$$= \frac{8 + 9}{2}$$

$$= 8.5$$

REMARKS

When no number in a data set occurs more often than others, there is no mode.

Example 9

The scores of seven students in three quizzes are as follows:

Quiz 1	3, 2, 7, 6, 7, 9, 5
Quiz 2	8, 0, 4, 0, 4, 0, 4
Quiz 3	9, 2, 5, 10, 8, 6, 1

Find the modal score in each quiz.

Solution

In Quiz 1, the score 7 occurs twice while other scores occur only once. Hence, the modal score of Quiz 1 is 7.

In Quiz 2, both scores 0 and 4 occur three times. Hence, the modal scores of Quiz 2 are 0 and 4.

In Quiz 3, no score occurs more than once. Hence, there is no modal score.

The pulse rates (beats per minute) of three groups of people are as follows:

$$A = \{75, 72, 76, 72, 72, 80, 71\}$$
$$B = \{83, 56, 70, 73, 76\}$$
$$C = \{78, 71, 82, 69, 71, 70, 78, 65\}$$

Find the modal pulse rate of each group of people.

B Comparison between Mean, Median, and Mode

 CLASS ACTIVITY 2

Objective: To compare between mean, median, and mode.

Questions

1. Consider the data set $A = \{3, 3, 7, 8, 9\}$.

   (a) Find its mean, median, and mode.

   (b) If the number 54 is included in the set, find the new mean, median, and mode.

   (c) Which measure in (a) is most affected by the addition of a large number?

   (d) Which measure in (a) do you recognize to be the most appropriate representation of the center of the data set A? Explain your choice briefly.

2. Consider the data set $B = \{1, 1, 3, 6\}$ and $C = \{1, 1, 4, 10, 10, 10\}$.

   (a) Find the mean, median, and mode of data set B, data set C and the combined data set D of data sets B and C. Copy and complete the following table.

Measure of Center	Mean	Median	Mode
Data set B			
Data set C			
Combined data set D			

   (b) Which measure of center involves all the data of a data set in its calculation?

   (c) Suppose you are given only the numbers of items for sets B and C, and their individual measures of center. Which measure can you derive for the combined data set D from the given values?

Based on Class Activity 2 and the previous sections, we can make a comparison among the three measures of center.

Mean
- Its calculation involves all the data. Hence, it is usually more representative of the center of a distribution.
- It is affected by extreme values. Hence, in some cases, it may give a misleading average value.
  For example, the mean of the data set {3, 3, 7, 8, 9, 54} is 14. It is not a good representation of the average. This is because it is higher than five out of the six observations.
- Two means can be combined to give an overall mean.

Median
- Its calculation involves just one or two middle values and does not take into consideration the rest of the data.
- It is not really affected by extreme values.
- Two medians cannot be combined to give an overall median.

Mode
- It is easy to find and understand but it does not take into consideration the bulk of the data.
- It is not affected by extreme values.
- Two modes cannot be combined to give an overall mode.

EXERCISE 15.5

 BASIC PRACTICE

1. Find the mode of each of the following data sets.
   (a) 4, 3, 5, 11, 4, 7, 5, 4
   (b) 9, 8, 2, 11, 8, 3, 2
   (c) 13, 16, 17, 9, 7, 6, 11, 5
   (d) 8.4, 3.6, 2.0, 7.5, 3.6, 5.7, 7.5, 3.6, 6.9

2. Find the mode of each of the following data sets.

(a)

0	4	3	2	2	1
0	2	1	0	1	3
2	0	2	0	1	5

(b)

20	30	20	25	35	15
35	20	15	30	25	20
25	20	25	15	20	30
20	15	25	20	25	25

3. The typing speeds, in words per minute, of 12 secretaries are

37, 46, 43, 39, 46, 51, 38, 47, 46, 40, 49, 43.

What is the modal typing speed?

4. The sizes of eight pairs of shoes sold are as follows:

$7\frac{1}{2}$, 6, 5, $5\frac{1}{2}$, 7, $7\frac{1}{2}$, $6\frac{1}{2}$, $7\frac{1}{2}$

(a) Find the modal size.
(b) Find the median size.
(c) Is the median size one of the available sizes?

5. The daily temperatures, in degrees Celsius, for eleven days in Juneau, Alaska, are shown below.

−2.5, −1.0, 1.2, 0, −3.8, 1.0, −2.5, −1.2, −1.0, −2.5, −3.1

Find
(a) the mode of these temperatures,
(b) the median temperature,
(c) the mean temperature.

6. The dot plot below shows the number of spelling mistakes in an essay made by each student in a class.

Dot Plot for the Number of Spelling Mistakes

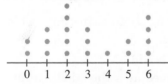

Number of Spelling Mistakes Made by Each Student

(a) How many students are there in the class?
(b) What is the modal number of spelling mistakes made by the students?
(c) Find the median number of spelling mistakes made by the students.
(d) Find the mean number of spelling mistakes made by the students.

7. The following table shows the number of traffic accidents on a road during each month in a particular year.

Month	Number of traffic accidents
January	19
February	17
March	15
April	13
May	11
June	10
July	18
August	17
September	12
October	17
November	15
December	28

(a) What is the total number of traffic accidents on the road in that year?
(b) Find the mean, median, and mode for the number of traffic accidents in that year.
(c) Which measure is the most appropriate as an average figure for public information?

8. The following table shows the number of pets of some households.

Number of pets in each household	Number of households
0	5
1	5
2	7
3	1
4	2

(a) What is the total number of pets in this sample?
(b) Find the median and mode of the data.
(c) Find the mean number of pets per household.
(d) Which one is the most appropriate as a measure of center in this case?

9. The numbers of working hours of 15 workers in a week are as follows:

41	36	43	58	8	40	45	50
51	45	40	49	35	45	44	

(a) Find the mean, median, and mode of the data.

(b) Would you use the mean or the median as a measure of center of the data? Why?

10. Construct a data set with seven items so that the mean, median, and mode are all equal to 8.

11. Construct a data set with eight items so that the mean is 4, the median is 3, and the mode is 2.

IN A NUTSHELL

Methods of Collecting Data

- Taking measurements in experiments
- Observing outcomes of events
- Conducting surveys
- Reading statistical publications

Mean

- For a data set of N items, $x_1, x_2, ..., x_N$,
$$\text{mean } \bar{x} = \frac{x_1 + x_2 + ... + x_N}{N}.$$
- Mean Absolute Deviation
$$\text{MAD} = \frac{\text{sum of absolute values of the deviations from the mean}}{\text{number of data values}}$$

Mode

The mode of a data set is the value that occurs most often.

Dot Plot

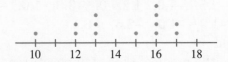

- Represent each data value as a dot above a number line.
- Show the shape and clusters of the distribution.

Median

- Arrange N items in a data set in ascending order.
- If N is odd,
  the median = the middle term.
  E.g., for {1, 3, 6, 8, 9, 10, 17},
  the median = 8.
- If N is even,
  the median = the mean of the two middle terms.
  E.g., for {4, 7, 10, 13, 15, 20},
  the median = $\frac{1}{2}(10 + 13)$
  = 11.5.

1. Parade organizers in a town conducted an online poll on its website about the complimentary items that were distributed during the parade. There were 7,200 votes. The poll and its results are shown below.

> Q. What is your favorite item?
> - Bag
> - Food
> - Interactive items
>
> **Vote**   **Reset**
>
> **View Result**

Results

Item	Percentage
Bag	25%
Food	9%
Interactive items	66%

(a) What kind of data-collection method was used?

(b) What problems might be inherent when using the Internet to collect data or perform polls?

(c) How can the problems in **(b)** be mitigated?

2. The following list shows the volume, in fluid ounces, of 25 cups of soda which are filled by a vending machine.

11.8	12.0	11.9	12.1	11.8
12.0	11.6	12.2	12.0	11.9
12.0	12.0	11.8	11.9	11.5
11.9	11.8	12.0	11.6	12.1
12.0	11.9	11.9	11.8	12.0

(a) Represent the data on a dot plot.

(b) Briefly describe the distribution of the volumes of soda.

(c) The cups of soda whose volumes are less than 11.8 fl oz are considered "below expectation". What is the percentage of the total number of cups which are below expectation?

(d) What are the modal and median volumes?

(e) Find the mean volume.

3. In a survey, the number of people in each of the 10 cars passing a certain traffic junction was tracked. The results are represented by the dot plot below.

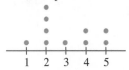

Dot Plot for the Number of People in a Car

Number of People in a Car

(a) Find the mean, median, and mode of the data.

(b) Find the mean absolute deviation of the data.

4. The masses of six women are as follows:
46 kg, 43 kg, 72 kg, 50 kg, 43 kg, 58 kg

(a) Find the mean, median, and mode of their masses.

(b) Which measure would give a fair gauge of the average mass of these women?

5. The mean age of five basketball players is 24 years.

(a) If the mean age of four of them is 23 years, find the age of the fifth player.

(b) Find the mean age of these players after three years.

6. Five boys participated in a fishing competition. None of them caught more than nine fish. The mean, median, and mode of the numbers of fish caught by them are 6, 5, and 4 respectively. Find the number of fish caught by each boy.

7. The table below shows the salaries of 25 employees of a company.

Salary ($)	2,000	2,500	3,000	3,500
Number of employees	3	9	x	5

Find
(a) the value of x,
(b) the modal salary,
(c) the median salary,
(d) the mean salary.

8. The weights (in pound) of 10 randomly selected bags of apples from Supermarket A and Supermarket B are presented in the following dot plots.

Dot Plot for the Weights of Bags of Apples from Supermarket A

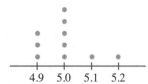

Weight (pound) of Each Bag of Apples

Dot Plot for the Weights of Bags of Apples from Supermarket B

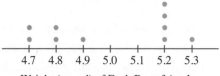

Weight (pound) of Each Bag of Apples

(a) Briefly describe the two distributions.
(b) Find the median weight of a bag of apples from each of the supermarkets.
(c) Find the mean weight of a bag of apples from each of the supermarkets.
(d) Find the mean absolute deviation (MAD) for each set of data.
(e) Compare the MADs. What conclusions can you draw?

9. A class of 32 students was randomly divided into two equal groups, A and B. Each group was taught a new mathematics topic using different methods. Their scores in a common test on that topic are as follows:

Group A	74	74	30	42	68	53	42	66
	29	64	96	70	68	85	53	30
Group B	69	80	72	27	60	60	55	80
	72	32	45	61	45	32	72	66

(a) Find the mean and median scores of Group A.
(b) Find the mean and median scores of Group B.
(c) Which group's performance is better? Why?
(d) Create a table showing the Data Value, Deviation from Mean, and Absolute Deviation for each set of data. Hence, find their respective mean absolute deviations (MAD).
(e) Compare the MADs. What conclusions can you draw?

10. The number of goals scored by soccer teams in the soccer league is shown in the following table.

Number of goals	0	1	2	3
Number of teams	5	6	3	y

(a) State the largest possible value of y if the mode is 1 goal.
(b) If the median is 1 goal, find the largest possible value of y.
(c) Find the value of y given that the mean is 1 goal.

Weighted Mean

Suppose in one academic semester, there are three tests and one examination on mathematics. The maximum points for each test or examination is 100. If the test points are x_1, x_2, and x_3, and the examination point is x_4, the overall mathematics points in the term is given by the **weighted mean** W, where

$$W = \frac{x_1 + x_2 + x_3 + 2x_4}{1 + 1 + 1 + 2}.$$

(a) If Wendy's points in the three tests are 62, 80, and 73, and her examination score is 65, find her weighted mean.

(b) Check the definition of weighted mean and write it down.

(c) For what purpose do you think we need to use the weighted mean?

WRITE IN YOUR JOURNAL

1. You have learned how to analyze and interpret dot plots. Describe some of the advantages and disadvantages of using these presentations.

2. How do you decide when to use the mean, the median, or the mode to describe a set of data?

16 PROBABILITY OF SIMPLE EVENTS

Playing

LET'S LEARN TO...

1. use set language and set notation to describe a set of objects, its elements, its subsets, and its complement

2. understand probability as a measure of chance

3. define the terms sample space, outcome, and event

4. list the sample space for a simple chance situation

5. find the probability of a single event

At amusement parks, we can usually see people trying their "luck" at the games stalls. What do you think are a player's changes of winning a game? Calculating the chances of winning a game involves a branch of mathematics known as "probability".

16.1 *Set Notation*

A Sets

We often come across different collections of objects in our daily life. For instance,

 a family of cats,

 a pod of dolphins,

and a pile of books.

DISCUSS

Consider the two sets below:

A = {teachers below 30 years of age in *XYZ* School}

B = {young teachers in *XYZ* School}.

Which set is well-defined? Why?

In mathematics, we use the term **set** to mean a collection of well-defined distinct objects. We use set notation to organize, classify, describe, and communicate in many branches of mathematics. The term set is also used in other disciplines, such as engineering and social science, to represent the relationship between things.

We usually denote sets by capital letters (e.g., A, B, C, ...). We may describe a set in words. For example,

 A = {calendar months beginning with the letter J},

 B = {states in the United States}.

The objects in a set are called **elements** or **members**. We can say that the months January and July are elements of the set A, while the states Ohio and Colorado are elements of the set B.

We may also describe a set by listing all its elements. For instance, we can list the elements of the set of four major compass directions

as D = {*North, East, South, West*},

and the set of all positive integers

as N = {1, 2, 3, 4, ...}.

A set may also be specified using **set-builder notation**, where the elements are described by the common properties that define them. For example, the set of positive integers can be defined as

$$N = \{x : x \text{ is a positive integer}\},$$

which is read as 'N is the set of all elements x such that x is a positive integer'.

In set notation, if x is an element of a set A, we write

$$x \in A,$$

and if x is not an element of a set A, we write

$$x \notin A.$$

$x \in A$ is read as 'x belongs to A' or 'x is an element of A'.

Do you know what the elements in this basket of fruits are?

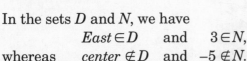

In the sets D and N, we have

$$East \in D \quad \text{and} \quad 3 \in N,$$
whereas $\quad center \notin D \quad \text{and} \quad -5 \notin N.$

The **number of elements** in a set A is denoted by $n(A)$. Therefore, we write $n(D) = 4$ since the set D has four elements. The set N has an infinite number of elements and we write it as $n(N)$ is infinity.

Example ❶   Given the set $S = \{$letters of the word '*BOOK*'$\}$,
  (a) list the elements of the set S,
  (b) find $n(S)$.

Solution   **(a)** $S = \{B, O, K\}$

  (b) The set S has three elements.
     $\therefore \; n(S) = 3$

Note: • A set only counts distinct elements. Therefore, each element is listed only once.
  • The order in which the elements appear is insignificant. We may write the set S as $S = \{O, B, K\}, S = \{B, K, O\}$, etc.

Try It! ❶   Given the set $C = \{$letters of the word '*STUDENT*'$\}$,
  (a) list the elements of the set C,
  (b) find $n(C)$.

Example 2

Given the set A = {five basic human senses},
(a) list the elements of the set A,
(b) state $n(A)$,
(c) is 'feeling' an element of A?

Solution

(a) A = {five basic human senses}
= {hearing, smell, sight, taste, touch}

(b) The set A has five elements.
∴ $n(A) = 5$

(c) No, 'feeling' is not an element of A,
i.e., feeling $\notin A$.

Try It! 2

Given the set B = {colors of the American flag},
(a) list the elements of the set B,
(b) state $n(B)$,
(c) is 'red' an element of B?

Example 3

Let $S = \{1^2, 2^2, 3^2, 4^2, 5^2\}$.
(a) Is 9 an element of S?
(b) Express S in set-builder notation.

Solution

(a) $S = \{1^2, 2^2, 3^2, 4^2, 5^2\}$
$= \{1, 4, 9, 16, 25\}$
Yes, $9 \in S$.

(b) $S = \{x : x$ is a positive square number not greater than 25}

DISCUSS

Is there only one way to express the set S in Example 3 in set-builder notation?

Try It! 3

Let $T = \{3, 4, 5, 6\}$.

(a) Is $\frac{1}{3}$ an element of T?

(b) Express T in set-builder notation.

B Equal Sets

Two sets A and B are **equal**, that is, $A = B$, if they have exactly the same elements. Let us find out if two sets with different expressions can be equal.

> **Example 4**
>
> Let A = {letters from the word '*parallel*'}
> and B = {letters from the word '*apparel*'}.
> Is $A = B$?
>
> **Solution**
>
> By listing the elements, sets A and B are as follows:
> $A = \{p, a, r, l, e\}$
> $B = \{a, p, r, e, l\}$
> Since both sets A and B have the same elements, $A = B$.
>
> **Try It! 4**
>
> Let $C = \{x : x$ is a digit from the phone number '92883388'}
> and $D = \{x : x$ is a digit from the phone number '92382238'}.
> Is $C = D$?

C Subsets

If every element of a set A is also an element of a set B, then A is said to be a **subset** of B and we write $A \subseteq B$. If A is not a subset of B, we write $A \nsubseteq B$.

If $A \subseteq B$ but $A \neq B$, then A is said to be a **proper subset** of B, and we write $A \subset B$. When A is not a proper subset of B, we write $A \not\subset B$.

Suppose $A = \{3, 5, 7\}$ and $B = \{3, 5, 7, 9\}$.

Then $A \subset B$ because all the elements (3, 5, and 7) in A are also contained in B but $A \neq B$ as there is an additional element 9 in B which is not an element in A.

Let us consider some other examples of subsets.

The set {*red, green*} is a proper subset of the set {*red, green, blue*}.
The set of all integers is a proper subset of the set of all rational numbers.
The set {*male, female*} is a subset (but not a proper subset) of {*female, male*}.

If we represent the above sets as

A = {*red, green*}, B = {*red, green, blue*},
C = {all integers}, D = {all rational numbers},
E = {*male, female*}, F = {*female, male*},

then the above relationships can be represented as $A \subset B$, $C \subset D$, and $E \subseteq F$.

Example 5

Let $A = \{-2, 2\}$, $B = \{2\}$, $C = \{1, 2, 3\}$, and $D = \{-2, 2\}$.
Using '$\subset$', '$\not\subset$', '$\not\subseteq$', and '$=$', describe the relationship between the following sets.

  (a) A and B **(b)** A and D

  (c) B and C **(d)** C and D

Solution

(a) Since $2 \in A$ and $2 \in B$, $-2 \in A$ but $-2 \notin B$,
$\therefore$ B is a proper subset of A, that is $B \subset A$.

(b) Since $A \subseteq D$ and $D \subseteq A$, we have $A = D$.

(c) $B = \{2\}$ and $C = \{1, 2, 3\}$.
Since all the elements of B are elements of C, but C has elements, 1 and 3, that are not elements of B, we have $B \subset C$.

(d) $C = \{1, 2, 3\}$ and $D = \{-2, 2\}$.
There is an element of C, say 1, that is not an element of D. C is not a subset of D.
Similarly, D is not a subset of C.
$\therefore$ $C \not\subseteq D$ and $D \not\subseteq C$.

> **DISCUSS**
>
> Is the statement "If $F \subseteq G$ and $G \subseteq F$, then $F = G$" correct? Why?

> **REMARKS**
>
> When $A \subseteq D$ and $D \subseteq A$, it means A and D have exactly the same elements.

Try It! 5

Let $P = \{1, 3\}$, $Q = \{1, 2, 3, 4\}$, $R = \{4, 3, 2, 1\}$, and $S = \{1, 3, 5\}$.
Using '$\subset$' '$\not\subset$', '$\not\subseteq$', and '$=$', describe the relationship between the following sets.

  (a) P and Q **(b)** Q and R

  (c) P and S **(d)** Q and S

D Universal Set and Empty Set

When considering sets for a certain problem, there is usually an overall set that every set is a subset of that set. We call the overall set the **universal set** of the problem. Note that different problems may have different universal sets. We usually use the Greek letter ξ (read as "xi") to denote a universal set.

> **REMARKS**
>
> There are two symbols for universal set – a symbol U and a Greek letter ξ.

Example 6

Suggest a universal set ξ for each of the following sets.

  (a) $A = \{carrot, cabbage, celery, lettuce\}$

  (b) $B = \{2, 4, 6, 8, 10\}$

Solution

(a) The universal set for A may be
$\xi = \{all\ vegetables\}$.

(b) If B is considered as a set of even numbers, the universal set is
$$\xi = \{x : x \text{ is an even number}\}.$$

If B is considered as a set of integers, the universal set is
$$\xi = \{x : x \text{ is an integer}\}.$$

Try It! 6 Suggest a universal set ξ for each of the following sets.
(a) $Q = \{drill, screwdriver, hammer, saw\}$
(b) $R = \{1, 3, 5\}$

DISCUSS
Do you think the set $A = \{x : x$ is an integer and $2x + 3 = 0\}$ is an empty set? Why?

There are some sets that do not contain any element at all. We call a set with no elements the **empty set**. It can be symbolized by ϕ (read as "phi") or { }. An empty set is also called a null set. For example, the set of months with 32 days is an empty set. We can write
$$\{\text{months with 32 days}\} = \phi.$$

Other examples include:
- The set of triangles with 4 sides.
- The set of integers which are both even and odd.

The solution set for an equation that has no solution is also called an empty set. For instance, for every real number x, we have $x^2 \geqslant 0$ and thus $x^2 + 1 > 0$. Hence,
$$\{x : x \text{ is a real number and } x^2 + 1 = 0\} = \phi.$$

Note that **the empty set ϕ is a subset of every set A**. This can be proven as follows:

Assume that the empty set ϕ is not a subset of a set A.
Then there must be an element of ϕ which is not an element of A.
But ϕ has no elements. So, this is a contradiction.

Therefore, the empty set ϕ must be a subset of A.

Hence, we have the following property:

> For every set A,
> $$\phi \subseteq A \subseteq \xi.$$

Example 7 Let $A = \{a, b, c\}$. List all the subsets of A.

Solution The subsets of A are
$\phi, \{a\}, \{b\}, \{c\}, \{a, b\}, \{a, c\}, \{b, c\},$ and $\{a, b, c\}$.

Note: In other words, $\phi \subset A, \{b\} \subset A, \{a, c\} \subset A$, etc.

Try It! 7 Let $B = \{1, 2, 3, 4\}$. List all the subsets of B.

E Complement of a Set

Suppose that the set A is a subset of a universal set ξ. Then the set of elements that does not belong to the set A is called the **complement** of the set A and is denoted by A'.

That is:

$$A' = \{x : x \in \xi \text{ and } x \notin A\}$$

REMARKS

A' is read as 'A prime' or 'A complement'. The complement of a set A can also be denoted by A^c.

Example 8

Let ξ = {*red*, *yellow*, *blue*, *green*, *black*},
A = {*red*, *yellow*, *green*},
and B = {*yellow*, *green*, *black*}.

(a) List the elements of A'.
(b) List the elements of B'.

Solution

(a) '*blue*' and '*black*' are the elements in ξ that do not belong to A, so the elements in A' are '*blue*' and '*black*'.
$\therefore$ A' = {*blue*, *black*}.

(b) '*red*' and '*blue*' are elements in ξ that do not belong to B.
$\therefore$ B' = {*red*, *blue*}.

Try It! 8

Let $\xi = \{a, b, c, x, y, z\}$,
$P = \{b, y, z\}$,
and $Q = \{x, y, z, c, b, a\}$.

(a) List the elements of
  (i) P',
  (ii) Q'.
(b) Describe the relationship between Q and ξ.
(c) What can you say about the complement of ξ?

EXERCISE 16.1

BASIC PRACTICE

1. Represent each of the following sets by listing its elements.
    (a) A = {letters in the word '*mathematics*'}
    (b) B = {consonants in the word '*WASHINGTON*'}
    (c) C = {the seasons in a year}
    (d) D = {days of a week}

2. List the elements in each of the following sets.
    (a) $P = \{x : x$ is a digit in the password '501314'$\}$
    (b) $Q = \{x : x$ is an even prime number$\}$
    (c) $R = \{x : x$ is a multiple of 9 less than 50$\}$
    (d) $S = \{x : x$ is a non-negative integer$\}$

3. Express each of the following sets in set-builder notation.
    (a) The set of factors of 12.
    (b) {3, 6, 9, 12, ...}
    (c) {2, 3, 5, 7, 11, 13, ...}

4. Let A = {1, 4, 7, 12, 16}. Determine whether each of the following statements is true or false.
    (a) $10 \notin A$
    (b) $1 + 4 \in A$
    (c) $\{12, 16\} \in A$
    (d) $\{1\} \subset A$

5. Let X = {a, e, i, o, u}. Determine whether each of the following statements is true or false.
    (a) $\phi \subset X$
    (b) $\{u, o, i, e, a\} = X$
    (c) $\{a, i, u\} \subset X$
    (d) $\{a\} \in X$

6. (a) List all the subsets of the set S = {*on, off*}.
    (b) Write down the subset of S which is not a proper subset.

7. (a) List all the subsets of the set T = {3, 6, 9}.
    (b) Write down the number of proper subsets of T.

8. Let ξ = {*fog, snow, cloud, rain, dew, ice*},
    M = {*cloud, rain*},
    and N = {*snow*}.
    List the elements of the set
    (a) M',
    (b) N'.

9. Let ξ = {letters in the word '*complement*'}
    and A = {letters in the word '*element*'}.
    (a) List the elements of ξ and A.
    (b) List the elements of A'.

10. Let ξ = {*sodium, potassium, calcium, magnesium, zinc, iron, lead*}
    and A = {*calcium, zinc, lead*}. Find
    (a) $n(\xi)$,
    (b) $n(A)$,
    (c) $n(A')$,
    (d) $n(\phi)$.

FURTHER PRACTICE

11. Let $A = \{x : x$ is an integer greater than 0 but less than 4$\}$,
    $B = \{x : x$ is a root of $5x - 10 = 0\}$,
    C = {3, 2, 1},
    and D = {0, 1, 2}.
    (a) Describe the relationship for each of the following sets using '$\subset$', '$\subseteq$', '$\not\subseteq$', and '='.
    (i) A and B (ii) A and C
    (iii) B and D (iv) C and D
    (b) Find the number of elements in each of the following sets.
    (i) A (ii) B

12. Let A = {a, b, c}. Determine whether each of the following is true or false.
    (a) $\{a, b\} \in A$
    (b) $A \in \xi$
    (c) $A \subseteq A$
    (d) $\{\phi\} = \phi$

13. A, B, and C are three sets such that $A \subset B$ and $B \subset C$.
  (a) If $x \in B$, is it necessary that
    (i) $x \in A$?
    (ii) $x \in C$?
  (b) What is the relationship between the sets, A and C?

14. Suggest a universal set for each of the following sets.
  (a) {birds, cats, dogs, fish}
  (b) {oxygen, hydrogen, nitrogen}
  (c) {Arizona, California, Oregon, Texas}
  (d) {1, 2, 3, 4}

15. Let $\xi = \{x : x \text{ is a whole number}\}$,
    $A = \{x : x \text{ is an odd integer}\}$,
  and $B = \{x : x \text{ is a multiple of } 4\}$.
  (a) Express ξ, A, and B by listing their elements.
  (b) Express A' by
    (i) listing its elements,
    (ii) using set-builder notation.

16. Let $R = \{$the seven colors of a rainbow perceived by human color vision$\}$
  and $P = \{black, cyan, magenta, yellow\}$,
  which is the set of colors used for four-color printing.
  (a) List the elements of the set R.
  (b) Is white $\in R$?
  (c) Is $P \subset R$?
  (d) Suggest a universal set for the sets R and P.

17. On a lunch menu, the choices of main dishes are chicken and fish, and the choices of beverages are coffee, tea, and fruit juice.
  (a) List the elements of
    (i) the set of choices of main dishes, M,
    (ii) the set of choices of beverages, B.
  (b) Suggest a universal set for each of the following sets.
    (i) M,
    (ii) B.
  (c) If $E = \{chicken, fish, lamb\}$, what is the relationship between E and M?

18. Let ξ be the set of all students in SMART School.
  Suppose $A = \{$all seventh grade students$\}$
  and $B = \{$all seventh grade female students$\}$.
  (a) Describe the sets A' and B'.
  (b) Describe the relationship for each of the following sets.
    (i) A and B
    (ii) A' and B'

19. Let $A = \{1, 3, 8\}$ and $B = \{3, 6, 8\}$.
  (a) Create a universal set ξ such that $A \subset \xi$ and $B \subset \xi$.
  (b) Create a set C such that $C \subset A$ and $C \subset B$.

16.2 The Meaning of Probability

A   Introduction

In our daily life, we use words such as "impossible", "50–50", and "certainly" to describe the chance of a phenomenon or result happening. How will you describe the chances of the following situations happening?

- My calculator will work properly during the next mathematics test.
- The sun will rise in the east tomorrow.
- There will be a tornado one year from now.

- Tomorrow will be a public holiday.
- It will snow tomorrow.
- I will visit my grandmother next month.

Probability is a branch of mathematics that studies the likelihood, or chance, of a phenomenon happening. The idea of probability was developed in the 17th century. This branch of mathematics has wide applications in business, science, and industries like in the fields of medicine, genetic theory, game strategy, and insurance.

B   Terms and Definitions

In probability, a **random experiment** is a process in which the result cannot be predicted with certainty. The result is called an **outcome** of the experiment. An experiment is likely to have more than one possible outcome.

The following activities introduce three random experiments which may give you a better idea of probability.

Objective: To understand the probability of a chance event by collecting data and observing the frequency of its happening.

Tasks

(a) Conduct a random experiment of tossing a coin 20 times.

Head

Tail

In tossing a coin, the results of getting a *head* or a *tail* are the two possible outcomes.

(b) Copy the following table. Record the result of each toss in it. Use the notation 'H' for *head* and 'T' for *tail*.

Trial	1st	2nd	3rd	4th	5th	6th	7th	8th	9th	10th
Outcome										

Trial	11th	12th	13th	14th	15th	16th	17th	18th	19th	20th
Outcome										

Questions

1. Before a coin is tossed, will you be able to predict with certainty the outcome of the toss?

2. In your result table, is there any trend in the outcomes?

3. Find the percentage of getting a *head* in your 20 tosses.

4. Compare and discuss your results with your classmates. What can you say about the nature of the results of tossing a coin?

5. In tossing a coin, what would you say about the chance of getting a *head*?

Objective: To collect data from another chance process and to predict the probability of a chance event from its relative frequency of occurrence.

Tasks

(a) Conduct a random experiment of rolling a die with six faces for 30 times. Each face denotes the numbers 1, 2, 3, 4, 5, and 6 respectively as shown below.

(b) Copy and complete the following table with the results obtained from rolling the die.

Trial	1st	2nd	3rd	4th	5th	6th	7th	8th	9th	10th
Outcome										

Trial	11th	12th	13th	14th	15th	16th	17th	18th	19th	20th
Outcome										

Trial	21st	22nd	23rd	24th	25th	26th	27th	28th	29th	30th
Outcome										

Questions

1. What are the possible outcomes?

2. Before a die is rolled, will you be able to predict with certainty the outcome of the throw?

3. In your result table, is there any trend in the outcomes?

4. Find the percentage of getting a '2' in your 30 throws.

5. Compare and discuss your results with your classmates. What can you say about the nature of the results of rolling a die?

6. In rolling a die, what can you say about the chance of getting a '2'?

Objective: To further study relative frequency of occurrence of a chance event and its probability of occurrence using random numbers generated from a spreadsheet program.

Microsoft Excel - random-decimals.xls

File   Edit   View   Insert   Format   Tools   Data   Window   Help

E14   =   =SUM(E4.E13)

	A	B	C	D	E	F	G	H	I
1	The Idea of Randomness								
2									
3	Random decimal	Tenth digit			Counts				
4	0.562532148	5		Number of 0 =	12				
5	0.053899929	0		Number of 1 =	9				
6	0.367665469	3		Number of 2 =	10				
7	0.236549877	2		Number of 3 =	10				
8	0.928217618	9		Number of 4 =	9				
9	0.868925455	8		Number of 5 =	13				
10	0.971963914	9		Number of 6 =	5				
11	0.991117059	9		Number of 7 =	9				
12	0.615189878	6		Number of 8 =	12				
13	0.416088368	4		Number of 9 =	11				
14	0.381244757	3		Total number of Trials	100				
15	0.965397609	9							
16	0.551548118	5							
17	0.828972632	8							
18	0.270300137	2							
19	0.285414823	2							
20	0.59994645	5							
21	0.392158499	3							
22	0.777535977	7							
23	0.982442339	9							
24	0.880742401	8							

Sheet1 / Sheet2 / Sheet3 /

Ready   NUM

The random number function RAND() of Excel generates an evenly distributed random number greater than or equal to 0 and less than 1 each time. You may imagine it as picking up a number x randomly between 0 and 1 on the number line, such that $0 \leq x < 1$.

Tasks

(a) Create the headers in the first three rows and the text at cells D4 to D14 on a spreadsheet as shown above.

(b) At the cell A4, enter the formula =RAND(). A random decimal between 0 and 1 will appear.

(c) At the cell B4, enter the formula =INT(A4*10). The tenth digit of the random decimal at the cell A4 will appear. It can be regarded as a random digit which may be 0, 1, 2, ..., or 9.

(d) Copy the cells A4 and B4 to the cells from A5 to B103. Then we will have generated 100 random digits in column B from cells B4 to B103.

(e) At the cell E4, enter the formula =COUNTIF(B4:B103, 0). This gives the number of 0's in column B.

(f) At the cell E5, enter the formula =COUNTIF(B4:B103, 1). This gives the number of 1's in column B.

(g) Similarly, complete the counts for the number of each random digit in column B.

(h) At the cell E14, enter the formula =SUM(E4:E13). This gives the total number of random digits generated. This should be 100.

(i) Enter a number at any empty cell, say E18. The random numbers will be regenerated.

Questions

1. Describe in your own words the random number generated from the spreadsheet program.

2. Can you observe any patterns of the random digits in column B?

3. What can you say about the count of each random digit in column B?

4. When you regenerate the random numbers, will the counts of individual random digits be unchanged?

5. If you generate 1,000 random digits in column B in the same way, how many 8's do you expect to get in these 1,000 random digits?

We say that a coin is **fair** or **unbiased** when the chance of getting a head is the same as the chance of getting a tail. In other words, "getting a head" and "getting a tail" are two **equally likely** outcomes of tossing a fair coin.

Similarly, can you now explain the meaning of a fair die in your own words?

Tossing a fair coin and rolling a fair die are experiments with equally likely outcomes.

A collection of outcomes is called an **event**. Consider the following cases.

1. When a coin is tossed, we may define getting a head as an event. This event consists of the outcome *head*.

2. When a die is rolled, we may define getting a prime number as an event and the outcomes are 2, 3, and 5.

3. When a random digit is generated, we may define getting a digit that is greater than 5 as an event and the outcomes are 6, 7, 8, and 9.

A measure of how likely an event E will take place is called the **probability** of that event, and it is denoted by $P(E)$. For example, if E = the event of getting a digit greater than 5, then $P(E)$ denotes the probability of getting a digit greater than 5.

Mathematically, $P(E)$ is defined as follows:

> The probability of an event E, $P(E)$, in a random experiment with equally likely outcomes is
>
> $$P(E) = \frac{\text{number of outcomes favorable to the event } E}{\text{total number of possible outcomes}}.$$

 **CLASS ACTIVITY 4**

Objective: To compare observed frequencies from a random experiment to the probabilities obtained from the definition of probability.

Tasks

1. A coin is tossed.
   (a) How many likely outcomes are there?
   (b) Use the definition of probability to determine the probability of getting a *head*.
   (c) Refer to your results of Class Activity 1. What fraction of your tosses resulted in *head*s?
   (d) How does the answer in **(c)** compare to that in **(b)**? Are they exactly the same?
   (e) If the results are different, why do you think they are different?

2. Collect the results for Class Activity 1 from the entire class.
   (a) Calculate the fraction of tosses that result in getting a *head*.
   (b) Compare the result in **2(a)** to your answers for **1(b)** and **(c)**. Explain any differences.

3. Design a probability experiment involving drawing a card from a deck or partial deck of playing cards. Conduct the experiment and record the results of the chance process.
   (a) Using the definition of probability stated earlier, find the probability of one random event of your experiment.
   (b) Compare the answer in **3(a)** to the probabilities obtained from your experimental results as well as from the entire class result. Explain any possible sources of discrepancy.

In Class Activity 4, we are observing what we refer to as **experimental probability** and **theoretical probability** in probability theory. Experimental probability refers to the probability of an event occurring when an experiment was conducted. In this case, an experiment is performed, like what you have done in the class activities, and an experimental probability of an event E is calculated as

$$P(E) = \frac{\text{number of times the event } E \text{ occurs}}{\text{number of trials}}.$$

For example, if a die is rolled 6,000 times and the number '2' occurs 990 times, then the experimental probability that '2' shows up on the die is $\frac{990}{6,000}$ (= 0.165).

On the other hand, theoretical probability or simply probability, $P(E)$, of an event E is determined by noting all the possible outcomes theoretically, and determining how likely the given outcome is. Mathematically, a theoretical probability is calculated as

$$P(E) = \frac{\text{number of outcomes favorable to the event } E}{\text{total number of possible outcomes}}$$

For example, the theoretical probability that the number '2' shows up on a die being rolled is $\frac{1}{6}$ ($\approx$ 0.167). This is because out of the six possible outcomes, 1, 2, 3, 4, 5, 6, only one outcome (die showing '2') is favorable.

In most experiments, the theoretical probability and experimental probability will not be equal but are relatively close to each other. If the experiment is fair, the theoretical and experimental probability should be very similar if a large number of trials are made.

REMARKS
The more trials that you conduct in your experiment, the closer your calculations will be for the experimental and theoretical probabilities.

Example 9 A fair die is rolled. Find the probability of getting
(a) a 6,
(b) an odd number,
(c) a number less than 3.

Solution
(a) In rolling a die, there are six equally likely outcomes, which are 1, 2, 3, 4, 5, and 6.
The event of getting a 6 consists of the one outcome '6'.
∴ the probability of getting a 6, P(getting a 6) = $\frac{1}{6}$

(b) There are three favorable outcomes of the event of getting an odd number; they are 1, 3, and 5.
∴ the probability of getting an odd number,
$$P(\text{getting an odd number}) = \frac{3}{6}$$
$$= \frac{1}{2}$$

(c) The favorable outcomes of the event of getting a number less than 3 are 1 and 2.

∴ the probability of getting a number less than 3,

$$P(\text{getting a number less than 3}) = \frac{2}{6}$$

$$= \frac{1}{3}$$

 Try It! 9

A fair die is rolled. Find the probability of getting

(a) a 5,

(b) a multiple of 3.

Example 10

A card is drawn randomly from a deck of 52 playing cards. The pack consists of four suits and each suit has 13 cards. The suits are Spade ♠, Heart ♥, Diamond ♦, and Club ♣. Find the probability that the card drawn is

(a) red, **(b)** a diamond,

(c) a picture card.

Solution **(a)**

Spade

Heart

Diamond

Club

The 13 cards from each suit are:
Ace, 2, 3, 4, 5, 6, 7, 8, 9, 10, Jack, Queen, and King.
There are 26 red cards (the hearts and the diamonds).

$$\therefore\ P(\text{a red card}) = \frac{26}{52}$$

$$= \frac{1}{2}$$

(b) There are 13 diamond cards.

$$\therefore\ P(\text{a diamond card}) = \frac{13}{52}$$

$$= \frac{1}{4}$$

REMARKS

For simplicity, the probability of getting a red card is denoted by P(a red card).

(c) The picture cards consist of four kings, four queens, and four jacks.

$$\therefore \text{P(a picture card)} = \frac{12}{52}$$

$$= \frac{3}{13}$$

Try It! 10

A card is drawn randomly from a deck of 52 playing cards. Find the probability that the card is

(a) black,
(b) an ace,
(c) a red queen.

Example 11

A bag contains two red balls, three yellow balls and four green balls. A ball is drawn at random from the bag. Find the probability that the ball drawn is

(a) green,
(b) blue.

DISCUSS
1. Refer to Example 11. Are the event of drawing a yellow ball and the event of drawing a green ball equally likely?

2. What is the range of the value of P(*E*) for any event *E*?

3. Can we have an event *E* such that P(*E*) = 1?

Solution

(a) The balls in the bag can be labeled as R_1, R_2, Y_1, Y_2, Y_3, G_1, G_2, G_3, and G_4, where R, Y, and G denote the color of the ball, which are red, yellow, and green respectively.

Total number of balls = 2 + 3 + 4
$$= 9$$

Each ball is equally likely to be drawn. The event of getting a green ball consists of the outcomes, G_1, G_2, G_3, and G_4.

$$\therefore \text{P(a green ball)} = \frac{4}{9}$$

(b) There are no blue balls in the bag.

$$\text{P(a blue ball)} = \frac{0}{9}$$

$$= 0$$

REMARKS
Drawing a blue ball from the bag is an impossible event.

Try It! 11

There are 40 students in a class. Six of them wear glasses, four of them wear contact lenses, and the rest can see without vision correction. A student is selected at random. Find the probability that the student selected

(a) does not have to correct his vision,
(b) is blind.

EXERCISE 16.2

BASIC PRACTICE

1. An unbiased coin is tossed. What is the probability of getting
   (a) a head,
   (b) a tail?

2. A fair die is rolled. Find the probability of getting
   (a) a 3,
   (b) an even number,
   (c) a number greater than 4.

3. A card is drawn at random from a deck of 52 playing cards. Find the probability that the card drawn is
   (a) green,
   (b) a king,
   (c) a number card.

4. A letter is chosen at random from the word 'PORTLAND'. Find the probability that the chosen letter is
   (a) the letter 'P',
   (b) a vowel.

5. There are 20 boys and 16 girls in a class. If one of the students is selected at random to present her solution of a mathematics question to the class, what is the probability that the student is
   (a) a boy?
   (b) a girl?

6. A bag contains 15 coins, of which 12 are silver coins and the rest are gold coins. A coin is drawn at random from the bag. Find the probability of drawing a
   (a) silver coin,
   (b) gold coin,
   (c) copper coin.

FURTHER PRACTICE

7. A box contains ten chips that are numbered from 1 to 10. A chip is drawn at random from the box. Find the probability that the number on the chip is
   (a) greater than 7,
   (b) a prime,
   (c) a multiple of 4.

8. There are 12 eggs in a basket, of which two are rotten. If an egg is picked randomly from the basket, what is the probability of getting an egg that is not rotten?

9. There are three yellow roses, four white roses, and five red roses in a bouquet of flowers. If a rose is selected at random from the bouquet, find the probability that the rose is
   (a) white,
   (b) red,
   (c) blue.

10. A letter is chosen at random from the word 'MATHEMATICS'. Find the probability that the chosen letter is
    (a) the letter 'M',
    (b) a consonant,
    (c) the letter 'K'.

MATH@WORK

11. There are 12 mathematics books and 8 science books on a shelf. Three of the science books are biology books. A book is taken at random from the shelf. Find the probability that the book is
    (a) a history book,
    (b) a mathematics book,
    (c) not a biology book,
    (d) a science book which is not a biology book.

12. A store has 15 LCD TV sets and n Smart TV sets on display. If a TV set is sold at random, the probability of selling a Smart TV set is $\frac{4}{9}$. Find the value of n.

13. In a batch of 20 vases, there are four defective ones. A quality control inspector checks the vases in the batch one by one without repetition.
   (a) Find the probability that the first vase checked is defective.
   (b) If the first vase checked is defective, find the probability that the second vase checked is also defective.

14. John and Navin will play a game of chess next week. There are three possible outcomes for John: win, draw, or lose. Is it true that the probability of John winning is $\frac{1}{3}$? Explain your answer.

15. Many studies have shown that a high percentage of lung cancer cases are caused by smoking. If a lung cancer patient is selected at random, would the probability that the patient is a smoker be the same as the probability that the patient is a non-smoker?

16.3 *Sample Space*

A Sample Space

We may use set notation to describe probability. The **sample space**, usually denoted by S, of a random experiment is the set of all its possible outcomes. Thus, each outcome is an element of the sample space. Each event, being a collection of some outcomes, is a subset of the sample space.

In tossing a coin,

the sample space $S = \{head, tail\}$

where $head \in S$ and $tail \in S$.

In rolling a die,

the sample space $S = \{1, 2, 3, 4, 5, 6\}$.
$1 \in S, 2 \in S, \dots, 6 \in S$.

If   event $E = \{x : x$ is an odd number$\}$
$= \{1, 3, 5\}$

and   event $F = \{x : x$ is less than 3$\}$
$= \{1, 2\}$,

we have $E \subset S$ and $F \subset S$.

If a random experiment has a finite number of equally likely outcomes, then the probability of an event E can be expressed as:

$$P(E) = \frac{n(E)}{n(S)}$$

where $n(E)$ is the number of outcomes in the event E
and $n(S)$ is the number of outcomes in the sample space S.

Example 12

A boy is selected at random and his month of birth is noted.
(a) What is the sample space S of the experiment?
(b) Let E be the event that the name of a month contains the letter 'r'. List all the possible outcomes of this event.
(c) If a boy is equally likely to be born in each month, find $P(E)$.

Solution

(a) The sample space consists of the months in a year.
∴ sample space S = {*January, February, March, April, May, June, July, August, September, October, November, December*}

(b) E = {names of the months that have the letter 'r'}
= {*January, February, March, April, September, October, November, December*}

(c) $P(E) = \dfrac{n(E)}{n(S)}$ From **(a)**, $n(S) = 12$; from **(b)**, $n(E) = 8$

$= \dfrac{8}{12}$

$= \dfrac{2}{3}$

> **REMARKS**
> Description of the event involves a listing of the outcomes.

Try It! 12

A multiple-choice question has five options, namely A, B, C, D, and E. A student marks an option at random.
(a) What is the sample space S of the experiment?
(b) Option B is the only correct answer for this question. Let F be the event that the option marked by the student is incorrect. List all the possible outcomes of this event.
(c) State the values of $n(S)$ and $n(F)$.
(d) Find $P(F)$.

Example 13

A telephone number is selected at random from a directory and the last two digits of the number are noted.
(a) List the sample space S.
(b) Let E be the event that at least one of the two digits is a 7. List all the possible outcomes of E.
(c) Find $P(E)$.
(d) Find $P(E')$.

Solution

(a) Each of the last two digits can be 0, 1, 2, ..., 9.

Sample space S = {00, 01, 02, ..., 09,
10, 11, 12, ..., 19,
20, 21, 22, ..., 29,
$\vdots$
90, 91, 92, ..., 99}

(b) $E = \{x : x \in S$ and at least one of the digits of x is 7}
= {07, 17, 27, 37, 47, 57, 67, 77, 87, 97, 70, 71, 72, 73, 74, 75, 76, 78, 79}

(c) $P(E) = \dfrac{n(E)}{n(S)}$ From (a), $n(S) = 100$;
from (b), we have $n(E) = 19$

$= \dfrac{19}{100}$

(d) $E' = \{x : x \in S$ and none of the digits is 7}
$n(E') = n(S) - n(E)$
$= 100 - 19$
$= 81$
$\therefore P(E') = \dfrac{n(E)}{n(S)}$
$= \dfrac{81}{100}$

Try It! 13

The reading in seconds of a digital clock is observed at random.
(a) List the sample space S.
(b) Let G be the event that at least one of the digits in the reading is '5'. List the event G.
(c) State the values of $n(S)$ and $n(G)$.
(d) Find $P(G)$.
(e) Find $P(G')$.

B Basic Properties of Probabilities

Suppose E is an event of a finite sample space S with equally likely outcomes. We know that

$$P(E) = \frac{n(E)}{n(S)}.$$

Since $E \subseteq S$, $\qquad\qquad 0 \leqslant n(E) \leqslant n(S).$

$$\frac{0}{n(S)} \leqslant \frac{n(E)}{n(S)} \leqslant \frac{n(S)}{n(S)}$$

Therefore,

$$0 \leqslant P(E) \leqslant 1 \text{ for any event } E$$

This means that the probability of any event E is between 0 and 1, both inclusive. When $P(E) = 1$, E is called a **certain event** as it must occur.

The sample space S itself is a certain event.

That is

$$P(S) = 1$$

When $P(E) = 0$, E is called an **impossible event** as it cannot occur.

If a ball is drawn at random from a bag containing 10 red balls,

$$P(\text{the ball drawn is red}) = \frac{10}{10} = 1$$

and $P(\text{the ball drawn is yellow}) = \dfrac{0}{10} = 0.$

The event that the ball drawn is red is a certain event while the event that the ball drawn is yellow is an impossible event.

For the complement event E' of an event E,

$$n(E') = n(S) - n(E)$$
$$\frac{n(E')}{n(S)} = \frac{n(S)}{n(S)} - \frac{n(E)}{n(S)}$$

Therefore,

$$\text{the probability of the event } E' \text{ is}$$
$$P(E') = 1 - P(E).$$

That is, the probability of an event E not occurring is 1 minus the probability of the event E occurring. You can verify this in Example 13**(c)** and **(d)**.

Example 14

There are six purple tulips, five red tulips, and four yellow tulips in a bouquet. A flower from the bouquet is selected at random. Find the probability that the flower is
(a) a tulip,
(b) a daisy,
(c) not a purple tulip.

Solution

(a) $n(S) = 6 + 5 + 4$
$ = 15$

Since every flower is a tulip, the probability of selecting a tulip,

$$P(\text{a tulip}) = \frac{15}{15}$$
$$= 1.$$

(b) Since no flower is a daisy,

$$P(\text{a daisy}) = \frac{0}{15}$$
$$= 0.$$

(c) $P(\text{a purple tulip}) = \frac{6}{15}$

$$= \frac{2}{5}$$

$P(\text{not a purple tulip}) = 1 - P(\text{a purple tulip})$

$$= 1 - \frac{2}{5}$$

$$= \frac{3}{5}$$

Try It! 14

There are 15 cats, 18 dogs, and 3 rabbits in a pet store. An animal is selected at random. Find the probability that the animal
(a) has four legs,
(b) is an insect,
(c) is not a rabbit.

EXERCISE 16.3

BASIC PRACTICE

1. List the sample space for each of the following:
   (a) Tossing two coins
   (b) Choosing a letter at random from the word 'SQUARE'
   (c) Choosing an odd number from 1 to 11 at random
   (d) Choosing a prime number less than 15 at random
   (e) Choosing a letter at random from the word 'DIVIDE'
   (f) Choosing one jelly bean at random from a jar containing five red, seven blue, and two green jelly beans

2. A boy picks a day of a week at random to clean his room.
   (a) List the sample space S.
   (b) Let F be the event that the day he picks begins with the letter 'T'. List all the possible outcomes of event F.
   (c) Find P(F).
   (d) Find the probability that the day he picks has the letter 'a' in its spelling.

3. Twenty cards are numbered 1 to 20. A card is selected at random and the number on it is noted.
   (a) List the sample space S.
   (b) Let M be the event that the number on the card selected is a multiple of 3. List all the possible outcomes of event M.
   (c) Find P(M).
   (d) Find P(M').

4. A spinner has four equal quarters colored red, yellow, blue, and green respectively. When the pointer on it is spun, the color of the quarter where the pointer stopped is noted.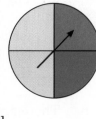
   (a) List the sample space S.
   (b) Find the probability that the color of the quarter where the pointer stopped is
   (i) red, (ii) white, (iii) not red.

5. A two-digit number is formed at random using the digits 1, 3, and 8 with repetition of digits allowed.
   (a) List the sample space S.
   (b) Let D be the event that the number formed is a double number (e.g., 33),
   (i) list all the possible outcomes of D,
   (ii) find P(D).
   (c) Let E be the event that the number formed is greater than 35,
   (i) list all the possible outcomes of E,
   (ii) find P(E),
   (iii) find P(E').

FURTHER PRACTICE

6. A quiz has 10 true/false questions and each question carries one point for a correct answer. A student's total score in the quiz is observed.
   (a) List the sample space S for the total score.
   (b) Let G be the event that the student's total score is above 7. List all the possible outcomes of
   (i) the event G,
   (ii) the event G'.
   (c) If a student attempts each question by guessing, are the events of getting a total score of 0 and a total score of 1 equally likely to occur?

7. A three-digit number is formed at random using the digits 0, 2, 5, and 8 without repetition of the digits.
  (a) List the sample space.
  (b) Let T be the event that the number formed is less than 300. Find
    (i) P(T),
    (ii) P(T').

8. There are 7 red, 10 green, 9 blue, 8 yellow, and 6 brown jelly beans in a bag. A bean is removed at random from the bag.
  (a) **(i)** List the sample space of the possible colors of the bean removed from the bag.
     (ii) Are the outcomes equally likely? Why?
  (b) Find the probability that the bean removed is
    (i) orange,
    (ii) brown,
    (iii) not orange,
    (iv) not brown.

9. A book consists of three volumes A, B, and C. These volumes are arranged on a shelf in a random order and the volume letters are read from left to right.
  (a) List the sample space.
  (b) Let H be the event that the first volume arranged is volume B. List all the possible outcomes of H.
  (c) Find P(H).

MATH@WORK

10. Richard randomly selects an ASEAN country to visit.
  (a) List all the ASEAN countries. Check your answers on the Internet.
  (b) Find the probability that the country Richard selects is
    (i) in Asia,
    (ii) Japan.
  (c) Find the probability that the name of the country he selects contains the letter 'p'.

11. A batch of computer chips comprises chips of grades A, B, and C. If a chip is selected at random from the batch, the probability that it is of grade A is $\frac{1}{4}$ and the probability that it is of grade B is $\frac{5}{12}$.

  (a) If a chip is selected at random from the batch, find the probability that it is of grade C.
  (b) If there are 72 grade C chips in the batch, find the total number of chips in the batch.

BRAIN WORKS

12. Describe a certain event in a sample space.

13. Describe an impossible event in a sample space.

14. Two fair dice are rolled. The sums of the scores obtained are recorded.
  (a) What is the sample space?
  (b) Are the outcomes in the sample space equally likely? Explain briefly.

IN A NUTSHELL

Sets

We can define a set in the following ways:

(a) Describe in words
   e.g., the set of girls in the class who wear contact lens.

(b) By listing its elements
   e.g., $E = \{2, 4, 6, 8, ...\}$

(c) In set-builder notation
   e.g., $P = \{x : x$ is a positive square number not greater than 36$\}$

Subsets

$A = \{1, 2, 3, 4, 5, 6\}$
$B = \{2, 5\}$

Since all the elements in B are in A and $B \neq A$, then B is a proper subset of A.

We write $B \subset A$.

Set Language	Set Notation
A is the set of positive integers	$A = \{1, 2, 3, 4, ...\}$
"... is an element of ..."	$\in$
"... is not an element of ..."	$\notin$
A is a subset of B	$A \subseteq B$
A is a proper subset of B	$A \subset B$
A is not a subset of B	$A \nsubseteq B$
A is not a proper subset of B	$A \not\subset B$
Number of elements in set A	$n(A)$
Universal set	ξ
Empty set	ϕ or $\{\ \}$
Complement of set A	A'

Terms in Probability

- A **sample space** is the set of all possible outcomes in a random experiment. It is usually denoted by the letter S and written using set notation.

- An **event** is a collection of outcomes from the sample space that we are considering in particular, that is, an event E is a subset of S.

- The probability of an event is a number that expresses the likelihood of the event occurring. Larger values of $P(E)$ indicates greater likelihood of occurrence.

Basic Properties of Probabilities

For a finite sample space S with equally likely outcomes,

- Probability of an event E, $P(E) = \dfrac{n(E)}{n(S)}$

- $0 \leqslant P(\text{any event } E) \leqslant 1$

- $P(\text{a certain event}) = 1$

- $P(\text{an impossible event}) = 0$

- $P(\text{event } E \text{ not occurring})$
  $= 1 - P(\text{event } E \text{ occurring})$
  that is $P(E') = 1 - P(E)$

1. A multiple-choice question has five options and only one of them is the correct answer. If a boy picks an option at random, what is the probability that it is not the correct answer?

2. A day of the week is chosen at random. Find the probability that the day chosen is
   (a) a Monday,
   (b) a day that has the letter 'u' in its spelling.

3. Let A = {*ruler, pencil, compasses, marker*}.
   (a) Find $n(A)$.
   (b) Is *pen* $\in A$?
   (c) Is {*marker*} $\subset A$?
   (d) Suggest a universal set for the set A.
   (e) If $B \subset A$, *compasses* $\notin B$, and $n(B) = 3$, find the set B.

4. Let A = {letters from the word '*later*'},
       B = {letters from the word '*latter*'},
   and C = {letters from the word '*letter*'}.
   (a) List the elements of the sets A, B, and C.
   (b) Find $n(C)$.
   (c) Describe the relationship between the sets using '$\subset$', '$=$', or '$\in$'
       (i) A and B,   (ii) B and C.

5. Let A = {quadrilaterals with four right angles},
       B = {quadrilaterals with four equal sides},
   and C = {quadrilaterals with two pairs of parallel sides}.
   (a) List the elements of the sets A, B, and C.
   (b) Suggest a universal set for these sets.
   (c) Describe the relationship between B and C.
   (d) Are all trapezoids elements of C?

6. Let ξ = {$x : x$ is an integer},
       P = {$x : x$ is a factor of 36},
   and Q = {$x : x$ is a factor of 60}.
   (a) List the elements of the sets P and Q.
   (b) Is P a subset of Q?
   (c) Describe a set R such that $R \subset P$ and $R \subset Q$.

7. A fair die has 12 faces, numbered 1 to 12. When it is rolled, find the probability of getting a prime number.

8. A bag contains some red balls and some green balls. A ball is drawn at random from the bag. If the probability of drawing a red ball is 0.55, what is the probability of drawing a green ball?

9. There are three bottles of barbecue sauce, two bottles of steak sauce, and one bottle of hot sauce on a shelf. A bottle is selected at random. Find the probability that the bottle
   (a) contains barbecue sauce,
   (b) does not contain hot sauce.

10. A box contains six red pens, nine blue pens, and three black pens. A pen is selected at random from the box. Find the probability that the pen is
   (a) green,
   (b) not green,
   (c) black,
   (d) not black.

11. A card is drawn at random from a deck of 30 cards, numbered 1 to 30. Find the probability that the number on the card is
   (a) a multiple of 4,
   (b) greater than 20,
   (c) a prime number.

12. A three-digit number is represented as 7*6, where * represents a digit from 0 to 9. Find the probability that the three-digit number is
    (a) an even number,
    (b) a multiple of 3,
    (c) is not a multiple of 3,
    (d) is divisible by 4.

13. A number is selected at random from the first 10 prime numbers.
    (a) List the sample space.
    (b) Find the probability that the number is
        (i) greater than 11,
        (ii) less than 11,
        (iii) 11.
    (c) What is the sum of the three probabilities found in (b)?

14. Two fair coins are tossed and their outcomes are noted.
    (a) List the sample space.
    (b) Find the probability of getting
        (i) two heads,
        (ii) one head and one tail.

15. Peter has one $2 bill, one $5 bill, one $10 bill, and one $50 bill in his wallet. Two of these bills are taken out at random and the total amount is recorded.
    (a) List the sample space of the total amount.
    (b) Find the probability that the total amount is
        (i) less than $5,
        (ii) more than $12,
        (iii) over $70.

16. There are three roads, A, B, and C, connecting City X and City Y, and four roads, P, Q, R, and S, connecting City Y and City Z.

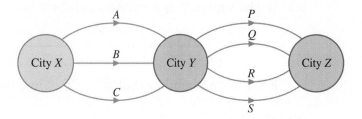

Mr. Wood selects these roads at random to drive from City X to City Z.
    (a) List the sample space of his routes.
    (b) Find the probability that Mr. Wood will drive along Road A and Road R.
    (c) Let E be the event that Mr. Wood will drive along Road Q.
        (i) Lst all the outcomes of this event.
        (ii) Find P(E),
        (iii) Find P(E').

17. During a fund raising event in a school, 1,000 raffle tickets priced at $20 each were sold. The tickets are numbered from 000 to 999. There are one first prize of $3,000, two second prizes of $1,000 each and three third prizes of $500 each.
    (a) If a ticket is drawn at random, find the probability that
        (i) its three digits are the same,
        (ii) the last digit is a '9',
        (iii) the last digit is not a '9',
        (iv) the last two digits are the same.
    (b) Find the total amount of money raised in the event.

Probability Involving Geometry

(a) In the figure, P is a random point on the line segment AB.

Find the probability that $AP : PB$ is less than $1 : 2$.

(b) The figure shows a circular target of radius 15 cm. The bull's eye is of radius 5 cm. Considering one of your throws which has hit the target, what is the probability that it will hit the bull's eye?

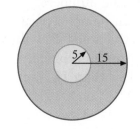

(c) What are the sample spaces in (a) and (b)? Are they finite?

In what ways can you apply your knowledge of probability in your daily life? Give examples of situations where probability is involved.

17 PROBABILITY OF COMBINED EVENTS

Playing

LET'S LEARN TO...

1. calculate the probability of a simple combined event using a possibility diagram or a tree diagram

2. identify mutually exclusive events

3. understand and apply the addition of probabilities for mutually exclusive events

4. identify independent events

5. understand and apply the multiplication of probabilities for independent events

The games at a casino are never fair. A casino ensures that it always has an advantage over its customers by setting the payouts using probability. If you think carefully about it – is winning a game at a casino a matter of probability, good luck or both?

17.1 *Probabilites of Simple Combined Events*

In this chapter, we will learn how to solve more complicated probability problems. In order to help us visualize the sample space and the events in such problems, we usually draw a diagram called a possibility diagram or a tree diagram.

A Possibility Diagram

We can use a rectangular grid, called a **possibility diagram**, to represent the sample space of a random experiment involving two stages.

- Tossing a coin twice
- Rolling two dice once
- Selecting two letters from a given word

are examples where possibility diagrams can be drawn to calculate their probabilities.

Example 1

An unbiased coin is tossed and a letter is selected at random from the word *NUMBER*. Find the probability of
(a) getting a head on the tossed coin and the letter *M* from the word,
(b) getting a vowel.

Solution

This experiment involves two stages: tossing a coin is a stage and selecting a letter from the word is another stage. The outcomes can be represented by the crosses in the possibility diagram as shown below.

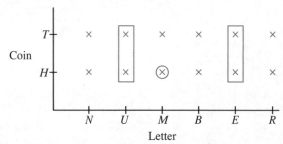

The sample space *S* = {*HN, HU, HM, HB, HE, HR, TN, TU, TM, TB, TE, TR*}, where the first letter represents the result of tossing a coin (*H* for head and *T* for tail), and the second represents the letter selected from the word *NUMBER*. There are 12 equally likely outcomes in *S*, that is $n(S) = 12$.
(a) There is one outcome, *HM* (shown enclosed by ◯ in the possibility diagram), favoring the event of getting a head on the tossed coin and the letter *M* from the word.

∴ P(a head on the tossed coin and the letter *M* from the word) = $\frac{1}{12}$

(b) There are four possible outcomes, *HU*, *TU*, *HE*, and *TE* (shown enclosed by ▯ in the possibility diagram), favoring the event of getting a vowel.

$$\therefore \; P(\text{a vowel}) = \frac{4}{12}$$
$$= \frac{1}{3}$$

Try It! **1**

A letter is selected at random from each of the words, *SURE* and *WIN*.
(a) Draw a possibility diagram to represent the sample space.
(b) Find the probability of getting
  (i) two vowels,
  (ii) the letter *W*.

RECALL

Of the 26 letters in the English alphabet, *a, e, i, o, u* are the vowels and the remaining 21 letters are called the consonants.

Example **2**

Two fair six-sided dice are rolled.
(a) Show all the possible outcomes using a possibility diagram.
(b) Find the probability that
  (i) the sum of the two numbers shown is 10,
  (ii) at least one die shows a 3.

Solution

(a) The possibility diagram showing the outcomes of rolling of two dice is as follows:

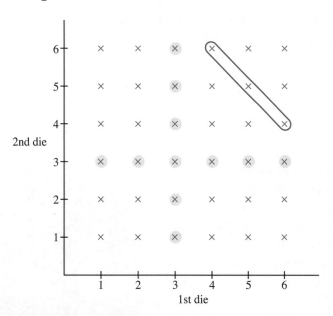

The sample space consists of all the ordered pairs represented by the crosses in the above diagram. For instance, (4, 6) refers to the outcome of getting 4 on the first die and getting 6 on the second die.

$\therefore$ sample space $S = \{(1, 1), (1, 2), (1, 3), ..., (1, 6),$
$(2, 1), (2, 2), (2, 3), ..., (2, 6),$
$(3, 1), (3, 2), (3, 3), ..., (3, 6),$
$\vdots \qquad\qquad\qquad\qquad \vdots$
$(6, 1), (6, 2), (6, 3), ..., (6, 6)\}$

There are 36 equally likely outcomes in S, thus $n(S) = 36$.

(b) (i) Let $E = \{$the sum of the two numbers is 10$\}$.
Then $E = \{(4, 6), (5, 5), (6, 4)\}$.
Thus, $n(E) = 3$.
$\therefore$ P(sum of two numbers shown is 10) = P(E)
$$= \frac{n(E)}{n(S)}$$
$$= \frac{3}{36}$$
$$= \frac{1}{12}$$

(ii) Let $F = \{$at least one die shows a 3$\}$.
Then $F = \{(3, 1), (3, 2), (3, 3), (3, 4), (3, 5), (3, 6),$
$(1, 3), (2, 3), (4, 3), (5, 3), (6, 3)\}$.
Thus, $n(F) = 11$.
$\therefore$ P(at least one die shows a 3) = P(F)
$$= \frac{11}{36}$$

Try It! 2 Two fair six-sided dice are rolled. Find the probability that
(a) the sum of the two numbers shown is 6,
(b) both dice show the same number.

B Tree Diagram

If a random experiment consists of two or more stages, we can use a **tree diagram** to represent the process. A tree diagram shows all the possible events. The first event is represented by a dot. From the dot, branches are drawn to represent all possible outcomes of the event. The probability of each outcome is written on its branch.

Example 3

Three unbiased coins are tossed. Find the probability of getting
(a) three heads,
(b) two heads and one tail.

Solution   **(a)** Here, the tossing of each coin is a stage.

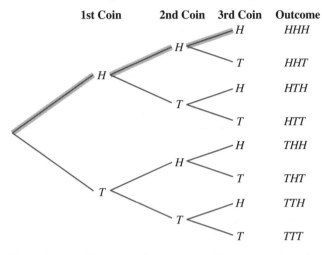

| 1st Coin | 2nd Coin | 3rd Coin | Outcome |

The above diagram is a tree diagram showing the outcomes of tossing three coins. In a tree diagram, the result of each stage is shown at the end of a branch for that stage. By reading along the branches, we get the outcomes of the experiment.

In this case, the outcome *HHH* means the first coin shows a head, the second coin shows a head, and the third coin shows a head (as indicated by the branches in orange color).

The eight outcomes are equally likely, that is $n(S) = 8$.
∴ P(three heads) = P(*HHH*)

$$= \frac{1}{8} \qquad n(E) = 1$$

(b) Let E = {outcomes showing two heads and one tail}
     = {*HHT*, *HTH*, *THH*}
$n(E) = 3$

∴ P(two heads and one tail) = $\frac{3}{8}$

Try It! 3

A family has two children.
(a) Draw a tree diagram to show the possible genders of the children.
(b) Assume that the probability of having a male child and the probability of having a female child are equal. Find the probability that
   (i) both children are boys,
   (ii) there is one boy and one girl.

DISCUSS

There is no effect on the outcome whether the three coins are tossed at the same time or one after another. Explain why.

Example 4

Bag A contains four chips numbered 1, 3, 5, and 7 respectively. Bag B contains three chips numbered 2, 4, and 6 respectively. A chip is drawn at random from each bag.

(a) Draw a tree diagram to show all the possible outcomes.

(b) Find the probability that the sum of the two chips drawn is

    (i) 7,   **(ii)** odd,   **(iii)** even.

Solution   **(a)**

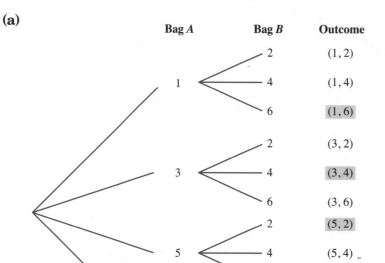

The above diagram is the required tree diagram. There are 12 equally likely outcomes in the sample space, that is $n(S) = 12$.

(b) **(i)** The favorable outcomes for a sum of 7 are (1, 6), (3, 4), and (5, 2).

$$\therefore \text{P(the sum is 7)} = \frac{3}{12}$$
$$= \frac{1}{4}$$

(ii) Since all the sums of the outcomes are odd,

$$\text{P(the sum is odd)} = \frac{12}{12}$$
$$= 1$$

(iii) There are no even sums.

$$\therefore \text{P(the sum is even)} = \frac{0}{12}$$
$$= 0$$

Note: • The event that the sum is odd is a certain event, while the event that the sum is even is an impossible event.
• Since there are only two stages in this experiment, we can also represent the sample space using a possibility diagram.

Try It! 4

Box A contains a red ball, a green ball, and a blue ball. Box B contains a red ball and a blue ball. A ball is drawn from each box at random.
(a) Draw a tree diagram to show all the possible outcomes.
(b) Find the probability that the two balls drawn are
   (i) both red,   (ii) both green,
   (iii) of the same color,   (iv) of different colors.

EXERCISE 17.1

⚙ BASIC PRACTICE

1. Two unbiased coins are tossed.
   (a) Represent the sample space using a possibility diagram.
   (b) Find the probability of getting
      (i) two heads,
      (ii) at least one head.

2. An unbiased coin is tossed and a fair die is rolled.
   (a) Represent the sample space using a possibility diagram.
   (b) Find the probability of getting
      (i) a head on the coin and an even number on the die,
      (ii) a number less than 5 on the die.

3. A letter is selected at random from each of the words, *NICE* and *ICE*.
   (a) Represent the sample space using a possibility diagram.
   (b) Find the probability that the two letters are
      (i) the same,   (ii) vowels.

4. On a console of a model helicopter, both the motion (up or down) and the direction (North, South, East, or West) are selected at random.
   (a) Represent the sample space using a tree diagram.
   (b) Find the probability of selecting the upward motion and the North direction.

5. A representative is chosen at random from a boy and a girl. A flag is chosen at random from a red one, a green one, and a yellow one. The chosen representative will carry the hoisted flag in a school parade.
   (a) Represent the sample space of choosing the representative and the flag using a tree diagram.
   (b) Find the probability that the chosen representative is a boy and the flag is not a red one.

6. A wallet contains a $5-bill, a $10-bill, and a $50-bill. One bill is taken out from the wallet at random and then replaced. A second bill is then taken out at random.
  (a) Represent the sample space using a tree diagram.
  (b) Find the probability that the sum of the bills taken out is
    (i) $20,
    (ii) more than $15.

FURTHER PRACTICE

7. A letter is selected at random from each of the words, *GOOD* and *APPLE*.
  (a) Represent the sample space using a possibility diagram.
  (b) Find the probability that the two letters selected are
    (i) both vowels,
    (ii) both consonants,
    (iii) a vowel and a consonant.

8. Two fair dice, each in the form of a regular tetrahedron as shown, are rolled. Each die has the numbers 1, 2, 3, and 4 marked on its faces. When the two dice are rolled, the number on the landing face of each die is observed.

  (a) Represent the sample space using a possibility diagram.
  (b) Find the probability that the numbers observed
    (i) are equal,
    (ii) add up to 6,
    (iii) are odd numbers.

9. There are going to be three newborn babies in a certain hospital. Assume that the probability of giving birth to a boy (*B*) is equal to the probability of giving birth to a girl (*G*).
  (a) Draw a tree diagram to show the possible genders of these three newborn babies.
  (b) Find the probability that there will be
    (i) three girls,   **(ii)** two girls,
    (iii) at least one girl.

10. Box *X* contains a gold coin and a silver coin. Box *Y* contain a copper coin, a gold coin, and a silver coin. Paul picks a coin at random from each box.
  (a) Show all the possible outcomes using a probability tree diagram.
  (b) Find the probability that he will pick
    (i) two gold coins,
    (ii) one gold coin and one silver coin,
    (iii) at least one silver coin.

MATH@WORK

11. Joanne plays a game on two spinners which are divided into four equal quadrants as shown below. The pointer of each spinner is equally likely to come to rest in any of the four equal quadrants. Each quadrant has been indicated by a number.

 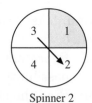

Spinner 1   Spinner 2

Joanne can only spin each pointer once.
  (a) Use a possibility diagram to show all the possible outcomes.
  (b) Find the probability that
    (i) the pointers will stop at the same number for both spinners,
    (ii) the first spinner shows a larger number,
    (iii) the sum of the two numbers is greater than 6.

12. Mrs. Lee is equally likely to read newspapers A, B, or C in the morning, and watch a TV program either on the Discovery channel or the Movie channel in the evening on a certain day.

(a) Draw a tree diagram to display the possible choices of the newspaper and the TV channel.

(b) Find the probability that she will read newspaper B and watch a program on the Movie channel on that certain day.

13. Box A contains 3 red balls and 1 green ball. Box B contains 1 red ball and 2 green balls. A ball is taken out at random from each box and its color is noted.

(a) Draw a possibility diagram to show the sample space.

(b) Find the probability of getting one red ball and one green ball.

(c) Discuss whether it is appropriate to draw a tree diagram as shown below, denoting a red ball by R and a green ball by G.

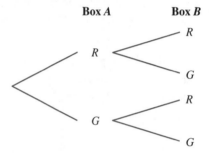

17.2 *Mutually Exclusive Events*

In some applications of probability, we may need to calculate the probability of a combination of two or more events. It is therefore necessary to know the relationship between those events and devise some rules to calculate the corresponding probabilities.

For any two events, A and B, we denote

    probability that both events A and B will occur as P(A and B);

    probability that either event A or event B will occur, or both will occur as P(A or B).

In a sample space, two events are **mutually exclusive** if they cannot occur at the same time.

For instance, in rolling a die,

event A = {the number shown is odd}
and   event B = {the number shown is even}

are mutually exclusive. This is because when the die shows an odd number, 1, 3, or 5, it definitely cannot show an even number, 2, 4, or 6.

Similarly, if a single card is drawn at random from a deck of 52 playing cards, the event of drawing an ace and the event of drawing a king are mutually exclusive.

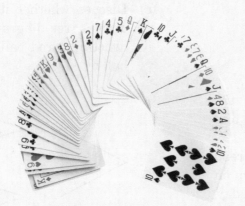

REMARKS

Mutually exclusive events have no outcomes in common.

DISCUSS

Is each of the following mutually exclusive?

- Getting a 5 and getting an odd number with one roll of a die

- Getting a club and getting a king when one card is drawn at random from a deck of 52 playing cards

CLASS ACTIVITY 1

Objective: To investigate the relationships between P(A), P(B), P(A and B), and P(A or B) for two mutually exclusive events, A and B.

Questions

1. A fair six-sided die is rolled.

   Let A be the event that the number is even,
       B be the event that the number is a multiple of 5,
   and C be the event that the number is a multiple of 3.

   (a) List the outcomes of the events A, B, and C.

   (b) **(i)** Are events A and B mutually exclusive?
   (ii) Are events A and C mutually exclusive?

   (c) Find the following probabilities:

   P(A), P(B), P(C), P(A or B), P(A or C), P(A and B), P(A and C)

   (d) Describe the relationship between
   (i) P(A), P(B), and P(A or B);
   (ii) P(A), P(C), and P(A or C).

2. Two unbiased coins are tossed.

Let A be the event that there are two heads,
B be the event that there is one head and one tail,
and C be the event that there is at least one head.

(a) List the outcomes of the events A, B, and C.

(b) (i) Are events A and B mutually exclusive?
(ii) Are events A and C mutually exclusive?

(c) Find the following probabilities:

$P(A)$, $P(B)$, $P(C)$, $P(A$ or $B)$, $P(A$ or $C)$, $P(A$ and $B)$, $P(A$ and $C)$

(d) Describe the relationship between
(i) $P(A)$, $P(B)$, and $P(A$ or $B)$;
(ii) $P(A)$, $P(C)$, and $P(A$ or $C)$.

3. If A and B are mutually exclusive events, what can you say about
(a) $P(A$ and $B)$,
(b) the relationship between $P(A)$, $P(B)$, and $P(A$ or $B)$?

Class Activity 1 illustrates the **addition** of probabilities for two mutually exclusive events.

> If A and B are two mutually exclusive events, then the probability of A or B occurring is
>
> $$P(A \text{ or } B) = P(A) + P(B).$$

Example 5

A club holds an election for the post of chairperson. The probabilities that the candidates, Monica and Roland, will be elected are 0.36 and 0.47 respectively. Find the probability that
(a) either Monica or Roland will be elected,
(b) neither Monica nor Roland will be elected.

Solution

(a) Let A be the event that Monica will be elected and B be the event that Roland will be elected.

Since there is only one chairperson, the events, A and B, are mutually exclusive.

P(either Monica or Roland will be elected)
$= P(A$ or $B)$
$= P(A) + P(B)$ Addition of probabilities of mutually exclusive events
$= 0.36 + 0.47$
$= 0.83$

(b) P(neither Monica nor Roland will be elected)

= 1 − P(either Monica or Roland will be elected)

= 1 − 0.83

= 0.17

Try It! **5** The probabilities of Serena, Sarah, and Stephy winning the tennis championship title is $\frac{1}{3}$, $\frac{5}{12}$, and $\frac{13}{36}$ respectively. Find the probability that

(a) Serena or Sarah will win the title,

(b) Sarah or Stephy will win the title,

(c) neither Sarah nor Stephy will win the title.

Example 6 A card is drawn at random from a deck of 52 playing cards. Find the probability that the card drawn is

(a) an ace or a 3,

(b) an ace or a red card.

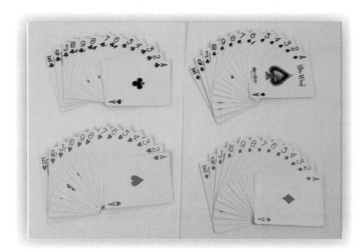

Solution **(a)** Let A be the event that the card drawn is an ace,

B be the event that the card drawn is a 3,

and C be the event that the card drawn is red.

Then, P(A) = $\frac{4}{52}$, P(B) = $\frac{4}{52}$, and P(C) = $\frac{26}{52}$.

We cannot draw a card which is both an ace and a 3.

∴ events A and B are mutually exclusive events.

P(an ace or a 3) = P(A or B)

= P(A) + P(B)

= $\frac{4}{52}$ + $\frac{4}{52}$

= $\frac{8}{52}$

= $\frac{2}{13}$

(b) As there are two red aces, the diamond ace and the heart ace, events A and C are not mutually exclusive events. Therefore, we cannot apply the addition of probabilities of mutually exclusive events to evaluate $P(A$ or $C)$. We have to find $P(A$ or $C)$ here by counting.

Apart from the two red aces, there are 24 red cards.

$P($an ace or a red card$) = P(A$ or $C)$

$$= \frac{4 + 24}{52}$$

Here, the 28 cards consist of 2 non-red aces, 2 red aces, and 24 remaining red cards (non-ace red cards).

$$= \frac{28}{52}$$

$$= \frac{7}{13}$$

Try It! **6**

Three unbiased coins are tossed. Draw a tree diagram to show all the possible outcomes and find the probability of getting
(a) three heads or two heads,
(b) three heads or the first coin being a head.

EXERCISE 17.2

BASIC PRACTICE

1. In each of the following, determine whether events A and B are mutually exclusive.
   (a) One card is chosen at random from a deck of 52 playing cards.
   $A = \{$getting a club$\}$;
   $B = \{$getting a jack$\}$
   (b) One month of the year is chosen at random.
   $A = \{$choosing July$\}$;
   $B = \{$choosing a fall month$\}$
   (c) $A = \{N, S, E, W\}$;
   $B = \{NE, NW, SE, SW\}$
   (d) $A = \{N, S, E, W\}$; $B = \{N, S, NE\}$
   (e) Two dice are rolled.
   $A = \{$a die shows a 3$\}$;
   $B = \{$sum of the resulting numbers is 10$\}$

   (f) Two dice are rolled.
   $A = \{$a die shows a 5$\}$;
   $B = \{$sum of the resulting numbers is 6$\}$

2. A bag contains 2 red balls, 3 white balls, and 15 yellow balls. A ball is drawn at random. Find the probability that the ball drawn is
   (a) red,
   (b) white,
   (c) red or white.

3. Twelve cards are numbered from 1 to 12. A card is drawn at random. Find the probability that the number on the card is
   (a) less than 4,
   (b) greater than 7,
   (c) less than 4 or greater than 7.

4. Thomas caught eight fish whose lengths were 18 cm, 21 cm, 22 cm, 26 cm, 27 cm, 31 cm, 35 cm, and 40 cm respectively. One of the fish is selected at random for cooking. Let A be the event that the selected fish is longer than 30 cm, and B be the event that the selected fish is between 25 cm and 30 cm. Find
(a) P(A),   (b) P(B),   (c) P(A or B).

5. A day of the week is chosen at random. Find the probability of choosing a Thursday or a weekend day.

6. There are 5 parents, 3 students, and 4 teachers in a room. If a person is selected at random, what is the probability that the person is a parent or a student?

7. A single letter is chosen at random from the word *SCHOOL*. What is the probability that an S or an O is chosen?

8. A card is drawn at random from a deck of 52 playing cards. Find the probability that the card drawn is
(a) a king or a queen,
(b) a queen or a spade.

![FURTHER PRACTICE]

9. One letter is chosen at random from the word *WASHINGTON*. Find the probability of choosing
(a) the letter N or a vowel,
(b) the letter W or a consonant,
(c) none of these three letters W, I, and N.

10. Michael has one penny, one nickel, one quarter, and one half-dollar in his right pocket. He has one nickel, one quarter, and one half-dollar in his left pocket. A coin is taken out at random from each pocket. Find the probability that the total value of the two coins taken out is
(a) 55 cents,
(b) more than 55 cents,
(c) 55 cents or more.

11. (a) List all the factors of 60.
(b) One of the factors is selected at random. Find the probability that it is
(i) less than 6,
(ii) greater than 10,
(iii) less than 6 or greater than 10.

12.

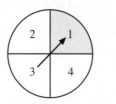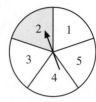

Spinner *X*   Spinner *Y*

The above diagram shows two spinners, X and Y. The pointer of each spinner is equally likely to come to rest in any of the section of the spinner that has been indicated by a number.
(a) Show the sample space using a possibility diagram.
(b) Let A be the event that the sum of the numbers indicated is 7 and B be the event that at least one of the numbers indicated is 1.
(i) List the outcomes of each event.
(ii) Are events A and B mutually exclusive?
(iii) Find P(A), P(B), and P(A or B).

13. Two fair dice are rolled. Show the sample space using a possibility diagram and hence find the probability that
(a) the sum of the two numbers shown is 9 or the numbers shown on the two dice are the same,
(b) the sum of the two numbers shown is 6 or the numbers shown on the two dice are even.

![MATH@WORK]

14. The probabilities that Yvonne and Joyce will win the championship title in a golf tournament are 0.32 and 0.25 respectively. Find the probability that
(a) either Yvonne or Joyce will win,
(b) neither Yvonne nor Joyce will win.

15. There are five service counters in a bank. The following table shows the probabilities of different numbers of service counters which will be opened to serve its customers at any one time.

Number of open counters	0	1	2	3	4	5
Probability	0	0.12	0.17	0.34	0.20	x

(a) Find the probability that two or three counters are open.

(b) Find the value of x.

(c) Find the probability that at least four counters are open.

16. A class has 40 students where 20 of them take geography and 25 take history. A student of the class is selected at random. Let G be the event that the student takes geography and H be the event that the student takes history.

(a) Are the events, G and H, mutually exclusive? Explain briefly.

(b) What other information is required in order to calculate P(G or H)?

17.3 *Independent Events*

Two events are said to be **independent events** if the occurrence or non-occurrence of one event does not affect the probability of occurrence of the other event.

For example, in tossing a fair coin twice, the event A that the first toss shows a head and the event B that the second toss shows a head are independent. That is, event A does not affect how likey event B will occur, and vice versa.

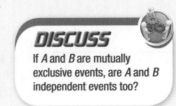

DISCUSS

If A and B are mutually exclusive events, are A and B independent events too?

 **CLASS ACTIVITY 2**

Objective: To investigate the relationship between P(A), P(B), and P(A and B) for two independent events, A and B.

Questions

1. An unbiased coin is tossed and an unbiased die is rolled. Let A be the event of getting a head and B be the event of getting a number greater than 4.

The sample space is shown below.

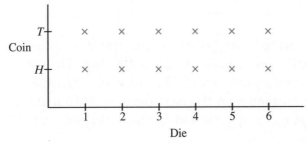

(a) Are the events, A and B, independent?

(b) Using the possibility diagram shown, find the following probabilities:
$P(A)$, $P(B)$, $P(A \text{ and } B)$.

(c) What is the relationship between $P(A)$, $P(B)$, and $P(A \text{ and } B)$?

2. A bag contains two red balls and one green ball. Two balls are drawn at random from the bag, one at a time with replacement (that is, the first ball drawn is put back into the bag before the second ball is drawn).

Let A be the event that the first ball drawn is red,
and B be the event that the second ball drawn is green.

	1st ball	2nd ball	Outcome
R_1 - red ball 1		R_1	$R_1 R_1$
R_2 - red ball 2	R_1	R_2	$R_1 R_2$
G - green ball		G	$R_1 G$
		R_1	$R_2 R_1$
	R_2	R_2	$R_2 R_2$
		G	$R_2 G$
		R_1	$G R_1$
	G	R_2	$G R_2$
		G	$G G$

(a) Are the events, A and B, independent?

(b) Using the tree diagram above, find the following probabilities:
$P(A)$, $P(B)$, $P(A \text{ and } B)$.

(c) What is the relationship between $P(A)$, $P(B)$, and $P(A \text{ and } B)$?

Class Activity 2 illustrates the **multiplication** of the probabilities of two independent events.

> If A and B are independent events, the probability of both events A and B occurring is the product of their individual probabilities, that is,
> $$P(A \text{ and } B) = P(A) \times P(B).$$

Consider the problem of drawing balls in Class Activity 2 Question 2. Imagine a similar problem with 10 red balls and 5 green balls in the bag. Then it would be very tedious to draw a tree diagram with 225 (= 15 × 15) branches. We can redraw the tree diagram as shown on the next page, such that the probabilities of the intermediate stages are indicated on the branches.

Total number of balls = 10 + 5 = 15, that is, $n(S) = 15$

$$P(R) = \frac{n(R)}{n(S)} = \frac{10}{15} = \frac{2}{3}$$

$$P(G) = \frac{n(G)}{n(S)} = \frac{5}{15} = \frac{1}{3}$$

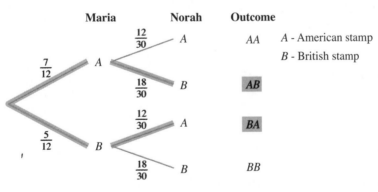

1st ball	2nd ball	Outcome	Probability	
	$\frac{2}{3}$ R	RR	$P(RR) = \frac{2}{3} \times \frac{2}{3} = \frac{4}{9}$	R - red ball
R				G - green ball
	$\frac{1}{3}$ G	RG	$P(RG) = \frac{2}{3} \times \frac{1}{3} = \frac{2}{9}$	
	$\frac{2}{3}$ R	GR	$P(GR) = \frac{1}{3} \times \frac{2}{3} = \frac{2}{9}$	
G				
	$\frac{1}{3}$ G	GG	$P(GG) = \frac{1}{3} \times \frac{1}{3} = \frac{1}{9}$	

To calculate the probability of an outcome, we **multiply** the probabilities along the branches leading to the outcome. This is a unique feature of a tree diagram.

Example 7

Maria has 7 American stamps and 5 British stamps. Norah has 12 American stamps and 18 British stamps. Each of them selects a stamp at random from her own collection. Find the probability that the two stamps selected are one American stamp and one British stamp.

Solution

Maria	Norah	Outcome	
	$\frac{12}{30}$ A	AA	A - American stamp
$\frac{7}{12}$ A			B - British stamp
	$\frac{18}{30}$ B	AB	
	$\frac{12}{30}$ A	BA	
$\frac{5}{12}$ B			
	$\frac{18}{30}$ B	BB	

P(one American stamp and one British stamp)
= P(AB or BA)
= P(AB) + P(BA)
$$= \frac{7}{12} \times \frac{18}{30} + \frac{5}{12} \times \frac{12}{30}$$
$$= \frac{31}{60}$$

Try It! 7

A letter is selected at random from each of the words, *BREAD* and *BUTTER*. Find the probability that both letters selected are vowels.

Example **8**

The probability that Jane will hit a target is $\frac{4}{5}$. The probability that Gary will hit the same target is $\frac{3}{4}$. If each of them fires once, find the probability that the target will be hit by
(a) both of them,
(b) only one of them.

Solution   **(a)** P(Jane will miss) = 1 − P(Jane will hit)

$$= 1 - \frac{4}{5}$$

$$= \frac{1}{5}$$

Similarly, P(Gary will miss) $= 1 - \frac{3}{4}$

$$= \frac{1}{4}$$

A tree diagram may be drawn to display the possible outcomes as shown below.

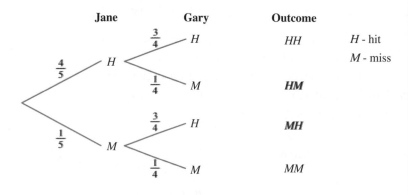

P(the target will be hit by both) = P(HH)

$$= \frac{4}{5} \times \frac{3}{4}$$

$$= \frac{3}{5}$$

(b) P(the target will be hit by only one of them)
    = P(Jane will hit and Gary will miss)
      + P(Jane will miss and Gary will hit)
    = P(HM) + P(MH)

$$= \frac{4}{5} \times \frac{1}{4} + \frac{1}{5} \times \frac{3}{4}$$

$$= \frac{4}{20} + \frac{3}{20}$$

$$= \frac{7}{20}$$

Sarah and Ryan work independently on a problem. The probabilities that the problem can be solved by Sarah and Ryan are $\frac{2}{3}$ and $\frac{4}{7}$ respectively. Find the probability that the problem can be solved by either Sarah or Ryan or both of them.

The multiplication of probabilities of two independent events can be extended to three or more independent events. Let us consider the following example.

Example **9**

The probability that a worker with occupational exposure to dust contracts a lung disease is 0.2. Three such workers are checked at random. Find the probability that
(a) none of the three workers contracted a lung disease,
(b) at least one of them contracted a lung disease.

REMARKS

A lung disease common to workers with occupational exposure to dust is chronic obstructive pulmonary disease.

Solution

(a) P(a worker does not contract a lung disease)
= 1 − P(a worker contracts a lung disease)
= 1 − 0.2
= 0.8

A tree diagram may be drawn.

1st worker	2nd worker	3rd worker	Outcome

```
                    0.2   C          CCC
              0.2 C
                    0.8   N          CCN      C - contracts
          C                                   N - does not contract
                    0.2   C          CNC
    0.2       0.8 N
                    0.8   N          CNN

                    0.2   C          NCC
              0.2 C
    0.8             0.8   N          NCN
          N
                    0.2   C          NNC
              0.8 N
                    0.8   N          NNN
```

P(none of them contracted a lung disease)
= P(*NNN*)
= 0.8 × 0.8 × 0.8   Multiplication of probabilities
= 0.512

(b) P(at least one of them contracted a lung disease)
= 1 − P(none of them contracted a lung disease)
= 1 − 0.512
= 0.488

RECALL

$P(A') = 1 - P(A)$
That is
$P(\text{not } A) = 1 - P(A)$
Hence,
$P(A) = 1 - P(\text{not } A)$

Try It! **9** The probability that a certain model of MP3 player fails within one year of purchase is 0.15. Mr. Hunter buys three such MP3 players. Find the probability that, within one year,

(a) all three MP3 players will fail,

(b) at least one MP3 player will not fail.

EXERCISE 17.3

⚙ BASIC PRACTICE

1. A box contains 3 yellow chips and 5 blue chips. Two chips are drawn at random one at a time from the box with replacement.

(a) Copy and complete the tree diagram.

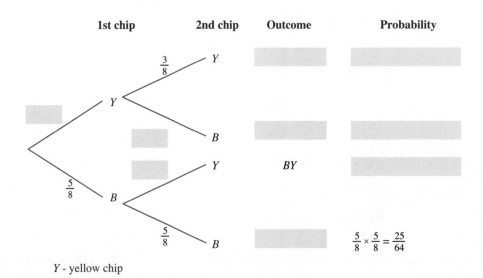

Y - yellow chip

B - blue chip

(b) Find the probability that

(i) both chips are yellow,

(ii) one chip is yellow and one chip is blue.

2. An unbiased die is rolled twice.

   (a) Copy and complete the tree diagram which shows all the possible events of 'six' and 'not six' occurring.

1st roll	2nd roll	Outcome	Probability

$\frac{1}{6}$ — six

— six

$\frac{5}{6}$ — not six   (six, not six) $\frac{1}{6} \times \frac{5}{6} = \frac{5}{36}$

— six

— not six

— not six

   (b) Find the probability of rolling
   - **(i)** double sixes,
   - **(ii)** no six,
   - **(iii)** at least one six.

3. A box contains 5 red balls, 3 green balls, and 7 yellow balls. Two balls are picked at random from the box, one at a time with replacement.

   (a) Copy and complete the tree diagram.

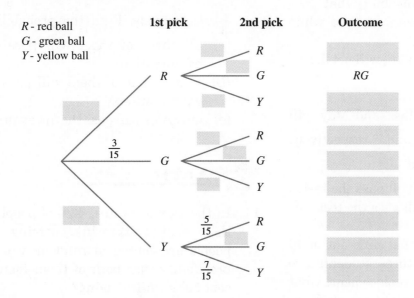

R - red ball
G - green ball
Y - yellow ball

1st pick	2nd pick	Outcome

R — R

R — G   RG

R — Y

$\frac{3}{15}$ — G — R

G — G

G — Y

$\frac{5}{15}$ — Y — R

Y — G

$\frac{7}{15}$ — Y

   (b) Find the probability that
   - **(i)** both balls are green,
   - **(ii)** one ball is red and one ball is yellow,
   - **(iii)** two balls are of different colors.

4. Seven cards are numbered from 1 to 7. A card is drawn at random and an unbiased coin is tossed. What is the probability of getting an odd number on the card and a tail on the coin?

5. Two cards are drawn at random from a deck of 52 playing cards one at a time with replacement. Find the probability of getting
(a) two hearts,
(b) one king and one queen.

6. In a 100-meter race, the probabilities that Michael and Shawn will break the national record are 0.1 and 0.15 respectively. Find the probability that the record
(a) will be broken by both Michael and Shawn,
(b) will not be broken by either of them or both.

7. The probabilities that airplane A and airplane B will arrive at Detroit International Airport on time are $\frac{3}{4}$ and $\frac{5}{6}$ respectively. Find the probability that
(a) airplane A will arrive on time while airplane B will not,
(b) both airplanes, A and B, will not arrive on time.

8. The probabilities that Lisa and May will pass a driving test are $\frac{2}{3}$ and $\frac{3}{8}$ respectively. Find the probability that
(a) both Lisa and May will pass the test,
(b) only one of them will pass the test.

9. A school survey found that nine out of 10 students like pizza. If three students are chosen at random with replacement, what is the probability that all three students like pizza?

10. One letter is selected at random from the word *PRINCETON* and one letter is selected from the word *UNIVERSITY*. Find the probability that
(a) both letters selected are I,
(b) neither of the letters selected is an I.

11. A rack contains 3 education CDs, 4 game CDs, and 5 music CDs. Two CDs are drawn at random one at a time from the rack with replacement. Find the probability that
(a) both CDs are game CDs,
(b) both CDs are of the same type,
(c) one is a music CD and the other is an education CD.

12. An unbiased die is rolled three times. Find the probability of getting
(a) three 6's,   (b) three 5's,
(c) three 6's or three 5's.

13. The probabilities that Alex, Bob, and Cliff will pass an art examination are $\frac{4}{5}$, $\frac{5}{7}$, and $\frac{2}{3}$ respectively. Find the probability that
(a) all three of them will pass the art examination,
(b) at least one of them will pass the art examination,
(c) only Alex will pass the art examination.

 **MATH@WORK**

14. In the United States, 43% of people fasten their seat belts while driving. If two people are chosen at random, what is the probability that both of them fasten their seat belts while driving?

15. A nationwide survey showed that 65% of all children in the United States dislike eating vegetables. If four children are chosen at random, find the probability that all of them dislike eating vegetables. Round your answer to the nearest percent.

16. A boat has two independent identical propellors. The boat will only move if at least one propellor is working. The probability that a propellor will fail during a trip is 0.05. Find the probability that
    (a) both propellors will fail during the trip,
    (b) the boat will complete the trip.

17. Based on a genetic theory, the probability that a first generation seed of a bean plant will yield red beans is $\frac{1}{4}$. Three of those seeds are germinated. Find the probability that
    (a) all three seeds will yield red beans,
    (b) none of the seeds will yield red beans.

18. The probability that a missile will hit a target is 0.9. The commander wants to ensure that the probability of hitting the target is more than 97%.
    (a) Find the least number of missiles that should be fired at the target.
    (b) Can we ensure a 100% hit? Why?

17.4 *Further Probabilities*

Consider drawing two balls at random from a bag containing 3 red balls and 5 green balls. Suppose the balls are drawn one by one *without replacement*.

Let A be the event that the first ball drawn is red
and B be the event that the second ball drawn is green.

At first, there are 8 balls in the bag. After drawing the first ball, there will be 7 balls left in the bag.

1. If event A happens (that is, the first ball drawn is red), the remaining balls are 2 red ones and 5 green ones.
$$\therefore\ P(B) = \frac{5}{7}$$

2. If event A does not happen (that is, the first ball drawn is not red), the remaining balls are 3 red ones and 4 green ones.
$$\therefore\ P(B) = \frac{4}{7}$$

That means, the probability of event B depends on whether event A will occur or not. Thus, A and B are not independent events. How do we calculate the probability of both events A and B occurring if they are not independent?

We may use a tree diagram to help us compute the probabilities. In the tree diagram, the probabilities indicating the second stage branches will depend on the results of the first stage.

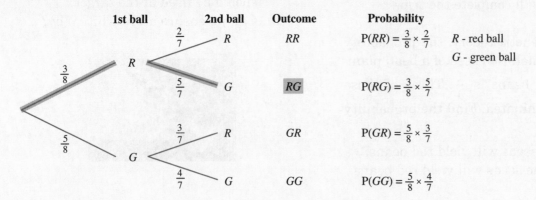

Hence, P(the first ball drawn is red and the second ball drawn is green)
$$= P(RG)$$
$$= \frac{3}{8} \times \frac{5}{7}$$
$$= \frac{15}{56}$$

REMARKS

When the outcome or occurrence of the first event affects that of the second event, the two events are said to be dependent.

Example 10

In a library, shelf A has 10 mathematics books and 6 science books, while shelf B has 8 mathematics books and 12 science books. Eva is equally likely to go to one of these shelves to pick up a book at random. Find the probability that the book she picked is a mathematics book.

• **Solution**

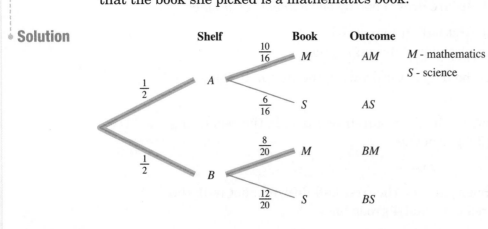

P(picking a mathematics book)
= P({shelf A and mathematics book} or
  {shelf B and mathematics book})
= P(AM) + P(BM)   Addition of probabilities
= $\dfrac{1}{2} \times \dfrac{10}{16} + \dfrac{1}{2} \times \dfrac{8}{20}$

Multiply the probabilities along the branches that lead to the outcome *BM*.

= $\dfrac{41}{80}$

Try It! 10

Box X contains 4 red pens and 2 black pens. Box Y contains 3 red pens and 7 black pens. Rex chooses one of the boxes at random and then selects a pen at random. Find the probability that the pen selected is a red one.

Example 11

The time taken by each of 60 men to replace a tire is recorded in the table below.

Time (t min)	$11 < t \leqslant 14$	$14 < t \leqslant 17$	$17 < t \leqslant 20$	$20 < t \leqslant 23$	$23 < t \leqslant 26$
Number of men	5	14	23	11	7

Two of these men are chosen at random. Find the probability that
(a) both men chosen took more than 20 minutes to replace a tire,
(b) one man took 14 minutes or less to replace a tire and the other took more than 20 minutes.

Solution

(a) Number of men who took more than 20 minutes
= 11 + 7
= 18
The situation of choosing two men at random is the same as the case of choosing two men at random, one at a time, without replacement.

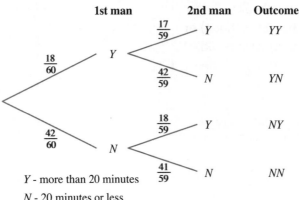

1st man   2nd man   Outcome

Y - more than 20 minutes

N - 20 minutes or less

P(both men chosen took more than 20 minutes)

$= \text{P}(YY)$

$= \dfrac{18}{60} \times \dfrac{17}{59}$

$= \dfrac{51}{590}$

(b) The time taken can be divided into three events.

L: 14 minutes or less, $n(L) = 5$

M: $14 < t \leqslant 20$, $n(M) = 37$

Y: more than 20 minutes, $n(Y) = 18$

1st man   2nd man   Outcome

P(one took 14 minutes or less and the other took more than 20 minutes)

$= \text{P}(LY) + \text{P}(YL)$

$= \dfrac{5}{60} \times \dfrac{18}{59} + \dfrac{18}{60} \times \dfrac{5}{59}$

$= \dfrac{3}{59}$

Note: Once we understand the rule for multiplication of probabilities, it is not necessary to draw a tree diagram.

The lengths of 50 fish in a pond are recorded in the table below.

Length (x cm)	$0 < x \leqslant 5$	$5 < x \leqslant 10$	$10 < x \leqslant 15$	$15 < x \leqslant 20$	$20 < x \leqslant 25$
Number of fish	10	15	13	8	4

Two fish were chosen at random. Find the probability that
(a) both fish chosen measured more than 5 cm but less than or equal to 15 cm,
(b) the length of one fish was 5 cm or less and of the other fish was more than 15 cm.

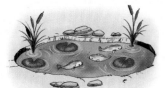

EXERCISE 17.4

BASIC PRACTICE

1. A bag contains 4 gold coins and 5 silver coins. Two coins are taken out at random from the bag, one at a time, without replacement.
   (a) Copy and complete the tree diagram.

1st coin	2nd coin	Outcome	Probability

$$\frac{4}{9} \quad G$$
$$\frac{3}{8} \quad G$$
$$\quad S \qquad GS$$
$$\quad G$$
$$\frac{5}{9} \quad S$$
$$\frac{4}{8} \quad S \qquad \qquad \frac{5}{9} \times \frac{4}{8} = \frac{5}{18}$$

G - gold coin
S - silver coin

   (b) Find the probability that
   (i) both coins are gold,
   (ii) the first coin is silver and the second coin is gold.

2. A box of 12 eggs contains 3 rotten ones. Two eggs are picked at random from the box.
   (a) Copy and complete the tree diagram.

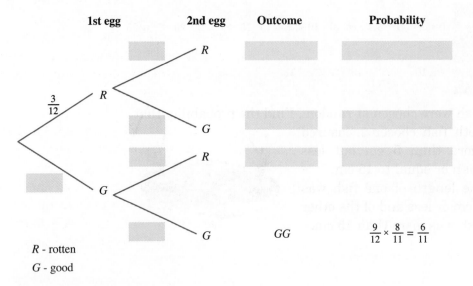

1st egg	2nd egg	Outcome	Probability

$\frac{3}{12}$ R

R

G

G

GG $\frac{9}{12} \times \frac{8}{11} = \frac{6}{11}$

R - rotten
G - good

   (b) Find the probability that
       (i) both eggs are rotten,
       (ii) one egg is good and one egg is rotten.

3. In a shipment of 25 tablet PCs, two of them are defective. If two tablet PCs are randomly selected and tested, what is the probability that both are defective if the first one is not replaced after it has been tested?

4. In a class consisting of 18 girls and 12 boys, Miss Mandy needs two students to assist her in a science demonstration. She randomly selects one student to come to the front of the classroom and then randomly selects another student from those still seated. Find the probability that both students selected are girls.

5. Two letters are selected at random from the word *CHICAGO*. Find the probability that
   (a) both letters are *C*,
   (b) only one letter is *C*.

6. Two cards are drawn at random from a deck of 52 playing cards, one at a time, without replacement. Find the probability that
   (a) both cards drawn are red,
   (b) the first card drawn is an ace and the second one is a king.

7. The Austin family has 3 boys and 1 girl. The Blake family has 2 boys and 3 girls. One of these two families is selected at random, and then a child is selected at random from the selected family to do a survey. Find the probability that the survey will be done by a boy.

8. Mrs. Costa has 6 grade A and 4 grade B tulip bulbs. The probability that a grade A tulip bulb will flower is $\frac{6}{7}$. The probability that a grade B tulip bulb will flower is $\frac{3}{5}$. If she selects one of the 10 tulip bulbs at random and plant it, find the probability that the tulip bulb will flower.

9. A box contains seven cards numbered 1 to 7. Two cards are drawn at random. Find the probability that the numbers on the two cards drawn give
(a) an odd product, **(b)** an odd sum.

10. A bag contains 1 red ball, 3 yellow balls, and 4 blue balls. Two balls are drawn at random from the bag, one at a time, without replacement. Find the probability that
(a) one ball is yellow and one ball is blue,
(b) both balls are of the same color,
(c) both balls are of different colors,
(d) the second ball is red.

11. The table below shows the number of members in a dancing club whose ages are categorized into different age ranges.

Age range (x years)	Number of members
$20 < x \leqslant 25$	9
$25 < x \leqslant 30$	21
$30 < x \leqslant 35$	25
$35 < x \leqslant 40$	17
$40 < x \leqslant 45$	8

Two members are selected at random. Find the probability that
(a) both members are 30 years old or less,
(b) one member is more than 40 years old and the other member is not more than 40 years old.

12. An office has 12 male and 18 female staff members. Two staff members are selected at random to attend a training course. Find the probability that
(a) both staff members are female,
(b) one staff member is male and the other is female.

13. In a country, 25% of the adults are smokers. The probability that a smoker will have lung cancer is 0.050. The probability that a non-smoker will have lung cancer is 0.002. If an adult from the country is selected at random, what is the probability that the person will have lung cancer?

14. A boy forgot his password for his Internet account. He has a total of 8 passwords for various accounts. If he tries these passwords at random, one at a time, without repetition, what is the probability that he will log in to his Internet account *within* two attempts?

15. There are 6 black cards and 1 red card in a box. Simon and Mary take turns to draw a card at random from the box, with Simon being the first to draw. The first person who draws the red card will win the game.
(a) If the cards are drawn without replacement, find the probability that Mary will win.
(b) If the cards are drawn with replacement, is it possible to work out the probability that Mary will win? If so, explain it briefly, with a diagram if necessary.

Basic Properties of Probability

- For a sample space S with a finite number of equally likely outcomes, the probability of an event E is
$$P(E) = \frac{n(E)}{n(S)}.$$

- $0 \leqslant P(E) \leqslant 1$

- $P(E') = 1 - P(E)$

Possibility Diagram

For example, a coin is tossed and a ball is drawn from a bag containing three balls, a red, a yellow and a blue one. The crosses (×) in the possibility diagram on the right represent the possible outcomes.

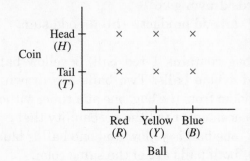

Tree Diagram

Using the same data as the possibility diagram, we have the following tree diagram.

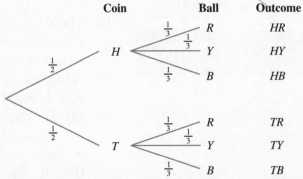

Computation of Probability

- **Addition of Probabilities**
  If A and B are mutually exclusive events,
  $$P(A \text{ or } B) = P(A) + P(B).$$

- **Multiplication of Probabilities**
  If A and B are independent events,
  $$P(A \text{ and } B) = P(A) \times P(B).$$

1. In a pet store, there are 6 puppies, 9 kittens, 4 gerbils, and 7 parakeets. If a pet is chosen at random, what is the probability of choosing a puppy or a parakeet?

2. In a basketball tournament, three of the participating teams, Knicks, Blazers, and Magic, have the probabilities $\frac{1}{5}$, $\frac{2}{15}$, and $\frac{3}{20}$ respectively of winning the tournament. Find the probability that
   (a) Magic will not win the tournament,
   (b) Knicks or Blazers will win the tournament,
   (c) neither Knicks nor Blazers will win the tournament,
   (d) none of these three teams will win the tournament.

3. Samuel has a deck of 52 playing cards and a bag containing one red marble, one black marble, and one white marble. He draws, at random, a marble from the bag and a card from the deck of playing cards. Find the probability that the two items drawn are
   (a) both red,
   (b) both black,
   (c) both red or both black,
   (d) of different colors.

4. A survey found that 47% of teenagers hold a part-time job and 78% plan to attend college. If a teenager is chosen at random, what is the probability that the teenager holds a part-time job and plans to attend college?

5. There are 10 blue hats and 8 black hats in a drawer. Two hats are taken out from the drawer at random. Find the probability that
   (a) both hats are black,
   (b) the two hats are of different colors.

6. In a city, 80% of the drivers fasten their seat belts. If three drivers are checked at random, find the probability that
   (a) none of the three drivers fastens his seat belt,
   (b) all three drivers fasten their seat belts,
   (c) at least one of the three drivers fastens his seat belt.

7. The dot plot shows the age distribution of a sample of students. If two students are selected at random from the sample, find the probability that
   (a) both their ages are 15,
   (b) the sum of their ages is more than 30.

Dot Plot for the Ages of Students

Age (Years)

8. John either walks or cycles to school every morning. The probability that he walks to school is $\frac{4}{9}$. When he walks, the probability that he is late for school is $\frac{5}{8}$. When he cycles, the probability that he is late for school is $\frac{3}{10}$. Find the probability that on a particular morning
   (a) he walks and is not late for school,
   (b) he is late for school.

9. Mr. Carter has 4 dimes, 10 quarters, and 2 half-dollars in his pocket. He takes two coins at random from his pocket, one after the other without replacement.
   (a) Draw a tree diagram to show all the possible outcomes.
   (b) Find the probability that
      (i) the first coin has a lower value than the second coin,
      (ii) the second coin he takes out from his pocket is a dime,
      (iii) the total value of the two coins is more than 60 cents.

Buffon's Needle Problem

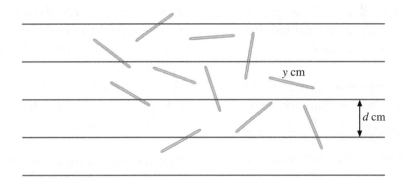

Buffon's needle problem in probability was first raised by a French mathematician Buffon in 1777. A needle of length y cm is dropped randomly on a sheet of paper with parallel lines equally spaced at d cm apart. The problem is to determine the probability that the needle will cross one of the parallel lines on the paper. It is interesting to note that the result is related to the value of π.

Find out more about Buffon's needle problem and do the experiment yourself by setting $d = y$ (for example, take $y = 3$).
Then determine if the value of the probability is close to $\dfrac{2}{\pi}$.

Suggestion: For the experiment, you can use a toothpick as an alternative to the needle.

WRITE IN YOUR JOURNAL

Mutually exclusive events and independent events do not mean the same thing. How would you differentiate between the two categories of events? Suggest a method that will help you understand and apply the addition of probabilities and the multiplication of probabilities better.

ANSWERS

Chapter 9 Number Patterns

Try It!

1. (a) 18, 22   (b) −17, −23
2. (a) 162, 486   (b) 16, −6.4
3. (a)

n	1	2	3	4
T_n	3	5	7	9
P_n	9	12	15	18

(b) $T_5 = 11$, $P_5 = 21$
4. $T_2 = 10$, $T_9 = 108$
5. (a) $T_n = 1 + 3n$ (b) $T_{15} = 46$
6. (a) $T_n = 4n - 3$ (b) $T_{18} = 69$

Exercise 9.1

1. (a) 19, 21   (b) 13, 16
   (c) 0, −4   (d) 5, −6
2. (a) 16, 32   (b) $\dfrac{3}{5}$, $\dfrac{3}{25}$
   (c) 1, −1   (d) −324, 972
3. (a) 125, 216   (b) 15, 21
   (c) $\dfrac{1}{16}$, $\dfrac{1}{32}$ (d) $\dfrac{5}{6}$, $\dfrac{6}{7}$
4. (a) 14   (b) 5
   (c) 320   (d) $\dfrac{512}{27}$
5. (a) 2, 8, 18, 32   (b) 128
6. (a) 2, 6, 12, 20   (b) 110
7. (b) $T_1 = 4$, $T_2 = 6$, $T_3 = 8$, $T_4 = 10$, $T_5 = 12$
   (c) $P_1 = 20$ cm, $P_2 = 24$ cm, $P_3 = 28$ cm, $P_4 = 32$ cm, $P_5 = 36$ cm
8. (a) $T_1 = 5$, $T_2 = 9$, $T_3 = 13$, $T_4 = 17$, $T_5 = 21$
   (b) $T_8 = 33$
   (c) $P_1 = 15$ cm, $P_2 = 24$ cm, $P_3 = 33$ cm, $P_4 = 42$ cm, $P_5 = 51$ cm
   (d) $P_8 = 78$ cm
9. 144
10. (a) Sum of previous two terms
    (b) 21, 34, 55
    (c) 1, 2, 3, 5, 8

Exercise 9.2

1. (a) 3, 5, 7   (b) 4, 1, −2
   (c) 0, 2, 8   (d) $\dfrac{1}{3}$, $\dfrac{1}{2}$, $\dfrac{3}{5}$
2. 154   3. 342
4. 32   5. 85
6. (a) $T_n = 41 - 2n$ (b) 5
7. (a) $a_n = n(n + 3)$ (b) $T_n = n^2 + 3n$
   (c) Yes
8. (a) 2, 3, 4   (b) 5^2 (c) n^2

9. (a)

n	Number of dots	Total number
1	1	1×2
2	$1 + 2$	2×3
3	$1 + 2 + 3$	3×4
4	$1 + 2 + 3 + 4$	4×5
5	$1 + 2 + 3 + 4 + 5$	5×6

(b) $1 : 2$ (c) $\dfrac{n(n+1)}{2}$ (c) 18,825
10. (a) $P_1 = 12$, $P_2 = 20$, $P_3 = 28$
    (b) $P_n = 2(2 + 4n)$
    (c) 124 cm
11. (a) (i) 16   (ii) n^2
    (b) (i) 20   (ii) $4 + 4n$
12. (b)

n	Number of carbon atoms	Number of hydrogen atoms
1	2	4
2	3	6
3	4	8
4	5	10

(c) $C_{n+1} H_{2n+2}$
13. (b)

n	1	2	3	4	5
T_n	0	1	3	6	10

(c) $T_6 = 15$, $T_7 = 21$
14. (b) Increase 1 block every time
    (c) $T_n = n$
15. 16

Review Exercise 9

1. (a) 33, 35   (b) 17, 11
   (c) 256, 1,024   (d) 80, −160
2. $T_3 = 15$, $T_{20} = 440$
3. $\dfrac{71}{105}$
4. (a) $T_n = n + 1$ (b) $T_n = 2 \times 3^{n-1}$
   (c) $T_n = \dfrac{n}{n + 3}$ (d) $T_n = n(n + 1)$
5. (b)

n	1	2	3	4
G_n	7	8	9	10
W_n	2	4	6	8

(c) $G_n = 6 + n$ (d) $W_n = 2n$

6. (a)

n	1	2	3	4
T_n	4	12	24	40

(b) $T_n = 2n(n + 1)$ **(c)** 220

7. (b)

n	1	2	3	4
T_n	1	4	9	16
P_n	7	14	21	28

(c) $T_n = n^2$

(d) $P_n = 7n$

Chapter 10 Coordinates and Linear Graphs

Try it!

1. (a) $P(3, 1)$, $Q(-2, -1)$

  (b) P: first quadrant, Q: third quadrant

2. (b) No

  (c) $y = 0.5$

3. (b) $t = 5$

4. Slope $PQ = 0$, Slope $PR = 1$, Slope $QR = -\frac{3}{2}$

5. (b) (i) -2 **(ii)** -2

     (iii) -2 **(iv)** -2

Exercise 10.1

1. (a) $A(3, 0)$, $B(5, 2)$, $C(2, 4)$, $D(0, 2)$, $E(-4, 3)$, $F(-5, -3)$, $G(-2, -4)$, $H(0, -1)$, $I(1, -3)$, $J(4, -2)$

  (b) B, C

  (c) I, J

  (d) D, H

2. (a) 3   **(b)** -2 **(c)** -1 **(d)** 0

3. (a) -5 **(b)** 2   **(c)** 7   **(d)** 0

5. (b) $C(-3, 3)$

  (c) $m\angle AOB = 45°$, $m\angle BOC = 45°$

  (d) Equal in length, i.e., $OA = OC$, Symmetric about y-axis, OA is perpendicular to OC

6. (b) fourth quadrant   **(c)** third quadrant

  (d) $m\angle POQ = 90°$ **(e)** $R(-4, 2)$

7. (b) 5 units^2 **(c)** $M(-2.5, 1)$

  (d) $MO = MS = MT$

8. (b) C and D

  (c) (i) Positive

     (ii) Negative

10. (a) Square 1: 2 units^2

     Square 2: 8 units^2

     Square 3: 18 units^2

  (b) Square 10: 200 units^2

  (c) area of Square n: $2n^2$ units^2

Exercise 10.2

1. (a) $-5, -2, 0, 2$

2. (a) $5, 1, -1, -5$

3. (b) No

4. (b) Yes   **(c)** $x = 3$

5. (b) $(1, 0)$

6. (b) x-axis: $(-2, 0)$, y-axis: $(0, 0.5)$

7. (b) $(1, 2)$, $(3, 2)$, $(1, -3)$, $(3, -3)$

  (c) 10 units^2

8. (b) All the lines cut through $(0, 1)$.

  (c) They all have 1 as the constant term.

9. (b) They are parallel.

  (c) The coefficient of x of each equation is -1.

10. (b) $a = 4$, $b = 9$, $c = 2\frac{1}{3}$

11. (b) 4 minutes

12. (b) 2.5 hours

Exercise 10.3

1. Slope $L_1 = 1$, Slope $L_2 = 3$, Slope $L_3 = -\frac{2}{3}$

2. Slope $L_4 = \frac{2}{5}$, Slope $L_5 = -2$, Slope $L_6 = -\frac{4}{9}$

3. Slope $AC = 0$, Slope $BC =$ undefined, Slope $AB = \frac{4}{9}$

4. (a) 1   **(b)** $\frac{1}{2}$ **(c)** $-\frac{1}{2}$

  (d) $-\frac{5}{6}$ **(e)** 0   **(f)** undefined

5. Slope $AB = -\frac{2}{5}$, Slope $BC = -\frac{4}{3}$, Slope $CA = 1$

6. (a) Slope $AB = \frac{1}{2}$, Slope $BC = -1$, Slope $CD = \frac{1}{2}$, Slope $DA = 5$

  (b) Slopes of one pair of opposite sides are equal.

7. (a) Slope $PQ = \frac{1}{3}$, Slope $QR = 3$, Slope $RS = \frac{1}{3}$, Slope $SP = 3$

  (b) Slopes of the opposite sides of a parallelogram are equal.

8. (a) $-\frac{3}{2}$ **(b)** $a = -2$, $b = -2.5$

9. (b) 0.5

  (c) Speed of the boy in m/s

10. (b) -3

  (c) rate of change of the volume of the piece of ice in cm^3/min

  (d) original volume of ice at $t = 0$

11. (b) $\frac{1}{12}$ **(c)** 6 m

Review Exercise 10

1. (a) $A(4, 0)$, $B(-1, 0)$, $C(-1, 5)$, $D(-4, -3)$

  (b) Point C

  (c) (i) Slope $AB = 0$ **(ii)** Slope $BC =$ undefined

     (iii) Slope $CD = \frac{8}{3}$

  (d) (i) $y = 0$ **(ii)** $x = -1$

2. (b) Slope of $AB = -1$

  (c) (i) $(2, 0)$ **(ii)** $(0, 2)$

3. (b) Slope of $AB = \frac{3}{5}$, Slope of $BC = -\frac{5}{9}$, Slope of $CA = -2$

4. (b) Slope of $PQ = \frac{1}{2}$, Slope of $QR = \frac{1}{2}$, Slope of $PR = \frac{1}{2}$

  (c) Yes

  (d) Slope of $OP = -\frac{1}{2}$, Slope of OQ is undefined

5. (b) Slope of $AB = -\frac{3}{2}$, Slope of $BC = \frac{2}{7}$,

     Slope of $CD = -\frac{3}{2}$, Slope of $DA = \frac{2}{7}$

6. (b) No   **(c)** $\frac{1}{3}$ **(d)** $(0, 2)$

7. (b) $\frac{2}{5}$

(c) cost per mile traveled

(d) the cost displayed at the fare meter at the start of journey

(e) $5.80

Chapter 11   Inequalities

Try it!

1. $x < 12$ **2.** $x \geq -21$ **3.** Yes

4. (a) $p - 1 < q - 1$ **(b)** $-4p > -4q$

     (c) $\frac{1}{5}p < \frac{1}{5}q$

5. $x < 6$ **6.** $x \geq -6$

7. $x \leq -11$ **8.** 1, 2, 3, 4, 5, 6, 7, 8

9. 2   **10.** 11 months

Exercise 11.1

1. (a) Yes   **(b)** No   **(c)** Yes   **(d)** Yes

     (e) No   **(f)** No   **(g)** Yes   **(h)** Yes

2. (a) $x < 5$ **(b)** $x > 6$ **(c)** $x \leq 1\frac{1}{2}$

     (d) $x \geq 2\frac{1}{5}$ **(e)** $x > -1\frac{1}{2}$ **(f)** $x \leq -3\frac{3}{4}$

     (g) $x \geq -2\frac{1}{2}$ **(h)** $x < -2\frac{2}{3}$

3. (a) $x > 10$ **(b)** $x < -12$ **(c)** $x < -6$

     (d) $x \leq \frac{2}{3}$ **(e)** $x \geq -1\frac{3}{4}$ **(f)** $x > 10$

4. (a) $x \geq 1\frac{1}{2}$ **(b)** $x < -8$

     (c) $x > -12$ **(d)** $x \leq 2\frac{11}{12}$

5. (a) 3   **(b)** 9   **(c)** -3   **(d)** -7

6. (a) 3   **(b)** 1   **(c)** -2   **(d)** -3

Exercise 11.2

1. (a) True   **(b)** False   **(c)** True   **(d)** False

2. (a) False   **(b)** True   **(c)** True   **(d)** False

3. (a) $<$ **(b)** $>$ **(c)** $\leq$ **(d)** $\leq$

4. (a) (i) $<$ **(ii)** $<$

     (b) (i) $\leq$ **(ii)** $\leq$

5. (a) $2p - 7 \leq 2q - 7$ **(b)** $-4 - \frac{1}{5}p \geq -4 - \frac{1}{5}q$

6. (a) (i) $a + c < b + c$ **(ii)** $b + c < b + d$

     (iii) $a + c < b + d$

     (b) Their combined monthly salary is more than $7,500.

7. not necessary

8. No

Exercise 11.3

1. (a) $x < 9$ **(b)** $x \geq 1$ **(c)** $x \leq 10$

     (d) $x < -3$ **(e)** $x \geq -1$ **(f)** $x < 2$

     (g) $x < 2$ **(h)** $x \leq 6$

2. (a) $x > -6$ **(b)** $x \leq 4\frac{5}{6}$ **(c)** $x \leq \frac{1}{2}$

     (d) $x > -\frac{1}{2}$ **(e)** $x > -2$ **(f)** $x \geq 2$

     (g) $x \leq -\frac{31}{33}$ **(h)** $x > 1\frac{21}{52}$ **(i)** $x < -17\frac{2}{3}$

     (j) $x \geq 7\frac{3}{4}$

3. 1, 2, 3, 4

Exercise 11.4

1. (a) $15x

     (b) She works for less than 5 hours.

2. (a) $50x   **(b)** 1, 2, 3, 4

3. (a) $1\frac{1}{5}x$ lb   **(b)** 16

4. 63

5. The speed must be more than 52 mi/hr.

6. 1, 2, 3, 4, 5, 6, 7, 8, 9   **7.** 15

8. 1, 2, 3, 4   **9.** after 5 hr

10. after 6 months

11. (a) $56.25   **(b)** 1, 2, 3, ..., 26

12. (a) $6x$ **(b)** 17   **(c)** $x < 20$

13. 11

14. 29, 31, 33 and 31, 33, 35

Review Exercise 11

1. (a) False   **(b)** False   **(c)** True   **(d)** True

     (e) ~~False~~ true

2. (a) True   **(b)** False   **(c)** True   **(d)** False

3. (a) $x < 8$ **(b)** $x \leq -15$ **(c)** $x > -6$

     (d) $x \geq 3\frac{1}{3}$

4. (a) 4   **(b)** -11

5. (a) -4   **(b)** 17

6. (a) 17   **(b)** $x \geq -3$

7. (a) $x < -5$ **(b)** $x \leq -4$

     (c) $x > 4\frac{5}{9}$ **(d)** $x \leq 6$

8. (a) $x > 1\frac{1}{9}$ **(b)** $x \geq -78$

     (c) $x \leq -6\frac{1}{3}$ **(d)** $x > -4$

9. 36   **10.** 11

11. (a) (i) $x > 5$ **(ii)** $y \leq -7$

     (b) fourth quadrant

12. (a) $4n$

     (b) 1, 2, 3, 4, 5

     (c) (i) $A(5,0), B(5,5), C(0,5)$

           (ii) Slope of AB = undefined

                  Slope of OB = 1

13. (a) $3n$ **(b)** 33   **(c)** 99

14. (a) 15%

     (b) (i) $170   **(ii)** $60

15. (a) (i) $y = 6$ **(ii)** $y = 0.75t$

     (c) 8 min

Chapter 12   Perimeters and Areas of Plane Figures

Try It!

1. (a) 400 cm^2 **(b)** 20   **(c)** 80 cm

2. (a) 6 cm^2 **(b)** 2.4 cm

3. Area = 706.86 cm^2, Circumference = 94.25 cm

4. (a) 6 cm   **(b)** 36π cm^2 **(c)** 3 cm

5. (a) 60 cm^2 **(b)** 10 cm

6. BE = 4.8 cm   **7.** 110 cm^2

8. (b) 1.4 m   **9.** 29.5 cm^2

10. (a) 109.13 cm   **(b)** 803.475 cm^2

11. 455 cm^2

Exercise 12.1

1. (a) Area = 25 in.^{2}, Perimeter = 20 in.
   (b) Area = $9x^2$ in.^{2}, Perimeter = $12x$ in.
2. (a) Area = 20 cm^2, Perimeter = 18 cm
   (b) Area = $(2x^2 - 3x)$ cm^2, Perimeter = $(6x - 6)$ cm
3. (a) 160 cm^2 (b) $1.5h^2$ cm^2
4. (a) 6 cm   (b) 36 cm^2
5. (a) 23 cm   (b) 92 cm
6. (a) 16 m   (b) 47 m
7. (a) 14 cm   (b) 490 cm^2
8. (a) $3\frac{1}{3}$ (b) 5
9. (a) 86 cm   (b) 188 cm^2
10. (a) 1,392 m^2 (b) 10.8%
11. (a) 6.5 m   (b) 8 m by 5 m
    (c) Square
13. (a) $420 = 2^2 \times 3 \times 5 \times 7$
    (b) Possible answers:
    20 cm by 21 cm, 15 cm by 28 cm

Exercise 12.2

1. (a) Area = 100π cm^2, Circumference = 20π cm
   (b) Area = $9x^2\pi$ cm^2, Circumference = $6\pi x$ cm
2. (a) Area = 379.94 mm^2, Circumference = 69.08 mm
   (b) Area = 38.5 m^2, Circumference = 22 m
   (c) Area = 113.10 in.^{2}, Circumference = 37.70 in.
3. (a) 9.00 cm   (b) 63.55 cm^2
4. (a) 14.00 cm   (b) 87.98 cm
5. Area = 5.97 m^2, Perimeter = 10.03 m
6. (a) 79.97 mm   (b) 384.85 mm^2
7. (a) 2.19 m   (b) 13.73 m   (c) 7.65 m^2
8. (a) 272.25 cm^2 (b) 346.64 cm^2
9. 29   10. 0.57 mi   11. 5.05
12. All the shaded figures have an equal area.
    Shaded figures (b) and (e) have the greatest perimeter.

Exercise 12.3

1. (a) 20 cm^2 (b) 54 cm^2
   (c) 49 cm^2 (d) $(3x^2 + 4x)$ cm^2
2.

	AB	DE	BC	DF	Area of ABCD
(a)	10	6	8	7.5	60
(b)	18	6	9	12	108
(c)	15	8	12	10	120
(d)	8	9	6	12	72

3. (a) 20 cm^2 (b) 4 cm
4. (a) 3 : 4   (b) 32 cm^2
5. (a) 12 cm   (b) 25 cm
6. (a) 90°   (b) 120 cm^2
   (c) $9\frac{3}{13}$ cm
7. (a) 3 m   (b) 11.4 m^2
8. (a) $MC = AN = 0.9$ m   (b) 1.62 m^2
   (c) 1 : 2

Exercise 12.4

1. (a) 108 cm^2 (b) 39 cm^2
   (c) 20 cm^2 (d) 72 cm^2
2.

	a	b	h	Area
(a)	7	10	8	68
(b)	5	9	6	42
(c)	13	20	14	231
(d)	6	11	10	85

3. (a) 2 in.   (b) 1 : 2
4. (a) 5 cm   (b) 45 cm^2
5. (a) 9 cm   (b) 5 : 7   (c) $83\frac{1}{3}$ cm^2
6. 210 cm^2
7. (a) 2.1 m   (b) 0.24 m^2 (c) $99
8. (a) $(20 - 2x)$ ft
   (b) (i) 225 ft^2 (ii) $x = 5$

Exercise 12.5

1. (a) Perimeter = 10 cm, Area = 4 cm^2
   (b) Perimeter = 52 cm, Area = 162 cm^2
   (c) Perimeter = 106 cm, Area = 205 cm^2
   (d) Perimeter = 97.13 cm, Area = 653.475 cm^2
   (e) Perimeter = 20 cm, Area = 19.6 cm^2
   (f) Perimeter = 26 cm, Area = 20 cm^2
2. (a) (ii) Perimeter = 32 cm, Area = 28 cm^2
   (b) (ii) Perimeter = 74.56 cm, Area = 151.64 cm^2
3. (a) 565 cm^2 (b) 416 cm^2
4. (a) 13.14 cm   (b) 9.30 cm^2
5. (a) 160 cm   (b) 336 cm^2
6. (a) 14.4 in.   (b) 7.2 in.^{2} (c) 12.43 in.^{2}
7. (a) 177.42 cm   (b) 848.55 cm^2
9. (c) 225 cm^2

Review Exercise 12

1. (a) 106 cm   (b) 672 cm^2 (c) 225.5 cm^2
2. 32.61 cm
3. (a) 18π cm   (b) 18π cm^2
4. (a) 14.00 cm   (b) 72.00 cm   (c) 11.46 cm
5. (a) 120 cm   (b) 720 cm^2 (c) 20 cm
6. (a) 63.66 m   (b) 9,549.30 m^2
7. (b) Perimeter = 12 cm, Area = 5 cm^2
   (c) 2.24 cm
8. (b) Perimeter = 117 cm, Area = 837 cm^2
9. (a) 100 cm   (b) 540 cm^2
   (c) 450 cm^2 (d) 1 : 5

Chapter 13   Volumes and Surface Areas of Solids
Try It!

1. Volume = 64 cm^3, Area = 96 cm^2
2. (a) 7 cm   (b) 343 cm^3
3. (a) 360 cm^3 (b) 332 cm^3 (c) 7.11 cm
4. (a) 8 cm   (b) 460 cm^2
5. 336 cm^3 6. 1,125 m^3
7. (b) 420 cm^3 (c) 480 cm^2
8. (a) 936 cm^3 (b) 464 cm^2 (c) $9.28

9. (a) (i) 200 m²   (ii) 2,072,600 cm²
   (b) (i) 200 m³   (ii) 199,221,100 cm³
10. (a) (i) 3,281.88 cm²   (ii) 0.3282 m²
    (b) (i) 1,146.6 cm³   (ii) 0.0011 m³
11. (a) 90 in.   (b) 485 in.²
    (c) 1,510 in.²   (d) 2,910 in.³
12. 12,300 cm³

Exercise 13.1

1. (a) No   (b) Yes
4. (a) Volume = 216 cm³, Area = 216 cm²
   (b) Volume = 1,331 in.³, Area = 726 in.²
   (c) Volume = 2.197 m³, Area = 10.14 m²
5. (a) Volume = 480 cm³, Area = 392 cm²
   (b) Volume = 420 in.³, Area = 344 in.²
   (c) Volume = 24 ft³, Area = 52 ft²
7. (a) 13 cm   (b) 1,014 cm²   (c) 2,197 cm³
8. (a) 9 cm   (b) 729 cm³

9.

Length	Width	Height	Volume	Total surface area
9 cm	6 cm	5 cm	270 cm³	258 cm²
11 cm	8 cm	5 cm	440 cm³	366 cm²
14 cm	11 cm	6 cm	924 cm³	608 cm²

10. (a) 140 cm³   (b) 5.19
11. (a) 50 cm   (b) 35 : 64
12. (a) 54,000 cm³   (b) 7,260 cm²   (c) 4 cm
13. (a) 944 cm²   (b) 2,688 cm³
14. (a) 12 cm by 7 cm by 5 cm
    (b) 780 cm³

Exercise 13.2

1. (a) (ii) Volume = 30 cm³, Area = 62 cm²
   (b) (ii) Volume = 21 cm³, Area = 54 cm²
   (c) (ii) Volume = 1,500 cm³, Area = 1,020 cm²
   (d) (ii) Volume = 300 cm³, Area = 300 cm²
2. (a) 3,150 cm³   (b) 1,308 cm²
3. (a) 28 in²   (b) 7.5 in.   (c) 236 in²
4. (a) (i) 15 cm
       (ii) Volume = 4,800 cm³, Area = 2,220 cm²
   (b) (i) 7 cm
       (ii) Volume = 2,520 cm³, Area = 1,848 cm²
5. (a) 2.52 m³   (b) 12.9 m²   (c) $387
6. (a) 12 m   (b) 312 m³
7. (a) 222 in.²   (b) 9,990 in.³   (c) 2,244 in.²
8. (a) 5 ft by 5 ft by 36 ft
       10 ft by 10 ft by 9 ft
   (b) 10 ft by 10 ft by 9 ft

Exercise 13.3

1. (a) 30,000 cm²   (b) 136,000 cm²
2. (a) 0.4 m²   (b) 2.56 m²
3. (a) 2,000,000 cm³   (b) 39,700,000 cm³
4. (a) 0.063 m³   (b) 9.28 m³
5. (a) 840 m²   (b) 8,400,000 cm²
6. (a) 2,000 cm³   (b) 0.002 m³

7. (a) Volume = 32 cm³, Area = 71.2 cm²
   (b) Volume = 12,960 cm³, Area = 3,336 cm²
8. (a) Volume = 110 cm³, Area = 174 cm²
   (b) Volume = 102,000 cm³, Area = 14,630 cm²
9. (a) 792 in.³   (b) 636 in.²
10. (a) 6,080 cm³   (b) 2,596 cm²
11. (a) (i) 1.12 m³   (ii) 1,120,000 cm³
    (b) (i) 15,625 cm³   (ii) 0.015625 m³
    (c) 71
12. (a) 314 cm   (b) 3,646 cm²
    (c) 6.3812 m²   (d) 0.65628 m³
13. (a) 1,280 ft³   (b) 1,088 ft²
    (c) 10   (d) 9

Review Exercise 13

1. (b) 10.5 cm³   (c) 30.5 cm²
2. (a) 14 in.   (b) 1,176 in.²   (c) 2,744 in.²
3. (a) triangular prism   (b) 4.33 cm³
   (c) 18.46 cm²
4. (a) Volume = 4,500 cm³, Area = 2,110 cm³
   (b) Volume = 420 cm³, Area = 330 cm²
5. (b) AD = 4.8 cm, CD = 6.8 cm
   (d) 91.2 cm³   (e) 128.48 cm²
6. (a) 8,000 cm³   (b) 16.67 cm   (c) 20 cm
7. (a) 340 cm   (b) 6,600 cm²
   (c) (i) 24,400 cm²   (ii) 2.44 m²
   (d) (i) 264,000 cm³   (ii) 0.264 m³
8. (a) 480 cm³   (b) 60 cm³   (c) 420 cm³
   (d) 12.5%   (e) No
9. (a) 4,196 cm³   (b) 4,384 cm²
10. (b) Volume = 2,184 cm³, Area = 856 cm²
    (c) 2.6 min

Chapter 14   Proportions
Try It!

1. (a) 1 : 1,800   (b) 1 : 3,500   (c) $1 : \frac{1}{4}$
2. (a) 1 : 50   (b) 48 cm
3. (a) 2.4 m by 2 m   (b) 4.8 m²
4. (b) 5.8 cm   (c) 13 m
5. (a) $\frac{1}{79,200}$ (b) 7.5 mi   (c) 4.8 in.
6. (a) 0.96 km²   (b) 12.5 cm²
7. (c) $w = 15t$ (d) $525   (e) 45 hours
8. 240 g
9. 2,250 g
10. $V = 120$ or $V = \frac{120}{P}$ (e) 15 cm³
11. 150 cm³
12. 6 in.

Exercise 14.1

1. (a) 1 : 240   (b) 1 : 20,000
   (c) $1 : \frac{1}{6}$ (d) 1 : 400
2. (a) 1 : 400   (b) 60 ft
3. (a) 1 : 600   (b) 12.5 cm
4. (a) $1 : \frac{1}{5}$ (b) 25 cm
5. (a) 6 in.   (b) 3.5 in.

6. Length = 22.5 cm, Width = 8.75 cm
7. 11.5 cm
8. (a) 1 : 50 (b) 42 cm
9. (a) $1 : \dfrac{1}{5}$ (b) 55 mm
10. (a) (i) 4 m by 5 m (ii) 3 m by 4 m
    (b) (i) 99 m^2 (ii) 36 m^2

Exercise 14.2

1. (a) 1 : 180,000 (b) 1 : 380,160
   (c) 1 : 30,000 (d) 1 : 400,000
2. (a) $\dfrac{1}{63,360}$ (b) $\dfrac{1}{158,400}$
   (c) $\dfrac{1}{25,000}$ (d) $\dfrac{1}{400,000}$
3. (a) $\dfrac{1}{50,000}$ (b) 6 km
4. (a) 350 m (b) 7 mi
5. (a) 8 cm (b) 50 cm
6. (a) 400 m^2 (b) 2,000 m^2
7. (a) 4 cm^2 (b) 60 cm^2
8. (a) $\dfrac{1}{300,000}$ (b) 15 km
9. (a) 1 : 40,000 (b) 2 cm^2
10. (a) 25 mi (b) 2 in.^{2}
11. (a) 1 : 1,500 (b) 9.6 in.
    (c) 9,375 ft^2
12. (a) $\dfrac{1}{300,000}$ (b) 2.25 km^2
13. (a) 900 m^2
    (b) (i) 9 cm, 36 cm^2 (ii) 22.5 cm, 225 cm^2
    (iii) 1.8 cm, 1.44 cm^2
14. (a) 17.83 cm (b) 0.58 cm^2
15. (a) 26.2 cm (b) 76.3 cm^2 (c) 1,605 km
16. (a) 1,260 km (b) 1 : 5,000,000

Exercise 14.3

1. (a) directly proportional
   (b) not directly proportional
   (c) directly proportional
   (d) not directly proportional
2. (a) not directly proportional
   (b) directly proportional
3. (a) directly proportional
   (b) not directly proportional
   (c) not directly proportional
   (d) directly proportional
4. $p = 12, q = 36$
5. (a) 30 (b) 9
6. (a) 48 (b) 7
7. (c) A straight line passing through the origin and slope is positive.
   (d) $P = 15x$ (e) 120
8. (a) No (b) Yes
   (c) $m = 0.65x^3$ (d) 473.85 g
9. $420
10. 525 g
11. (a) 2.0 gal (b) 37.0 mi
12. (a) 1.78 s (b) 0.25 m
13. (a) 180 m (b) 7 s

Exercise 14.4

1. (a) not inversely proportional
   (b) inversely proportional
   (c) inversely proportional
   (d) not inversely proportional
2. (a) No (b) Yes
3. (a) inversely proportional
   (b) not inversely proportional
   (c) inversely proportional
   (d) not inversely proportional
4. $p = 8, q = 10$
5. (a) 21 (b) 7
6. (a) 96 (b) 36
7. (d) $m = \dfrac{600}{d}$ (e) 24
8. (a) No (b) Yes
   (c) $x^2y = 900$ (d) 400
9. (a) 1.92 (b) 4
10. (a) 2 (b) 3.6, 10
11. 1.5 mins 12. 8 mins
13. (a) 320 Hz (b) 32 cm
14. (a) 126 units (b) 6 in.
15. (a) $746\dfrac{2}{3}$ m/s (b) 64 g

Review Exercise 14

1. (a) 1 : 5 (b) 0.76 cm
2. (a) 1 : 200 (b) 5 m (c) 3 m by 4 m
3. (a) 1 : 200 (b) 3 in. (c) 1,250 ft^2
4. (a) 140 m (b) 12.5 cm^2
5. (a) 10 cm
   (b) (i) 16,200 m^2 (ii) 6.48 cm^2
6. (c) $y = 5x$ (d) 35 carats
7. (a) 225 in. (b) $16
8. (a) 9 cm
   (b) (i) 8 cm (ii) 228 g
9. (c) y is directly proportional to x^2.
   (d) $y = 2x^2$ (e) 12.5
10. (a) 0.5 kg (b) 75
11. (a) $y = \dfrac{720}{x}$ (b) 30 (c) 48
    (d) The area of the rectangle is always 720 in.^{2}
12. (a) 576 units (b) 3 m
13. (a) 4 hours (b) 48 workers
14. 2.4 lb

Chapter 15   Data Handling

Try it!

2. 42 kg 3. 13 4. 1.1 kg
5. (b) Basketball: 80 inches, Soccer: 71 inches
6. (c) Jamie: 2, Brenda: 0.75
7. 27.5 cm
8. (a) 74.5 m^2 (b) 88 m^2 (c) 80 m^2
9. A: 72, B: No mode, C: 71, 78

Exercise 15.1

1. (a) Conducting Surveys (b) Reading Publications
   (c) Taking Measurements (d) Taking Measurements
   (e) Conducting Survey (f) Conducting Survey
   (g) Observing Outcomes (h) Observing Outcomes

(i) Taking Measurements   **(j)** Reading Publications

2. (a) Observing Outcomes
    (b) No
3. (a) (i) Reading Publications
       (ii) Conducting Surveys
       (iii) Conducting Surveys
    (b) Method **(iii)**
4. (a) Conducting Survey   **(b)** Question 1

Exercise 15.2

1. (a) 12   **(b)** 3 to 11
2. (a) 13   **(b)** 6 to 11
3. (a) A: 56 g to 63 g
       B: 56 g to 63 g
    (b) A: Cluster around 60 g and 61 g and are quite spread out
       B: Cluster around 60 g to 63 g with only one value at 56 g
4. (a) 40%
5. (a) Yes

Exercise 15.3

1. (a) $17\frac{1}{3}$ **(b)** 11.25   **(c)** 10.4   **(d)** 18.5
2. 145   **3.** 63
4. (a) 32.75   **(b)** 15.3
5. (b) Set A: 1.78, Set B: 0.444, Set C: 4
6. $22.40   **7.** 23°C
8. 260 g   **9.** 39 years old
10. (a) 21   **(b)** 23   **(c)** 47
11. 2
12. (b) Sixth grade: 53 kg   **(d)** Sixth grade: 0.8
       Seventh grade: 57 kg   Seventh grade: 2.4
13. 62   **14.** 50 kg
15. (a) 8.8   **(b)** 8.7
    (c) Bryan   **(d)** Bryan: 0.7, Josh: 0.6
16. 275 mi

Exercise 15.4

1. (a) 17   **(b)** 41   **(c)** 159   **(d)** 28.5
2. (a) 21.5 s   **(b)** 24 °C   **(c)** 21 m   **(d)** 4.5 g
3. (a) 12 m²   **(b)** 11 m²
4. (a) 3.27   **(b)** 3.19
5. (a) 7   **(b)** 14
    (c) 11   **(d)** No
6. (a) 34 cm   **(b)** 33 cm   **(c)** median
7. (a) 0.93%   **(b)** 0.92%
8. (a) $4,630   **(b)** $4,760   **(c)** median

Exercise 15.5

1. (a) 4   **(b)** 2, 8   **(c)** No mode
    (d) 3.6
2. (a) 0, 2   **(b)** 20
3. 46
4. (a) $7\frac{1}{2}$ **(b)** $6\frac{3}{4}$ **(c)** No
5. (a) −2.5°C   **(b)** −1.2°C
    (c) −1.4°C
6. (a) 20   **(b)** 2   **(c)** 2.5   **(d)** 3
7. (a) 192
    (b) mean = 16, median = 16, mode = 17
    (c) median and mean

---

8. (a) 30
    (b) median = 1.5, mode = 2
    (c) mean = 1.5
    (d) mean
9. (a) mean = 42 hr, median = 44 hr, mode = 45 hr
    (b) median

Review Exercise 15

1. (a) Conducting Survey
2. (c) 12%
    (d) mode = 12.0 fl oz
         median = 11.9 fl oz
    (e) mean = 11.9 fl oz
3. (a) mean = 3
         median = 2.5
         mode = 2
    (b) 1.2
4. (a) mean = 52 kg
         median = 48 kg
         mode = 43 kg
    (b) median
5. (a) 28 years old   **(b)** 27 years old
6. 4, 4, 5, 8, 9
7. (a) 8   **(b)** $2,500
    (c) $3,000   **(d)** $2,800
8. (b) A: 5.0 pounds, B: 5.05 pounds
    (c) A: 5.0 pounds, B: 5.0 pounds
    (d) A: 0.06 pounds, B: 0.22 pounds
9. (a) mean: 59
         median: 65
    (b) mean: 58
         median: 60.5
    (d) Group A: 17
         Group B: 14
    (e) Scores in Group A vary more and are more spread out.
10. (a) 5   **(b)** 7   **(c)** 1

Chapter 16   Probability of Simple Events

Try It!

1. (a) $\{S, T, U, D, E, N\}$ **(b)** 6
2. (a) {$red, blue, white$}   **(b)** 3
    (c) Yes
3. (a) No
    (b) $\{x : x$ is an integer and $2 < x < 7\}$
4. Yes
5. (a) $P \subset Q$ **(b)** $Q = R$
    (c) $P \subset S$ **(d)** $Q \not\subset S, S \not\subset Q$
6. (a) {all carpentry tools}   **(b)** $\{x : x$ is an odd number$\}$
7. ϕ, {1}, {2}, {3}, {4}, {1, 2}, {1, 3}, {1, 4}, {2, 3}, {2, 4}, {3, 4}, {1, 2, 3}, {1, 2, 4}, {1, 3 ,4}, {2, 3, 4}, {1, 2, 3, 4}
8. (a) (i) $P' = \{a, c, x\}$ **(ii)** ϕ
    (b) $Q = \xi$
    (c) ξ' is an empty set.
9. (a) $\frac{1}{6}$ **(b)** $\frac{1}{3}$
10. (a) $\frac{1}{2}$ **(b)** $\frac{1}{13}$ **(c)** $\frac{1}{26}$
11. (a) $\frac{3}{4}$ **(b)** 0

12. (a) $S = \{A, B, C, D, E\}$ **(b)** $\{A, C, D, E\}$

(c) $n(S) = 5, n(F) = 4$ **(d)** $P(F) = \dfrac{4}{5}$

13. (a) $S = \{00, 01, 02, ..., 59\}$

(b) $G = \{05, 15, 25, 35, 45, 50, 51, 52, 53, 54, 55, 56, 57, 58, 59\}$

(c) $n(S) = 60, n(G) = 15$

(d) $P(G) = \dfrac{1}{4}$

(e) $P(G') = \dfrac{3}{4}$

14. (a) 1 **(b)** 0 **(c)** $\dfrac{11}{12}$

Exercise 16.1

1. (a) $A = \{m, a, t, h, e, i, c, s\}$
(b) $B = \{W, S, H, N, G, T\}$
(c) $C = \{Summer, Spring, Autumn, Winter\}$
(d) $D = \{Monday, Tuesday, Wednesday, Thursday, Friday, Saturday, Sunday\}$

2. (a) $P = \{5, 0, 1, 3, 4\}$ **(b)** $Q = \{2\}$
(c) $R = \{9, 18, 27, 36, 45\}$ **(d)** $S = \{0, 1, 2, 3, 4, ...\}$

3. (a) $\{x : x \text{ is a factor of } 12\}$ **(b)** $\{x : x \text{ is a multiple of } 3\}$
(c) $\{x : x \text{ is a prime number}\}$

4. (a) True **(b)** False **(c)** False **(d)** True
5. (a) True **(b)** True **(c)** True **(d)** False
6. (a) $\phi, \{on\}, \{off\}, \{on, off\}$
(b) $\{on, off\}$
7. (a) $\phi, \{3\}, \{6\}, \{9\}, \{3, 6\}, \{3, 9\}, \{6, 9\}, \{3, 6, 9\}$
(b) 7
8. (a) $\{fog, snow, dew, ice\}$
(b) $\{fog, cloud, rain, dew, ice\}$
9. (a) $\xi = \{c, o, m, p, l, e, n, t\}, A = \{e, l, m, n, t\}$
(b) $A' = \{c, o, p\}$
10. (a) 7 **(b)** 3 **(c)** 4 **(d)** 0
11. (a) (i) $B \subset A$ **(ii)** $A = C$
  (iii) $B \subset D$ **(iv)** $C \not\subseteq D, D \not\subseteq C$
(b) (i) 3 **(ii)** 1
12. (a) False **(b)** False **(c)** True **(d)** False
13. (a) (i) Not necessary **(ii)** Necessary
(b) $A \subset C$
14. (a) $\{all\ animals\}$ **(b)** $\{all\ gases\}$
(c) $\{All\ U.S.\ states\}$ **(d)** $\{all\ integers\}$
15. (a) $\xi = \{0, 1, 2, 3, ...\}, A = \{1, 3, 5, 7, ...\}$, $B = \{4, 8, 12, 16, ...\}$
(b) (i) $A' = \{0, 2, 4, 6, ...\}$
  (ii) $A' = \{x : x \text{ is not an odd integer}\}$
16. (a) $R = \{red, orange, yellow, green, blue, indigo, violet\}$
(b) No
(c) No
(d) $\{all\ colors\}$
17. (a) (i) $M = \{chicken, fish\}$
  (ii) $B = \{coffee, tea, fruit\ juice\}$
(b) (i) $\{all\ main\ dishes\}$ **(ii)** $\{all\ beverages\}$
(c) $M \subset E$
18. (a) $A' = \{all\ non\text{-}seventh\ grade\ students\}$, $B' = \{all\ students\ who\ are\ not\ seventh\ grade\ female\ students\}$
(b) (i) $B \subset A$ **(ii)** $A' \subset B'$
19. (a) $\xi = \{1, 2, 3, 6, 7, 8\}$ **(b)** $C = \{3, 8\}$

Exercise 16.2

1. (a) $\dfrac{1}{2}$ **(b)** $\dfrac{1}{2}$

2. (a) $\dfrac{1}{6}$ **(b)** $\dfrac{1}{2}$ **(c)** $\dfrac{1}{3}$

3. (a) 0 **(b)** $\dfrac{1}{13}$ **(c)** $\dfrac{9}{13}$

4. (a) $\dfrac{1}{8}$ **(b)** $\dfrac{1}{4}$

5. (a) $\dfrac{5}{9}$ **(b)** $\dfrac{4}{9}$

6. (a) $\dfrac{4}{5}$ **(b)** $\dfrac{1}{5}$ **(c)** 0

7. (a) $\dfrac{3}{10}$ **(b)** $\dfrac{2}{5}$ **(c)** $\dfrac{1}{5}$

8. $\dfrac{5}{6}$

9. (a) $\dfrac{1}{3}$ **(b)** $\dfrac{5}{12}$ **(c)** 0

10. (a) $\dfrac{2}{11}$ **(b)** $\dfrac{7}{11}$ **(c)** 0

11. (a) 0 **(b)** $\dfrac{3}{5}$

  (c) $\dfrac{17}{20}$ **(d)** $\dfrac{1}{4}$

12. $n = 12$

13. (a) $\dfrac{1}{5}$ **(b)** $\dfrac{3}{19}$

14. No **15.** No

Exercise 16.3

1. (a) $\{HH, HT, TH, TT\}$ where T is tail and H is head
(b) $\{S, Q, U, A, R, E\}$
(c) $\{1, 3, 5, 7, 9, 11\}$ **(d)** $\{2, 3, 5, 7, 11, 13\}$
(e) $\{D, I, V, E\}$
(f) $\{red\ jelly\ bean, blue\ jelly\ bean, green\ jelly\ bean\}$
2. (a) $S = \{Sunday, Monday, Tuesday, Wednesday, Thursday, Friday, Saturday\}$
(b) $F = \{Tuesday, Thursday\}$
(c) $\dfrac{2}{7}$ **(d)** 1
3. (a) $\{1, 2, 3, 4, 5, 6, 7, 8, 9, 10, 11, 12, 13, 14, 15, 16, 17, 18, 19, 20\}$
(b) $\{3, 6, 9, 12, 15, 18\}$
(c) $\dfrac{3}{10}$
(d) $\dfrac{7}{10}$
4. (a) $S = \{red, yellow, blue, green\}$
(b) (i) $\dfrac{1}{4}$ **(ii)** 0 **(iii)** $\dfrac{3}{4}$
5. (a) $S = \{11, 13, 18, 31, 33, 38, 81, 83, 88\}$
(b) (i) $D = \{11, 33, 88\}$
  (ii) $\dfrac{1}{3}$
(c) (i) $E = \{38, 81, 83, 88\}$
  (ii) $\dfrac{4}{9}$ **(iii)** $\dfrac{5}{9}$
6. (a) $S = \{0, 1, 2, 3, 4, 5, 6, 7, 8, 9, 10\}$
(b) (i) $G = \{8, 9, 10\}$
  (ii) $G' = \{0, 1, 2, 3, 4, 5, 6, 7\}$
(c) No

7. **(a)** $S = \{205, 208, 250, 258, 280, 285, 502, 508, 520, 528,$
$580, 582, 802, 805, 820, 825, 850, 852\}$

   (b) **(i)** $\dfrac{1}{3}$ **(ii)** $\dfrac{2}{3}$

8. **(a)** **(i)** $S = \{red, green, blue, yellow, brown\}$
      (ii) No

   (b) **(i)** 0   **(ii)** $\dfrac{3}{20}$

      (iii) 1   **(iv)** $\dfrac{17}{20}$

9. **(a)** $S = \{ABC, ACB, BAC, BCA, CAB, CBA\}$
   (b) $H = \{BAC, BCA\}$
   (c) $\dfrac{1}{3}$

10. **(a)** $S = \{Brunei, Cambodia, Indonesia, Laos, Malaysia,$
$Myanmar, Philippines, Singapore, Thailand,$
$Vietnam\}$

   (b) **(i)** 1   **(ii)** 0

   (c) $\dfrac{1}{5}$

11. **(a)** $\dfrac{1}{3}$ **(b)** 216

14. **(a)** $\{2, 3, 4, 5, 6, 7, 8, 9, 10, 11, 12\}$
   (b) No

Review Exercise 16

1. $\dfrac{4}{5}$

2. **(a)** $\dfrac{1}{7}$ **(b)** $\dfrac{4}{7}$

3. **(a)** 4   **(b)** No   **(c)** Yes
   (d) {all stationeries}
   (e) $B = \{ruler, pencil, marker\}$

4. **(a)** $A = \{l, a, t, e, r\}, B = \{l, a, t, e, r\}, C = \{l, e, t, r\}$
   (b) 4
   (c) **(i)** $A = B$ **(ii)** $C \subset B$

5. **(a)** $A = \{square, rectangle\},$
$B = \{square, rhombus\},$
$C = \{square, rectangle, parallelogram, rhombus\}$
   (b) {all types of quadrilaterals}
   (c) $B \subset C$
   (d) No

6. **(a)** $P = \{1, 2, 3, 4, 6, 9, 12, 18, 36\},$
$Q = \{1, 2, 3, 4, 5, 6, 10, 12, 15, 20, 30, 60\}$
   (b) No
   (c) $R = \{1, 2, 3, 4, 6, 12\}$

7. $\dfrac{5}{12}$

8. 0.45

9. **(a)** $\dfrac{1}{2}$ **(b)** $\dfrac{5}{6}$

10. **(a)** 0   **(b)** 1   **(c)** $\dfrac{1}{6}$ **(d)** $\dfrac{5}{6}$

11. **(a)** $\dfrac{7}{30}$ **(b)** $\dfrac{1}{3}$ **(c)** $\dfrac{1}{3}$

12. **(a)** 1   **(b)** $\dfrac{3}{10}$ **(c)** $\dfrac{7}{10}$ **(d)** $\dfrac{1}{2}$

13. **(a)** $S = \{2, 3, 5, 7, 11, 13, 17, 19, 23, 29\}$

   (b) **(i)** $\dfrac{1}{2}$ **(ii)** $\dfrac{2}{5}$ **(iii)** $\dfrac{1}{10}$

   (c) 1

14. **(a)** $S = \{HH, HT, TH, TT\}$

   (b) **(i)** $\dfrac{1}{4}$ **(ii)** $\dfrac{1}{2}$

15. **(a)** $S = \{\$7, \$12, \$52, \$15, \$55, \$60\}$

   (b) **(i)** 0   **(ii)** $\dfrac{2}{3}$ **(iii)** 0

16. **(a)** $S = \{AP, AQ, AR, AS, BP, BQ, BR, BS, CP, CQ, CR, CS\}$

   (b) $\dfrac{1}{12}$

   (c) **(i)** $\{AQ, BQ, CQ\}$ **(ii)** $\dfrac{1}{4}$

      (iii) $\dfrac{3}{4}$

17. **(a)** **(i)** $\dfrac{1}{100}$ **(ii)** $\dfrac{1}{10}$

      (iii) $\dfrac{9}{10}$ **(iv)** $\dfrac{1}{10}$

   (b) $\$13,500$

Chapter 17   Probability of Combined Events

Try It!

1. **(b)** **(i)** $\dfrac{1}{6}$ **(ii)** $\dfrac{1}{3}$

2. **(a)** $\dfrac{5}{36}$ **(b)** $\dfrac{1}{6}$

3. **(b)** **(i)** $\dfrac{1}{4}$ **(ii)** $\dfrac{1}{2}$

4. **(b)** **(i)** $\dfrac{1}{6}$ **(ii)** 0

      (iii) $\dfrac{1}{3}$ **(iv)** $\dfrac{2}{3}$

5. **(a)** $\dfrac{3}{4}$ **(b)** $\dfrac{7}{9}$ **(c)** $\dfrac{2}{9}$

6. **(a)** $\dfrac{1}{2}$ **(b)** $\dfrac{1}{2}$

7. $\dfrac{2}{15}$ 8. $\dfrac{6}{7}$

9. **(a)** 0.003375   **(b)** 0.996625

10. **(a)** $\dfrac{29}{60}$

11. **(a)** $\dfrac{54}{175}$ **(b)** $\dfrac{24}{245}$

Exercise 17.1

1. **(b)** **(i)** $\dfrac{1}{4}$ **(ii)** $\dfrac{3}{4}$

2. **(b)** **(i)** $\dfrac{1}{4}$ **(ii)** $\dfrac{2}{3}$

3. **(b)** **(i)** $\dfrac{1}{4}$ **(ii)** $\dfrac{1}{3}$

4. **(b)** $\dfrac{1}{8}$

5. **(b)** $\dfrac{1}{3}$

6. **(b)** **(i)** $\dfrac{1}{9}$ **(ii)** $\dfrac{2}{3}$

7. **(b)** **(i)** $\dfrac{1}{5}$ **(ii)** $\dfrac{3}{10}$ **(iii)** $\dfrac{1}{2}$

8. **(b)** **(i)** $\dfrac{1}{4}$ **(ii)** $\dfrac{3}{16}$ **(iii)** $\dfrac{1}{4}$

9. **(b)** **(i)** $\dfrac{1}{8}$ **(ii)** $\dfrac{3}{8}$ **(iii)** $\dfrac{7}{8}$

10. (b) (i) $\dfrac{1}{6}$ (ii) $\dfrac{1}{3}$ (iii) $\dfrac{2}{3}$

11. (b) (i) $\dfrac{1}{4}$ (ii) $\dfrac{3}{8}$ (iii) $\dfrac{3}{16}$

12. (b) $\dfrac{1}{6}$

13. (b) $\dfrac{7}{12}$

Exercise 17.2

1. (a) No   **(b)** Mutually exclusive
(c) Mutually exclusive   **(d)** No
(e) Mutually exclusive   **(f)** No

2. (a) $\dfrac{1}{10}$ **(b)** $\dfrac{3}{20}$ **(c)** $\dfrac{1}{4}$

3. (a) $\dfrac{1}{4}$ **(b)** $\dfrac{5}{12}$ **(c)** $\dfrac{2}{3}$

4. (a) $\dfrac{3}{8}$ **(b)** $\dfrac{1}{4}$ **(c)** $\dfrac{5}{8}$

5. $\dfrac{3}{7}$ **6.** $\dfrac{2}{3}$ **7.** $\dfrac{1}{2}$

8. (a) $\dfrac{2}{13}$ **(b)** $\dfrac{4}{13}$

9. (a) $\dfrac{1}{2}$ **(b)** $\dfrac{7}{10}$ **(c)** $\dfrac{3}{5}$

10. (a) $\dfrac{1}{6}$ **(b)** $\dfrac{1}{4}$ **(c)** $\dfrac{5}{12}$

11. (a) 1, 2, 3, 4, 5, 6, 10, 12, 15, 20, 30, 60

    (b) (i) $\dfrac{5}{12}$ (ii) $\dfrac{5}{12}$ (iii) $\dfrac{5}{6}$

12. (b) (i) A: 2 and 5, 3 and 4, 4 and 3
             B: 1 and 1, 1 and 2, 1 and 3, 1 and 4, 1 and 5,
             2 and 1, 3 and 1, 4 and 1

    (ii) Mutually exclusive

    (iii) $P(A) = \dfrac{3}{20}$, $P(B) = \dfrac{2}{5}$, $P(A \text{ or } B) = \dfrac{11}{20}$

13. (a) $\dfrac{5}{18}$ **(b)** $\dfrac{1}{3}$

14. (a) 0.57   **(b)** 0.43

15. (a) 0.51   **(b)** 0.17   **(c)** 0.37

16. (a) No. There are students who take both history and geography.

    (b) Number of students who take both geography and history, or the number of students taking geograpy and not history, or the number of students taking history but not geography

Exercise 17.3

1. (b) (i) $\dfrac{9}{64}$ (ii) $\dfrac{15}{32}$

2. (b) (i) $\dfrac{1}{36}$ (ii) $\dfrac{25}{36}$ (iii) $\dfrac{11}{36}$

3. (b) (i) $\dfrac{1}{25}$ (ii) $\dfrac{14}{45}$ (iii) $\dfrac{142}{225}$

4. $\dfrac{2}{7}$

5. (a) $\dfrac{1}{16}$ **(b)** $\dfrac{2}{169}$

6. (a) 0.015   **(b)** 0.765

7. (a) $\dfrac{1}{8}$ **(b)** $\dfrac{1}{24}$

8. (a) $\dfrac{1}{4}$ **(b)** $\dfrac{13}{24}$

9. $\dfrac{729}{1,000}$

10. (a) $\dfrac{1}{45}$ **(b)** $\dfrac{32}{45}$

11. (a) $\dfrac{1}{9}$ **(b)** $\dfrac{25}{72}$ **(c)** $\dfrac{5}{24}$

12. (a) $\dfrac{1}{216}$ **(b)** $\dfrac{1}{216}$ **(c)** $\dfrac{1}{108}$

13. (a) $\dfrac{8}{21}$ **(b)** $\dfrac{103}{105}$ **(c)** $\dfrac{8}{105}$

14. 0.1849

15. 18%

16. (a) 0.0025   **(b)** 0.9975

17. (a) $\dfrac{1}{64}$ **(b)** $\dfrac{27}{64}$

18. (a) 2   **(b)** No

Exercise 17.4

1. (b) (i) $\dfrac{1}{6}$ (ii) $\dfrac{5}{18}$

2. (b) (i) $\dfrac{1}{22}$ (ii) $\dfrac{9}{22}$

3. $\dfrac{1}{300}$ **4.** $\dfrac{51}{145}$

5. (a) $\dfrac{1}{21}$ **(b)** $\dfrac{10}{21}$

6. (a) $\dfrac{25}{102}$ **(b)** $\dfrac{4}{663}$

7. $\dfrac{23}{40}$ **8.** $\dfrac{132}{175}$

9. (a) $\dfrac{2}{7}$ **(b)** $\dfrac{4}{7}$

10. (a) $\dfrac{3}{7}$ **(b)** $\dfrac{9}{28}$

    (c) $\dfrac{19}{28}$ **(d)** $\dfrac{1}{8}$

11. (a) $\dfrac{87}{632}$ **(b)** $\dfrac{72}{395}$

12. (a) $\dfrac{51}{145}$ **(b)** $\dfrac{72}{145}$

13. 0.014   **14.** $\dfrac{1}{4}$

15. (a) $\dfrac{3}{7}$ **(b)** Yes

Review Exercise 17

1. $\dfrac{1}{2}$

2. (a) $\dfrac{17}{20}$ **(b)** $\dfrac{1}{3}$ **(c)** $\dfrac{2}{3}$ **(d)** $\dfrac{31}{60}$

3. (a) $\dfrac{1}{6}$ **(b)** $\dfrac{1}{6}$ **(c)** $\dfrac{1}{3}$ **(d)** $\dfrac{2}{3}$

4. 0.3666

5. (a) $\dfrac{28}{153}$ **(b)** $\dfrac{80}{153}$

6. (a) $\dfrac{1}{125}$ **(b)** $\dfrac{64}{125}$ **(c)** $\dfrac{124}{125}$

7. (a) $\dfrac{1}{5}$ **(b)** $\dfrac{7}{15}$

8. (a) $\dfrac{1}{6}$ **(b)** $\dfrac{4}{9}$

9. (a) (i) $\dfrac{17}{60}$ (ii) $\dfrac{1}{4}$ (iii) $\dfrac{7}{40}$